Praise for

Just War Reconsidered: Strategy, Ethics, and Theory

"Dubik's new book, *Just War Reconsidered*, examines conduct in war not
in the traditional terms of the morality of war; or of a given war, per se;
or from a primarily tactical point of view, e.g., whether civilian casualties
can be justified; but from a new perspective—the morality of executing
strategies not capable of meeting the war aims. Given America's
experience in most major ground wars since World War II—
Korea, Vietnam, Iraq, Afghanistan—this perspective is profoundly
useful. Diplomats and statesmen and stateswomen will benefit from his
insights as much as military officers, as the ultimate determination of
war aims is a civilian responsibility, and determining the proper strategy
to execute it a combined military-civilian endeavor. I wish we had had
such insights before we made fateful decisions on Vietnam and Iraq."
—James Jeffrey, former U.S. Ambassador to Iraq,
Turkey, and Albania

"Although much has been written about the ethics of fighting wars,
much less attention has been paid to the ethical responsibilities of senior
military and political leaders who plan those wars. This work, written by
a distinguished general with vast experience across a range of American
conflicts, remedies this omission. Clearly written and persuasively
argued, *Just War Reconsidered* will be treasured by ethicists, historians,
and the interested public."
—Steven R. David, Johns Hopkins University

"*Just War Reconsidered* examines a timeless topic: moral leadership at
the strategic level of war. Dubik's five principles for waging war justly
provide a framework for judging the moral agency of senior leaders,
civilian and military, in their war-waging responsibilities."
—Lance Betros, author of *Carved from Granite: West Point since 1902*

"Dubik's own experience as a military leader has clearly given him a keen sense of civil-military leadership dynamics and of the practical realities of war that is not available to most academics or business experts, and this lends great authority to his perspective."

—Scott Segrest, author of
America and the Political Philosophy of Common Sense

Just War Reconsidered

BATTLES AND CAMPAIGNS

The Battles and Campaigns series examines the military and strategic results of particular combat techniques, strategies, and methods used by soldiers, sailors, and airmen throughout history. Focusing on different nations and branches of the armed services, this series aims to educate readers by detailed analysis of military engagements.

SERIES EDITOR: Roger Cirillo

An AUSA Book

JUST WAR

RECONSIDERED

Strategy, Ethics, and Theory

JAMES M. DUBIK

Foreword by
General Martin Dempsey, USA (Ret.)

UNIVERSITY PRESS OF KENTUCKY

Published by the University Press of Kentucky

Scholarly publisher for the Commonwealth,
serving Bellarmine University, Berea College, Centre College of Kentucky,
Eastern Kentucky University, The Filson Historical Society, Georgetown
College, Kentucky Historical Society, Kentucky State University, Morehead
State University, Murray State University, Northern Kentucky University,
Transylvania University, University of Kentucky, University of Louisville,
and Western Kentucky University.

Editorial and Sales Offices: The University Press of Kentucky
663 South Limestone Street, Lexington, Kentucky 40508-4008
www.kentuckypress.com

Library of Congress Cataloging-in-Publication Data

Names: Dubik, James M., author.
Title: Just war reconsidered : strategy, ethics, and theory / James M. Dubik.
Description: Lexington, Kentucky : University Press of Kentucky, [2016] |
    Series: Battles and campaigns | Includes bibliographical references and
    index.
Identifiers: LCCN 2016025073| ISBN 9780813168296 (hardcover : alk. paper) |
    ISBN 9780813168302 (pdf) | ISBN 9780813168319 (epub)
Subjects: LCSH: Just war doctrine.
Classification: LCC U21.2 .D73 2016 | DDC 172/.42--dc23
LC record available at https://lccn.loc.gov/2016025073

ISBN 978-0-8131-7501-0 (pbk. : alk. paper)

This book is printed on acid-free paper meeting the requirements of the American
National Standard for Permanence in Paper for Printed Library Materials.

Manufactured in the United States of America.

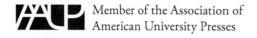 Member of the Association of
American University Presses

Contents

Foreword

Thirty years ago, Major Jim Dubik and Major Marty Dempsey would often run together through the hills of the Hudson valley when we weren't teaching English composition and philosophy classes at West Point. We would talk about the military profession, about the use of force, about the relationship of the military with our society, and about the nature of war. Those conversations remain among the highlights of my professional education.

Those were formative days for two young majors who would go on to serve the nation in positions of significant responsibility. Therefore, it was no surprise to me that Jim Dubik would reflect not only on his own experiences but also on the experiences of our nation and its military over the past decade and write a book—an important book—on the ethics of war at both the point of execution on the battlefield and the point of decision in our nation's capital.

In a period of history that is being defined by persistent conflict, ubiquitous information, yet near-extreme uncertainty, Dubik offers us seven war-waging responsibilities that provide an important intellectual framework and a useful ethical road map for military leaders and elected officials alike.

Just War Reconsidered is a book not about personalities but about principles. It is a book that examines the ethics of the nation's choices, decisions, and consequences over time. It is pragmatic. It is innovative. Dubik asserts that the principles of *jus in bello* are no longer confined to actions on the battlefield. That is an assertion with obvious and profound implications.

Just War Reconsidered will surprise, discomfort, and ultimately enlighten those interested in how the nation wields the military instrument of power. Dubik challenges us to understand and confront our responsibility not only to fight wars ethically but also to wage wars ethically.

As he cautions us: "The difficulty of conditions that may mitigate responsibility does not erase it."

We will be better prepared to live up to our ethical responsibilities in waging war with this book in our rucksack or briefcase.

Martin E. Dempsey
General, USA (Retired)
Eighteenth Chairman of the Joint Chiefs of Staff

Prologue

America may be tired of war, but war does not yet seem to be tired of America. As I wrote *Just War Reconsidered,* the United States entered its fourteenth year of war. America "reengaged" in the Iraq war that President Obama once declared was over, and in Syria it has still not decided what to do even as it conducts air strikes and attempts to arm selected rebels. The administration has been forced to delay its decision to withdraw from Afghanistan. Libya is a divided state, even after a NATO humanitarian intervention that ended in regime change—and some say because of it. In other Middle East countries, the hope of the "Arab Spring" has been replaced with spreading flames of violence, insurgency, and civil war. ISIS (the Islamic State in Iraq and Syria) has declared an Islamic state formed out of parts of Iraq and Syria and is in competition with al-Qaeda for leadership of radical Islamists. None of this will end by itself.

This book was written also as a crisis erupted in the wake of Russia's intervention in and annexation of Crimea as well as what could become a de facto annexation of Eastern Ukraine and a Baltic region feeling threatened. Now the Russians are in league with the Iranians, Hezbollah, and some of the Iraqi Shia militias to support the Assad regime. North Korea continues its bellicose attitude, threatening new forms of nuclear testing; a nuclear capable Iran will likely remain regionally assertive despite an international agreement; an emerging China has a tense relationship with Japan and others in the Pacific; unrest remains in North Africa, the Middle East, and Central Asia; and "cyber war" is becoming a growing threat. No one knows how any of these developments will evolve, nor can anyone anticipate other areas where the potential for conflict may emerge. War, in several forms, will remain a condition of our contemporary strategic environment for the foreseeable future.

Some of the ideas in this book came from my reflections on how we have fought and waged war over the past decade—to include my own experience during the Surge of 2007–2008 as the commanding general of the Multi-National Security and Transition Command, Iraq, and the NATO Training Mission, Iraq, and as a special adviser to several commanding generals in Iraq and Afghanistan. Other ideas came from my thirty-seven years of experience in the US Army. I was an infantryman, a paratrooper, and a ranger. I had the privilege of commanding soldiers in a variety of units as small as twenty and as large as forty-six thousand. In addition to commanding in Iraq as a lieutenant general, as a brigadier general I was the deputy commanding general of Task Force Eagle and the First Cavalry Division in Bosnia, and as a colonel I commanded a Joint and Multinational Brigade Combat Team during the 1994 intervention in Haiti. Each assignment caused me to delve deeper into the moral dimension of using force. Throughout my career, I was also fortunate to have had great senior commanders, mentors, peers, and subordinates who shared my interest in and concern for the moral aspects of our profession. Conversations and arguments with them helped shape many of the ideas in this book.

I was also fortunate to have received a master of arts in philosophy from Johns Hopkins before teaching ethics and just war theory at West Point and the theory and application of military force at the army's School of Advanced Military Studies at Fort Leavenworth, Kansas. These teaching opportunities gave me the time to study war's moral dimension in more detail. Shortly after retiring from the army in 2008, I returned to Johns Hopkins to finish my doctoral work, which allowed me to reflect on a lifetime of service to our nation and to the men and women whom I commanded.

There are a number of people who helped me shape the ideas and improve the arguments put forth in this book. In particular, Dr. Hilary Bok as well as Drs. Richard Bett, Steven David, and Eliot Cohen all raised insightful questions, probed my rationale, and offered challenging alternative arguments. I am grateful for their significant contributions of time and substance. I am also grateful to General Stanley McChrystal, whose experience and wisdom pushed my thinking. I must also thank other readers of earlier drafts: Professor Nancy Sherman of Georgetown University as well as friends, retired general officers, and former government officials whose comments helped me better form my arguments and ideas. All faults in and shortcomings of this book, however, are mine alone. Finally, I am grateful to Dr. Kim Kagan, president of the Institute for the Study of War, where I am a senior fellow. She allowed me the time to focus on producing this book.

The motivation to complete *Just War Reconsidered* came from three sources. The first is found in the soldiers whom I served. These sons and daughters of America are the ones who bear the final burden of war. Soldiers and their families pay the costs of the war aims, strategies, policies, and military campaigns for which senior political and military leaders are responsible. If this book can help increase the probability that their sacrifices will be made on behalf of better-thought-out aims, strategies, policies, and campaigns, then I will have done my duty to them. The second is found in my wife, Sharon Basso, whose encouragement and support gave me the time and space necessary to research, think, write, and edit. Her challenges and insights sharpened the final product. For this reason and so many others, I will always be in her debt. The final source of motivation comes from my mom, Sylvia Rzodkiewicz Dubik, who died in 2004. She and my dad, Sam Dubik, are responsible for my values and work ethic. Without their example, I would have attained little.

What follows is an argument for a new addition to the *jus in bello* component of just war theory. The current theory is deficient. It omits a major part of the conduct of war. Chapter 1 identifies the omission: just war theorists have overly restricted the conduct of war to fighting—war's tactical dimension—in their treatment of *jus in bello*. Fighting—what happens in combat and as a result of combat—is the most visible aspect of war's conduct. It is certainly the subject of most media reporting and what comes to anyone's mind first when asked, What is war? The conduct of war, however, involves more than fighting. War is also conducted at the strategic level, the level at which senior political and military leaders set war aims, identify strategies and policies, approve the military and nonmilitary campaigns necessary to achieve those war aims, and establish the coordinative bodies necessary to translate plans into actions and adapt as the vagaries of war unfold. This strategic level of war has a direct effect on how a war is fought, how long it lasts, and whether the lives used and risked are used well and risked appropriately. Yet few—if any—accounts of *jus in bello* include it.

Chapter 2 describes the war-waging dimension of *jus in bello* more completely, setting it apart from the traditional war-fighting dimension. It lays out the tripartite moral tension inherent in waging war as the tension among (1) achieving coherence by setting war aims and making strategy, policy, and campaign decisions that increase the probability of achieving those war aims, (2) generating organizational capacity by translating those aims and decisions into action to achieve war aims at the least cost, in terms of lives and resources, and the least risk to the innocent and to one's political community and then adapting decisions and actions as the vagaries of war unfold, and (3) maintaining legitimacy by doing all the foregoing while observing the conventions of war, sustaining public support of the war effort, and ensuring proper subordination of the military to civilian leadership. The chapter ends by describing seven war-waging responsibilities of senior political and military leaders.

Chapters 3 and 4 analyze two alternative accounts of how senior political and military leaders interact at the strategic level. The first is a principal-agent account; the second is an account based on an unequal dialogue between senior political leaders and their military subordinates. These two chapters find important insights in both views but ultimately conclude that neither is sufficient to account for *jus in bello* war-waging responsibilities. The principal-agent account relies too heavily on obedience, compliance, and control to adequately account for the range of *jus in bello* responsibilities that senior political and military leaders share at the war-waging level. The unequal dialogue approach provides a much richer account of the relationship between senior political and military leaders and the responsibilities they share. It does not, however, capture the full extent of the sets of dialogues that must be conducted to wage war; it is incomplete in its treatment of the conditions necessary for the dialogue to work; and it does not discuss how decisions that result from the dialogue get translated into action, an important war-waging responsibility.

Chapter 5 attempts to provide a full account of the *jus in bello* strategic, war-waging responsibilities, and chapter 6 presents five principles that govern those responsibilities. Chapter 5 suggests that war cannot be waged justly using a discrete dialogue in which military leaders provide episodic advice or input. Rather, what is required to wage war justly is a performance-oriented, decision-execution regime consisting of sets of dialogues and actions rather than a single unequal dialogue within a small group of leaders. Such a regime is necessary to identify the initial war aims, strategies, policies, and military campaigns as well as to adapt to the dynamic nature of war. Chapter 6 adduces five principles—the principles of continuous dialogue, final decision authority, managerial competence, legitimacy, and resignation—as those that govern *jus in bello*'s war-waging activities. It also describes the sources and purposes of these principles.

Throughout, I use historical and contemporary illustrations to clarify and explain the ideas and arguments that I present.

Just war theory is a theory of practical morality applied in the most complex of human activities.[1] War is the realm of ambiguity, whether for the soldiers and their military leaders who are fighting it or for the senior political and military leaders who are waging it. Decisions and actions, whether tactical or strategic, are often taken under conditions of near extreme uncertainty. Those responsible to decide and act—from soldiers and their immediate military leaders to senior generals and political officials—often do not have the luxury of time or anything close to complete information or understanding. Under fire, soldiers sometimes stare at their sergeants and lieutenants for what seems eternal seconds awaiting orders. The battlefield rarely provides the time to get more information, to reflect a bit longer, or to understand more completely. For a different set of reasons, time is often not on the side of senior political leaders and generals either. Nor do these senior leaders always have the information they would like to have before making important and consequential decisions. Mistakes, misjudgments, and misunderstandings are rife at both the tactical and the strategic levels. In every war, learning takes place at both the tactical and the strategic levels. Any practical morality, and certainly a theory of responsibility designed to explain and guide the conduct of war, whether war fighting or war waging, must take into consideration these actual conditions under which moral agents decide and act. Equally certain, however, is this: the difficulty of conditions that may mitigate responsibility does not erase it.

Moral philosophers have the luxury of time, and they have the luxury of not being responsible for deciding and acting under conditions of extreme ambiguity and with lives at stake. In this book, I take advantage of those luxuries to help those responsible for waging war as well as those responsible for evaluating war-waging decisions and actions.

1

Jus in Bello's Missing Piece

The prevailing view of just war theory recognizes the responsibilities of soldiers and leaders in combat[1] but omits an adequate account of the *jus in bello* responsibilities that senior leaders have in the conduct of war. Governments who conduct war necessarily use the lives of their citizens and risk the lives of innocents and sometimes even the life of their political community. Those who use and risk lives in war include both the soldiers and leaders on the battlefield and the senior political and military officials who send them there. Strategic responsibilities in the conduct of war, though less direct and apparent than those on the battlefield, are no less important. This book attempts to identify, describe, and fill the gap in the traditional account of *jus in bello*.

In its second decade at war, America has relearned that the moral dimension is as much a part of war's essence as are its other dimensions. It is also finding out once again that war is one of the most complex and, in many ways, the most inscrutable of human activities. The public discussion in the United States about its post-9/11 wars reflects that complexity.

The American Dialogue

Some of the dialogue about the post-9/11 wars is technical, continuing Americans' fascination with machines and technology and the hope that somehow technology will offset the ugliness of war. Some is strategic and fiscal, wondering about our role in the world and our ability to pay the costs of a nation with global interests and responsibilities. Some is sociopolitical, questioning the kind of community America is or ought to be. And some is pragmatic, assessing how we are doing and why, after so much sacrifice and spending, we are not in a better place. This dialogue has also resurrected the language and logic of just war theory, that portion of philosophy responsible for studying war from its moral perspective. Perennial questions have arisen: Are these wars justified? (concerns of *jus ad bellum*) and Have we conducted these wars justly? (matters of *jus in bello*) as well as Are we ending these wars justly? and What do we as a political community owe those who have fought on our behalf? (issues of *jus post bellum*).

At various times, the public dialogue in the United States concerning the conduct of its wars has focused on the justification for the US intervention in Iraq, the Abu Ghraib prison abuses, rendition and secret prisons, interrogation techniques and torture, the use of armed drones, the complexities of fighting these kinds of wars, the difficulties involved in distinguishing combatants from noncombatants, crimes committed by US combatants, the atrocities committed by our enemies, our rules of engagement for combat, collateral damage caused by area-effects weapons, what *proportionality* means in the kinds of wars the nation is fighting, and what a just end to this war might look like. These matters all concern the principles governing various aspects of just war theory. An understanding of the framework of this theory, its principles, and their application is important, for the concept and tools of war are changing, as are its methods. By definition, war has been understood as a state-versus-state phenomenon. That is no longer the case. What counts as war has expanded. War is, once again, being recognized as "more than a true chameleon," as it was first described by Carl von Clausewitz.[2]

Moral philosophers have an important role in this time of change,[3] and they have risen to this occasion. A brief survey of some of the salient discussions illustrates the depth of the philosophical community's reexamination of just war theory.

One of the bedrock principles of just war theory is that aggression can be rightly resisted. *Jus ad bellum* rests on this foundation: a state is justified in defending itself against aggression. "Wars are not self-starting," Michael Walzer points out. "They may 'break out' . . . under conditions difficult to analyze and where the attribution of responsibility seems impossible. But usually they are more like arson than accident: war has human agents as well as human victims."[4] The agents of aggression are not justified, but the victims coming to their own defense or that of others are.

David Rodin, however, subjects this seemingly intuitively obvious belief to intense analysis and commentary in his *War and Self-Defense*. In his treatment of the subject, he questions the validity of "the domestic analogy"—that the right to national self-defense is analogous to the right of personal self-defense. He also questions "proportionality"— the comparative judgment about value and harm—as a useful concept in deciding *jus ad bellum* issues. His analysis includes looking at both wars between nation-states and civil war within a state. Additionally, he questions the supposed separation between *jus ad bellum* and *jus in bello*—that the justice of fighting a war can be logically and morally separated from the justice of the war itself.

In the end, Rodin concluded that "the tendency to view all conflict through the lens of aggression and defense is at once morally misleading and dangerous." It is misleading because, to the extent that conflicts are infected by the politics of brinkmanship, the application of the categories of aggression and defense is often nothing more than an exercise in moral bad faith. It is dangerous because it may actually encourage participation in the game of brinkmanship. Further, the lens of aggression and defense fails to address the problems of civil war and internal oppression. Rodin then goes on to adduce alternative frameworks and principles, ones that give strength to the final conclusion that "our traditional conceptions of international law and international ethics need to be fundamentally rethought."[5]

Another of the central foundations of traditional just war theory holds that fighting is a rule-governed activity and that the rules apply equally to soldiers fighting on either side of the conflict. The main *jus in bello* rules generally accepted among nations include the principal upholding of the distinction between combatants and noncombatants, where the former are legitimate targets of war and the latter are, under most circumstances, not; the principle of double effect and double intent, outlining when the killing of noncombatants is morally permissible; the principle of due care and due risk, which describes how combatants must assume risk in executing combat actions, thus providing due care for the rights of the innocent who might be caught up in the

fighting; and the principle of proportionality, which dictates that soldiers use only proportionate force against legitimate targets. The net
result of the equal applicability of these *jus in bello* principles is a "moral
equality of soldiers," which, as Jeff McMahan puts it in *Killing in War,*
produces a belief that no one does wrong or acts impermissibly merely
by fighting in a war—even an unjust one.[6] McMahan presents powerful challenges to this traditional approach.

McMahan examines the details of the moral arguments that under-
gird the intuition that a just war can be fought unjustly and an unjust
war fought justly. His analysis drives to the very heart of traditional just
war theory, a theory that uses the individual rights of life and liberty as
well as the communal dimension of these rights, political sovereignty,
and territorial integrity as the ultimate moral foundation of *jus ad bellum* and *jus in bello.* Those who are rightly liable to attack have no right
of defense, McMahan explains. He argues that this is true in relations
among individuals not only in civil society but also in war. By engaging in morally justified self- and other defense, soldiers do nothing to
forfeit their right not to be attacked or killed. McMahan goes on to
say: "Even though just combatants are 'doing harm' and 'pose a danger
to other people' . . . , they do not thereby become legitimate targets of
attack." Why? Because, like police officers, they are not subject to justified attack, even in self-defense. McMahan admits to exceptions to his
new rule—just combatants who pursue their cause by impermissible
means—and he admits that it is morally important to get unjust combatants to exercise restraint in their military operations.[7] His analysis
shows, however, the inadequacy of the arguments traditionally used in
just war theory to explain how classes of people—soldiers of either side
in a war—can lose their rights against deliberate attack and become
liable to be attacked.

McMahan admits that this is a perplexing conclusion with respect
to the intuitions of traditional just war theory. He examines proportionality, discrimination, supreme emergency, and other principles and
concepts commonly accepted among traditional just war theorists, and
he comes to equally perplexing—although powerfully convincing—
conclusions. In the end, he rejects the idea of the moral equality of soldiers and presents an alternative, responsibility-based understanding of
what it means to be liable to attack. In that process, he hopes to deepen

"our understanding of the morality of participation in war" and provide a moral framework for soldiers and others to use before signing up to fight in a war.[8]

Traditional just war theory also contains the *jus in bello* principle of due care and due risk, which holds that soldiers and commanders must assume risk to safeguard civilians. This "trade-off" of risk, David Luban says in "Risk Taking and Force Protection," is even more pronounced when the fighting is between "regular forces with superior technology and non-state adversaries who live, work, and fight in the midst of civilians."[9] Luban recognizes that the traditional principles of *jus in bello* provide no direct answer to the questions of how much risk, or how much care, or how to balance the two. In fact, in *Just and Unjust Wars*, Walzer admits that the laws of war say nothing about the degree of care to be provided to civilians and the amount of risk to be incurred by soldiers.[10] Luban initiates, therefore, a detailed analysis of the morality of risk transfer.

Luban argues for the general principle, If a person A is creating a risk for another, innocent person B, A may not transfer that risk to B or other innocents. He then uses this general principle to investigate a variety of risk-transfer situations between two poles. At one pole, there is zero risk to soldiers, and all risk is transferred to civilians; at the other pole, the soldier accepts so much risk that he is certain to die and the legitimate military action is certain to fail. Luban seeks to establish the minimum standard of acceptable care soldiers owe civilians—whether the civilians are "enemy" or "their own."[11]

In the end, Luban concludes, with Walzer, that "no precise answer can be given to the 'how much risk?' question," but, en route to that conclusion, he adds clarity to the traditional *jus in bello* principle. Force protection, he agrees, is a concrete and direct military advantage. Protecting a soldier's "asset value," however, does not outweigh the moral requirement for soldiers to provide the minimum standard of care even to enemy civilians.[12]

America's post-9/11 wars have also highlighted a glaring deficiency inherent in the traditional approach of dividing just war theory into two parts: *jus ad bellum*, which focuses on the justice of going to war, and *jus in bello*, which covers justice in the conduct of war. Left out, Brian Orend reminds us in *The Morality of War*, is *jus post bellum*—

the issue of justice after a war. Orend rightly points out that sticking
only to the two traditional parts of just war theory is "a decrepit state
of affairs that must be remedied, both for conceptual and concrete historical reasons."[13]

Orend suggests that, at a minimum, a proper account of *jus post bellum* would include analyses of what an "ethical end state" might consist
of and of what are just ends for a war. Also included must be some discussion of discrimination and proportionality with respect to postwar
sanctions, punishments, or compensations as well as a proper understanding of what military and political rehabilitation of the aggressor
state actually entails. Orend demonstrates, too, that a complete account
of *jus post bellum* would necessarily include an understanding of war-
crimes trials and the responsibilities not only of soldiers and their leaders but also of heads of state and collective political bodies. He provides
at least a first cut at each of the elements he believes should be part of
jus post bellum.

That first cut goes a long way toward sketching out a general blueprint for postwar justice. Orend then looks at several historical examples and includes a discussion of when regime change is justified and
how "rights-violating aggressor regimes" might be transformed.[14] Mona
Fixdal goes a bit further in *Just Peace*, although she too admits that
her work is far from a blueprint or design. Rather, she hopes only to
"untangle" the elements of peace and justice that, ultimately, make up
any judgment of a war's outcome. "Although recent years have seen
somewhat of a proliferation of discussion of this topic," Fixdal says, "it
is fair to say that *jus post bellum* is still largely ignored."[15]

Nancy Sherman's focus on *jus post bellum* is from a completely different perspective from Orend's and Fixdal's. Her start point concerns
"how soldiers themselves, in their most reflective, personal, and sometimes anguished moments, experience war as a moral enterprise and
hold themselves accountable."[16] From here, she goes on to ask what a
nation owes its citizens-who-become-soldiers. She is seeking an answer
deeper than "thank you for your service" or the current public discussion of medical, institutional, and financial support for wounded
veterans.

Sherman does not diminish the importance of saying thank you,
providing continuing care for veterans, or identifying *jus post bellum*

principles that apply to states or other warring entities. She takes on, however, much more profound tasks: understanding the injuries war inherently causes to a person's moral sense and the implications of those injuries. In giving voice to "moral injury," she adds an important dimension to *jus post bellum*. She brings to the fore topics previously either left unsaid or spoken of only among veterans and a small handful of others. She pulls back the curtain of war and exposes us, the political community on whose behalf soldiers fight, to the moral injuries war necessarily produces.

Not satisfied with simply reminding us of our communal responsibility toward those whom we send to fight for us, Sherman combines her training in both psychology and philosophy to describe approaches to moral healing. Self-empathy, self-forgiveness, reexperiencing troubling wartime events, and reenvisioning one's moral frameworks are several of the ways in which postwar moral reparative work gets done. She also examines the roles of trust, resentment, betrayal, hope, meaning, and purpose in healing the soldier's soul. She also examines the role that a network of relationships (one's community)—the very network that is injured by alienation and separateness—plays in each of these healing processes.

These are brief illustrations of just a few of the central issues being examined, but they show that the update to traditional just war theory is an active field for moral philosophers and that the discussion is far from finished. My purpose in this book, however, is not to enter any of these debates, for these are being thoroughly examined by others.

Rather, I want to identify yet another deficiency in traditional just war theory. What follows is an argument for a new addition to *jus in bello*. Current just war theory omits a major part of the conduct of war. Just war theorists have overly restricted the conduct of war to fighting—war's tactical dimension—in their treatment of *jus in bello*. Fighting—what happens in combat and as a result of combat—is the most visible aspect of war's conduct. The conduct of war, however, involves more than fighting. War is also conducted at the strategic level, the level at which senior political and military leaders set war aims, identify strategies and policies and conduct campaigns to achieve those aims, and establish the coordinative bodies necessary to translate plans into actions. This strategic level of war has a direct effect on how a war is fought, how long that war lasts, and whether the lives used and risked in it are used well and risked appropriately. Yet few—if any—accounts of *jus in bello* consider its strategic dimension.

The Gap in Traditional *Jus in Bello*

The discussion presented thus far builds on the continuing influential work done by Michael Walzer in *Just and Unjust Wars* and his other writings on war. As Brian Orend points out: "Walzer's *Just and Unjust Wars*, of 1977, remains the breakthrough work of that decade, directly inspired by Vietnam. It's not much of an exaggeration to say this work has been to current just war theory what Grotius's *The Laws of War and Peace* was to prior centuries."[17] I will use the same start point.

What initially motivated Walzer to delve into just war theory was political activism, not moral philosophy. He thought that, even though there was a rich tradition in just war theory, Americans in the 1960s and 1970s were insufficiently prepared to understand and use it because of "an education which taught . . . [that morality] had no proper descriptive use and no objective meaning." So he set out to show that there is a structure—a language and a logic—to the ways in which citizens, soldiers, and political leaders talk about war's moral dimension. This structure, he demonstrates, is evident in the ways in which those responsible for the conduct of war justify and explain their actions and the ways in which those judging their conduct argue.[18] The structure of his theory remains in place and has provided the framework for much of the moral thinking about America's post-9/11 wars.

Some moral philosophers who have written since 9/11 amplify or provide further explanation of Walzer's principles. Others have been critical, pointing to areas where Walzer has been incomplete, inconsistent, or incorrect. They then provide alternatives to his approaches. This body of work has advanced our understanding of the moral dimension of war. It has, however, missed an important gap in Walzer's approach to *jus in bello,* a gap that results from overly restricting the conduct of war to fighting.

Fighting—combat and the result of combat—takes place within the context of political and military strategy. In fact, individual battles and engagements gain their meaning only relative to campaign objectives and the political war aims that campaigns help achieve. War aims, strategies, and the policies and the associated campaigns necessary to execute strategies and achieve war aims are devised and promulgated by senior political and military leaders. The strategic dimension of war's conduct includes weaving both military and nonmilitary elements of national power together into a coherent whole. Further, strategies, policies, and campaigns must be translated into action. This translation occurs through the effective use of both the military chain of command and the machinery of civil and military bureaucracies. Fighting a war concerns the tactical dimension of war's conduct; waging a war concerns the conduct of war's strategic dimension.

The invasion of North Africa during World War II is a clear example of the gap that I am talking about.

A World War II Illustration

The decision to invade North Africa in 1942 emerged from extended correspondence, dialogue, debate, and argument among four key figures—President Franklin D. Roosevelt, Prime Minister Winston Churchill, General George C. Marshall, and General Sir Alan Brooke—as well as the bureaucracies, staffs, and subordinates serving each. Although informed and shaped by military factors, that decision was, in the final analysis, made—and correctly so—as much on the basis of political considerations as on military considerations.

The context of this decision is important. In 1942, the war was not going well for the Allies. Western Europe was under Nazi occupation, and the Japanese were on the offensive in the Pacific. In January, the Japanese invasion of the Philippines forced the withdrawal of American forces toward Bataan. The Japanese laid siege to the Bataan Peninsula and cut off all help and supplies.[19] Their success in Malaya forced the withdrawal toward Singapore and the eventual surrender in February of the British. By April, American forces in the Philippines had surrendered to the Japanese, who also forced the British to withdraw from Burma into India. In June 1942, the German army's Africa Corps pushed British forces out of Libya and threatened Egypt. That same month, nearly two hundred German divisions invaded the Soviet Union. Within a day, their attacks had demolished one-quarter of the Soviets' air forces. Within four months, the Germans had occupied 600,000 square miles of Russian soil, captured three million Red Army troops, and closed within sixty-five miles of Moscow.[20] The Soviet Union was on the ropes.

When Germany invaded Russia, the United States was fighting in the Pacific but not yet in Europe. The defeats Russia suffered gave rise to a powerful movement for a second front that would return the Allies to the Continent and draw German troops from the Russian front.[21] Great Britain ultimately won the air battle over its skies but did not have the capacity to create a second front alone, nor were the conditions ripe for a successful Allied invasion of the Continent. Whether a second front would be undertaken—when, where, by whom, and under whose command—ultimately became decisions facing President Roosevelt, Prime Minister Churchill, and Generals Marshall and Brooke.

Soon after Pearl Harbor, December 1941, the Americans and British met in Washington. US military leaders wanted to invade Europe in 1942. "We've got to get to Europe and fight," wrote General Eisenhower in January 1942, "and we've got to quit wasting resources all over the world—and worse—wasting time."[22] The United States was thinking about an invasion of Europe in two phases: first, a buildup of troops and materiel in England; then, an invasion to seize Antwerp followed by a move east toward Berlin. Both the British prime minister and his chiefs of staff opposed such a course, believing—correctly as it turned out—that a 1942 invasion of Europe would be folly. As the historian John Keegan puts it: "Churchill feared the [early] Second Front [in Europe] because it would succeed only if it was launched in such overwhelming force . . . that the Atlantic Wall and its defenders would be crushed by the impact; and he knew that neither the force nor the support would be available in 1942."[23] After several months of active analysis, intense and sometimes acrimonious debate, aboveboard and behind-the-scenes maneuvering, contentious reanalysis, and final argument, the four key leaders decided to delay a direct invasion of Europe in favor of an invasion of and subsequent campaign in North Africa.

Roosevelt ultimately cast the deciding vote when he realized that an invasion of Europe was not actually possible in 1942 but that some action was both militarily and politically necessary that year. So, in mid-July, active planning and preparation of forces, shipping, equipment, and supplies for an invasion of North Africa began. The invasion took place in November 1942.[24] "The rationale for the president's decision," Williamson Murray and Allan Millett report in *A War to Be Won*, "stemmed from domestic politics. The United States had to involve its forces in combat with the Germans in 1942 or else the political pressures for a 'Japan First' strategy might become intolerable."[25]

This individual decision took place within the context of other, even broader strategic discussions and decisions among the four key civil-military leaders. In March 1941, after fourteen sessions in Washington over two months, American and British planners agreed to the strategy that would be adopted in the event of the United States entering the war. Germany would be defeated first, Allied interests in the Mediterranean would be maintained, and the Pacific Theater would stay on the defensive until victory was secured in the West.[26] Over the following years, there would be subsequent debates over exact priorities, operational and logistic, and how active the defense in the Pacific would be, but the general outline of this strategy held throughout the war.

How to react, what would be the overall war aims and strategies, where and how to begin counteroffensives, and what priorities to establish in terms of personnel, force size and composition, logistics, and manufacturing, all these were decisions that Roosevelt and Churchill had to make. All were decisions that had both domestic and international consequences. None were solely military decisions. The fate of nations was at stake. Each political leader needed the advice of his senior military leaders, Marshall and Brooke, but, in the end, each had responsibility for these decisions. In *Masters and Commanders*, Andrew Roberts sums it up this way: "Each of the four men was strong willed, tough minded and certain he knew the best way to win the war. Yet, in order to get his strategy adopted, each needed at least two of the other three. Occasionally the politicians would side together against the soldiers, and vice versa."[27] The decisions to demand unconditional surrender, use the United States as the industrial base, place the defeat of Germany ahead of that of Japan, and begin with a campaign in North Africa exemplify, like so many others of World War II, final, strategic, war-waging decisions that rightfully lay with the political leadership.

While final decision authority rests on a very small group—sometimes a single individual—decisions of this magnitude are preceded by detailed analysis of alternatives, feasibility studies, and reams of paper reflecting the arguments that had been conducted by numerous committees and study groups as well as subordinate organizations and staff agencies. The quality of the final decisions often reflected the quality of the preparatory work. Adequate organizational capacity matters. Finally, decisions must be executed and adapted as the war unfolds. Execution and adaptation require that civil and military bureaucracies work together well enough to carry out the decisions made, then alter those initial decisions, if necessary, as opportunities and/or obstacles arise. In a very real way, therefore, it is a set of senior political and military leaders who share responsibility for war-waging decisions and actions. The reality of war is not, as Walzer presents it, a line "between the war itself, for which soldiers are not responsible, and the conduct of the war, for which they are responsible."[28] Rather, war-waging decisions are examples of the shared responsibilities associated with those senior civil and military leaders who contribute to the dialogue concerning war aims, strategies, policies, military campaigns, and nonmilitary activities that are all means toward achieving the declared aims.

Roosevelt, Churchill, Marshall, and Brooke had to create new organizations and processes to prepare them for their personal dialogue and the decisions that flowed from it as well as supervise the execution of those decisions. Two of these organizations were the Joint Staff Mission and the Combined Chiefs of Staff. The Joint Staff Mission was located in Washington, DC, and consisted of members of the British and US chiefs of staff. It became the forum in which the British chiefs were represented in regular meetings with their American counterparts. In October 1941, the mission was staffed with about two hundred military personnel. By the end of the war, it had grown to no fewer than three thousand personnel. The Combined Chiefs of Staff—US and British—was an instrument designed to create close cooperation and direct Anglo-American strategy until the war's end.[29] Other combined organizations and command structures were created as requirements emerged.

For example, Roosevelt created several new agencies: the National Defense Advisory Commission (spring 1940); the Office of Production

Management (winter 1940–1941); and the Supply Priorities and Allocations Board (summer 1941). This group of agencies was to acquire raw materials, set production targets, let out contracts, and estimate the requirements of various national efforts as well as their sequence and priority.[30]

Marshall also had organizational work to do internal to the War Department. The bureaucracy that he inherited in the department was simply incapable of efficient and effective action. He knew that the United States would have to raise an army and expand the army air corps as well as build a navy capable of global operations. In the early part of 1940, for example, the year of the German blitzkrieg, the American army was antique enough. There were only two regular divisions in the continental United States that could be said to be reasonably ready for combat. One was traditional horse cavalry, the other an infantry division. Both were under Eighth Corps headquarters in Texas to guard against trouble spilling across the Rio Grande.[31] Marshall also knew that the policies of conscription, troop and industrial mobilization, and pace and prioritization of industrial production and distribution would require not only changes to the nonmilitary government departments but also those departments' close coordination with the War Department. The president directed many of these changes in the years leading up to and immediately following US involvement in World War II.[32]

Marshall's assessment was that the War Department's planning and coordinating organization had lost track of the purpose of its existence. It had become a huge, bureaucratic, red-tape-ridden operating agency. It slowed down everything. The changes were sudden, massive, and radical. Marshall downgraded general staff positions, eliminated chiefs of arms, subordinated formerly independent organizations to the chiefs of staff, and abolished a number of headquarters all together. In less than a week, he had his recommendations, but such changes had political implications, and the decisions were not just his to make, so he explained them to the secretary of war, who gave his approval. A few days later, the president put the changes into effect by executive order. The pressure of war and the shock of Pearl Harbor made it possible to stifle the heated protests of the officers whose authority was being eliminated or sharply curtailed. Only because he believed that ruthless changes were vital to the effective waging of war did Marshall demand the immediate adoption of a program that might otherwise have been debated for months.[33]

Like the "Europe-first" strategy of World War II, the "don't involve China" strategy of the Korean War, the "stop communism in Southeast Asia" strategy in Vietnam, the "handover to Iraqi control" strategy of 2003–2007, and the debate over a counterterrorist or counterinsurgency strategy in Afghanistan that started in 2008 are all examples of civil-military decisions where the military advice of a select number of senior generals played an important role but political considerations often outweighed or modified purely military factors. Military factors play an essential part in making these kinds of decisions, as do nonmilitary factors. The final decisions rightfully fall to political leaders since decisions concerning strategies and campaigns are a far cry from solely military activities.

In World War II, war aims and strategy as well as the policies associated with industrial capacity and priorities, logistic preparedness, industrial and personnel mobilization plans, and domestic and Allied organizational effectiveness in execution all fell within the realm of civil-military shared war-waging responsibility. All had a direct effect on how the war was fought. Fighting—the tactical dimension of war's conduct—takes place within war's strategic, war-waging context.

The history of World War II shows that decisions made at the strategic level have consequences. They either increase or decrease the probability of success in war, increase or decrease war's duration, increase or decrease the probability that lives will be well used or wasted. None of the foregoing World War II decisions were easy, nor were they perfectly conceived and executed. All, however, were the result of continual, often heated, civil-military exchanges. All included reasonable alternatives. Many initial decisions needed modifications to adapt to the dynamics of war. Further, all needed both military and government mechanisms—organizations and processes—to increase the quality of final decisions and translate plans into action. Furthermore, all illustrate that *jus in bello* has at least two dimensions: a tactical dimension, which concerns fighting a war, and a strategic dimension, which concerns waging a war.

These two dimensions could have been equally illustrated by the campaign to break out of the Pusan Perimeter and conduct the Inchon landing in Korea, the air campaign against North Vietnam, and the decisions to surge in Iraq in 2007 and Afghanistan in 2009. For each of these are examples of decisions that commit significant resources of a nation—troops, funds, supplies, and equipment as well as political capital. Each is also an example of civil-military decisions where political considerations sometimes outweighed military factors and political leaders rightly held the final decision authority. Further, each had a significant impact on the conduct of war.

War's Reality and Its Associated Theory of Responsibility

In some ways, the omission of an account of *jus in bello*'s strategic dimension and the gap that results from this omission are understandable. They begin with a common misunderstanding of war's conduct and end with an equally common and misconstrued theory of responsibility. Following the conventional understanding of war's conduct—that war equals fighting—Walzer draws a line "between the war itself, for which soldiers are not responsible, and the conduct of the war, for which they are responsible," a line that Orend reinforces and the authors of *The Law of Armed Conflict* follow.[34]

Walzer, representing traditional just war theory, uses this line to separate *jus ad bellum*, or matters concerning the justice of the war itself, which is the realm of political responsibility, from *jus in bello*, or matters concerning the justice of the conduct of war, which is the realm of military responsibility. This stark separation of responsibilities does not correspond to the realities of conducting a war, where, as we have seen, responsibilities are twofold, fighting and waging. The war-waging dimension demonstrates that political leaders have responsibilities in the conduct of war and, therefore, that just war theory's *jus in bello* should include an account of these responsibilities.

War springs from political purpose, political goals form war's aim, and violent force is an important means by which to attain that aim—these propositions are basic to the understanding of war.[35] The military and nonmilitary means of war cannot be understood in isolation from the political purpose. Waging war is, therefore, essentially a political *and* a military act; it is neither solely military nor solely political, especially in democratic nations.

In drawing his line between war and its conduct as he does, Walzer employs the traditional view that strategy, war policy, and military operations are aligned by civilian leaders deciding to go to war, with generals and other officers conducting that war. Such strict role differentiation is too simplistic and results in a gap not only in his treatment of *jus in bello,* but also in his theory of responsibility. Not recognizing that the conduct of war includes more than fighting, he leaves out the mutually related responsibilities among those senior civil and military leaders who must wage war—that is, the responsibility to figure out war aims, identify and promulgate war strategies and policies, ensure that military and nonmilitary campaigns are means toward the declared aims, and make both civil and military bureaucracies work well enough that they help achieve the aims set.

Generals, by themselves, simply do not "plan and organize campaigns" and "decide on strategy," as Walzer believes. Nor do all generals, as he holds, "straddle the line" between those responsible for the war itself and those responsible for the conduct of war.[36] Both claims are overstated. The reality of war is that strategies, policies, and campaigns are civil-military decisions that require a robust and continual interaction between selected senior political leaders and generals.

Some generals do straddle the line between officers and political leaders, but some do not. The distinguishing marks are often rank and position. Some generals have as little to do with the war itself as do common soldiers or other officers. Others have significant input into consequential decisions as to war policy. In World War II, for example, General Eisenhower certainly did straddle the line, but Brigadier General Darby, who led a regiment of rangers and was responsible solely for successful tactical operations, did not. Generals MacArthur and Ridgway straddled the line during the Korean War, but the commanding generals of the various infantry divisions who fought the war did not. The same is true of Generals Westmoreland and Abrams in Vietnam and their subordinate combat division commanding generals. Generals Casey and Petraeus in Iraq and Generals McNeill, McKiernon, and McChrystal in Afghanistan also straddled this line, but the generals commanding tactical troops in the various provinces of both countries did not. The distinction has moral consequences. Those generals who have significant input into consequential war-waging decisions have responsibilities different from those of generals who do not.[37]

In some senses, Walzer seems to grasp this distinction among general officers. In his discussion of the Nuremberg trials and of the Vietnam War, for example, he lays the responsibility for war policy decisions not only on heads of state but also on inner circles of advisers—those who play a major role in making or executing strategy and policy—and a nation's foreign policy elite.[38] Some generals may be in this inner circle, but not all are.

In sum, however, Walzer's theory of responsibility concerning generals is inadequate. First, it is factually inaccurate, for the final authority for those decisions that Walzer attributes to generals actually lies with political leaders. Second, not all generals are alike. Some are involved in decisions of strategy, campaigns, and policy; others are not. Third, Walzer omits in his theory of responsibility any recognition of the ongoing, mutual dialogue necessary to align war aims, strategy, policy, military campaigns, and other related nonmilitary operations. Nor does his theory address the positional responsibilities of those who are, or should be, in this dialogue, responsibilities that "significantly affect the interests of others"—life, death, the protection of the innocent, and the protection of the political community—and result from the voluntary assumption of morally relevant roles.[39] Finally, his account of generals does not discuss their part of the responsibility to translate aims, strategies, and policies into action.

These inadequacies emerge both from the strict role differentiation that derives from drawing too firm of a line between the war itself and the conduct of war and from addressing the conduct of war from only its tactical dimension. Inadequacies emerge again in Walzer's account of the wartime responsibilities of political leaders.

Walzer holds political leaders responsible for three major wartime decisions. First, governments decide to go to war. Whether the war is aggressive or defensive, whether a justified intervention or not, preventative or preemptive, the decision to go to war is, according to Walzer, one of the burdens of political office.[40] Second, governments can be held responsible if they establish policies that result in war crimes.[41] Third, political leaders decide whether their states face a supreme emergency, a rare condition that would temporarily justify overriding the rules of war.[42] The first responsibility that Walzer presents concerns *jus ad bellum*. The second and third concern *jus in bello*. As the World War II example offered above demonstrated, however, some political leaders have a wider role in the conduct of war.

Political leaders do not, as the conventional view Walzer employs suggests, just decide to go to war, then hand off the responsibility to conduct that war to generals. At least some subset of political leaders sets war aims—the goals or objectives that give war its purpose. These political leaders also establish strategies and policies governing the conduct of the war—strategies and policies necessary to mobilize the political, economic, diplomatic, industrial, psychological, fiscal, and logistic resources necessary to achieve the war aims and conduct military campaigns. They also have responsibilities for policies that govern actions following the termination of major hostilities, responsibilities that sometimes include fighting—policies of occupation, temporary guardianship of a conquered nation, or other political arrangements that may result from active combat. Further, they are also coresponsible for the quality of the dialogue among senior civil and military leaders that affects the war's aim as well as the strategies and policies that govern that war.

Finally, executing policies—whether those associated with *jus ad bellum, jus in bello,* or *jus post bellum*—requires a government that is sufficiently capable of generating and orchestrating the military and nonmilitary means available in ways that increase the probability of success. Winning a war—as defined by achieving the strategic aims of a war or some other employment of military force—requires that political leaders make their governments work well enough to succeed. This responsibility is embedded in the claim that a state has a right to win wars it is forced to fight. As Walzer notes: "When soldiers believe themselves to be fighting against aggression, war is no longer a condition to be endured. It is a crime they can resist. . . . And once one is fighting for purposes of this sort, it becomes terribly important to win."[43] Of course, a state cannot do anything to win—moral limits are spelled out in the war convention and rules of war—but inherent in the right to win are two key assumptions: first, that one has the military and nonmilitary means to win, and, second, that a government has the capacity to use those means efficiently and effectively enough to win. "Lyndon Johnson and Robert McNamara failed as war leaders," explains Eliot Cohen, "not so much because they micro-managed the war, but because they failed to manage it properly."[44]

Conclusions: A Search for Understanding and Clarity

Just war theory is a theory of practical morality applied in the most complex of human activities. War is the realm of ambiguity, whether for the soldiers and their military leaders who are fighting it or for the senior political and military leaders who are waging it. Decisions and actions, again whether tactical or strategic, are often taken under conditions of near extreme uncertainty. Those whose responsibility it is to decide and act—from soldiers and their immediate military leaders to senior generals and political officials—often do not have the luxury of time or anything close to complete information or understanding. Under fire, soldiers sometimes stare at their sergeants and lieutenants for what seems eternal seconds awaiting orders. The battlefield rarely provides the time to get more information, to reflect a bit longer, or to understand more completely. For a different set of reasons, time is often not on the side of senior political leaders and generals either. Nor do these senior leaders have the information they would like to have before making important and consequential decisions. Mistakes, misjudgments, and misunderstandings are rife at both the tactical and the strategic levels. In every war, learning takes place at both the tactical and the strategic levels. Any practical morality and certainly a theory of responsibility designed to explain and guide the conduct of war—whether war fighting or war waging—must take into consideration these actual conditions in which moral agents decide and act. Equally certain, however, is this: the difficulty of conditions may mitigate responsibility, but it does not erase it.

American citizens, however, expect their leaders to account for their decisions and actions. American leaders, political and military, understand this. Explanation and justification—whether during a political campaign, before the media, in front of a congressional committee, at a memorial service with the family of a veteran killed in combat, or among those with whom one just fought—go with the territory of leadership.

Explanation and justification, however, first require understanding, and a complete understanding of the conduct of war reveals that *jus in bello* concerns more than "right conduct in the midst of battle, after the war has started," as Orend claims.[45] *Jus in bello* also has a larger, war-waging scope. Success in war is an outcome, partially related to what military units do in battle, but it is equally related to what senior political and military leaders do in their capital.[46] The absence of the strategic, war-waging dimension of *jus in bello* forms the gap in traditional just war theory.

Jus in bello must include not only the responsibilities of soldiers and their leaders in battle but also the responsibilities that senior political and military leaders have at the strategic level. These are the responsibilities to establish proper war aims, strategies, policies, and campaigns and set in place processes for cross–government department coordination as well as coordination among allies, methods to adjudicate conflicts in priorities, and procedures to ensure departmental support for important war policies meant to achieve sufficient unity of effort and coherence in action throughout the war. These responsibilities apply equally to planning and execution, for strategy fails as much in execution as it does in formulation.[47]

The standard is certainly not perfection, for every war is replete with examples of mistakes and missteps. Morality should demand, however, that there be some way to assess the number and frequency of mistakes made by those who wage war as well as the speed or slowness with which those who wage war learn and improve.

Soldier and leader responsibilities on the battlefield are clear. The immediacy of combat provides this clarity. Less clear because of the distance from the battlefield, but no less important, is the senior political and military leader's responsibility to get decisions concerning war aims, strategies, policies, and campaigns as right as possible, then execute those decisions sufficiently well and adapt as the war unfolds. The next chapter aims to make clear what the strategic level of waging war involves.

2

Describing *Jus in Bello*'s War-Waging Dimension

The American Civil War and the post-9/11 wars in Afghanistan and Iraq serve as good examples spotlighting the gap in the traditional just war theory account of *jus in bello*. Thus, they are clear windows through which we can see and understand strategic, war-waging responsibilities, responsibilities that are essential to conducting war but that lie far beyond fighting and "right conduct in the midst of battle." They are also useful in clarifying the central tension inherent in the strategic, war-waging dimension of war's conduct as tripartite: (1) achieving coherence by setting war aims and making strategy, policy, and campaign decisions that increase the probability of achieving those aims; (2) generating organizational capacity by translating those aims and decisions into action that achieves those aims at the least cost, in lives and resources, and the least risk to the innocent and to one's political community, then adapting decisions and actions as the vagaries of war unfold; and (3) maintaining legitimacy by doing all the foregoing while observing the war convention, sustaining public support of the war effort, and ensuring proper subordination of the military to civilian leadership.

Waging War in the American Civil War

"The Civil War was the first of the modern total wars, and the American democracy was almost totally unready to fight it," writes the historian T. Harry Williams. The same could be said of the US military at the time, for, at the start of the war, no officer—not even Robert E. Lee, whom both sides courted to lead their causes—was capable of efficiently administering and fighting a large army.[1] The outbreak of the Civil War found President Lincoln equally unprepared for his duties as a war president. Yet his success or failure as president and the very survival of the United States depended on how he performed his duties as commander in chief.[2] Lincoln worked hard to master his new role as a war president. What he learned and the actions he and his senior political and military leaders took as a result laid the foundation for the shared civil and military war-waging responsibilities that continue today—but that the traditional view of *jus in bello* omits.

While article 2, section 2, of the Constitution identifies the president as the commander in chief, the powers, responsibilities, and limitations of this role are not defined. Additionally, his role as commander in chief was, as Lincoln would learn, shared with Congress. Article 1, section 8, of the Constitution gave Congress the power to declare war; raise, fund, and regulate the army and the navy; and provide for the capture of enemy property.[3] Ultimately, Lincoln settled on five wartime functions to exercise his role as commander in chief. The Civil War historian James McPherson describes those functions as follows:

1. *Policy* refers to war aims—the political goals of the nation in a time of war.
2. *National Strategy* refers to mobilizing the political, economic, diplomatic, and psychological as well as military resources of the nation to achieve these war aims.
3. *Military Strategy* concerns plans for the employment of armed forces to win the war and fulfill the goals of policy.
4. *Operations* concerns the management and movement of armies in particular campaigns to carry out the purposes of military strategy.
5. *Tactics* refers to the formations and handling of an army in actual battle.[4]

Whether these five functions are exactly right is immaterial. They illustrate that the strict role differentiation between political and military

leaders in war that is used in traditional just war theory is inaccurate. Lincoln came to realize that the conduct of war included fighting
(tactics), but it also included more—policy, national strategy, military
strategy, and operations. Lincoln's five functions make clear that conducting war cannot be solely the concern of military leaders.

To conduct the Civil War, the Lincoln administration had to identify its war aims. Then, together with Congress, government departments and agencies, and the military leadership, it had to devise a
strategy—more accurately, a set of military and nonmilitary strategies—to attain those aims. Then it had to raise an army and navy
capable of victory and secure the funds to sustain that force. A special
session of Congress, held in July 1861, eventually authorized all the
emergency actions that Lincoln had taken, including calling up troops
and instituting a naval blockade of the South. In this session, Congress
appropriated funds to put 500,000 soldiers in the field. The Militia Act
of 1862 bolstered Union forces by allowing the president to employ
persons of African descent in military and naval service. Finally, the
Conscription Act of 1863 created the first draft in American history.

With respect to war aims, as Andrew Polsky notes in *Elusive Victories:* "Lincoln first established national preservation as the goal for
which the North would fight, putting aside the question of slavery. In
doing so, he chose the approach that plainly commanded the broad-
est public support. . . . Although Lincoln made the prudent choice at
the start, he faced a more difficult task in reevaluating war aims as the
conflict progressed."[5] By 1862, sentiments had changed, and the war
had evolved into a nation-rending struggle that few had anticipated.
An August 1862 letter that Senator John Sherman wrote to his brother
General William T. Sherman said as much: "A year ago men might have
faltered at the thought of proceeding to this extremity [but now] they
are in great measure prepared for it." Emancipation became a "military
necessity . . . to the preservation of the Union."[6] War aims changed
when the Emancipation Proclamation went into effect in 1863.

War costs money. As gold and silver coin became increasingly
scarce, the government's ability to finance the war was at risk. In addition to loans,[7] and again working with Congress, the Lincoln administration used the Legal Tender Act to create paper money. The act also
established the Internal Revenue Bureau within the Department of the

Treasury and levied a federal income tax for the first time in American history.[8]

War involves diplomacy. One of the main diplomatic efforts of the Civil War was designed to keep European powers from recognizing the South. The Confederate States tried to withhold cotton as an economic weapon. As one southern newspaper wrote: "Keep every bale of cotton on the plantation. Don't send a thread to New Orleans or Memphis till England and France have recognized the Confederacy." To counter the threat of recognition, one that would certainly have prolonged the war, the Union executed both a naval strategy of blockade and a diplomatic engagement strategy in London and Paris. British and French officials opined about the probable impact of a cotton famine. Textile magnates in Lancashire and Lyons forecast shutdowns, and British and French diplomats discussed the possibility of joint military action to lift the blockade.[9] As Doris Kearns Goodwin has noted: "History would give Secretary of State [William H.] Seward high marks for his role in preventing Britain and France from intervening in the war."[10]

War requires managerial capacity. The sheer scale of the Civil War was beyond any previous US military or political experience. Initial management efforts simply failed. Secretary of War Edwin M. Stanton came to realize that to wage a war as massive as the one he faced "everything had to be done systematically and in order." As if a harbinger of what President Franklin Roosevelt, Secretary of War Henry Stimson, and General George Marshall faced in World War II, some of the most important innovations of the Civil War concerned more efficient techniques, procedures, organizations, and processes to manage personnel and logistics and execute strategy.[11]

Stanton and his quartermaster general, Montgomery Meigs, put in place a number of new organizations and management procedures. For example, the War Board was created to help manage the broad undertaking demanded of the Civil War. Though an informal body, not functioning as a source of command, the War Board ultimately created a unity of effort that facilitated logistics; coordinated rail, water, and road transport as well as telegraph and industrial actions; and recommended priorities and strategies. In establishing this board and running it as he did, Stanton strengthened the administration of the Union war effort.

After he established the board, Stanton "gathered together the heads of several bureaus of the army 'to effect an *informal organization* for his own instruction, and in order . . . to bring to bear the whole power of the Government'" on the operations involved in the Civil War. This gathering included the adjutant general, the quartermaster general, the chief engineer, and the commissary general. The War Board and its informal committee of bureau heads facilitated control of and coordination in operations, often prescribing the strategy of particular campaigns. Following suit, Lincoln's secretary of the navy created several boards—the Navy Board, the Board of Strategy, and the Ironclad Board—to orchestrate the actions of the navy, the government, and private industry.[12]

None of these managerial innovations worked immediately, and none worked perfectly. They did, however, contribute significantly to translating aims, strategies, policies, and campaigns into action, and they helped the civil and military bureaucracies adapt to both opportunities and obstacles that emerged as the Civil War unfolded. Thus, they helped make Lincoln's government work well enough toward his common goal—that is, at least better than the Confederate government. In sum, the Union developed the superior managerial talent to mobilize and organize its resources for victory in the modern industrialized conflict that the Civil War became.[13] In *How the North Won*, Herman Hattaway and Archer Jones agree. Effective civil and military leadership, efficient civil and military staffs, and innovative management of both the military and the civil dimensions of the overall war effort—all were key to Lincoln's success.[14]

War, at least when waged by a democracy, requires legitimacy. Lincoln understood that, if he were to attain his war aims, his decisions concerning strategy and military operations had to be made with "a keen awareness of their political implications." He had to come to grips with maintaining the war's legitimacy among a variety of political factions, competing views, geographic regions, and ethnic constituencies.[15] For example: "Lincoln appointed 'political generals' whose chief recommendation was their prominence as politicians or as leaders of . . . ethnic communities. The rationale . . . was . . . to mobilize maximum support and recruitment for the war."[16] Of course, some of the political generals' inability to command caused problems, but, recognizing the strategic value of their service in generating and sustaining popular support for the war, the president found ways to work around these problems.

Sustaining public support was a daunting challenge in the face of heavy losses and battlefield setbacks. Morale slumped in the wake of defeats.[17] Following the 1861 Union defeat in the Battle of First Manassas came the failure of General George B. McClellan's Peninsula Campaign, which started in May 1862 and ended with a Confederate victory in the Battle of Seven Days. Then came Jackson's success in his Shenandoah Valley Campaign and the Union defeats in the Battle of Second Manassas in August 1862 and Fredericksburg in December 1862. All were shocks to the North's resolve. Its success at Antietam in September 1862 helped dissuade the French and British from recognizing the Confederacy and, thus, provided some hope to the Lincoln administration.[18]

Success in the battle of Antietam—even though the North let Lee's army escape destruction—and Grant's initial progress along the Tennessee, Cumberland, and Mississippi Rivers were bright spots in an otherwise dim year of fighting. In general, 1862 brought the Union high casualties and little progress toward success, putting the legitimacy of the war at risk. In fact, part of the rationale for the 1862 Emancipation Proclamation was to bolster support for the war. The twin Confederate defeats in the summer of 1863 at Vicksburg and Gettysburg and the beginning of the final set of campaigns that began in the spring of 1864 increased northern support for the war. Even then, however, Lincoln had to attend to the relationship among support for the war, casualties, and progress. Union troops, fresh from the Gettysburg battlefield, for example, had to rush to New York City to help quell draft riots in July 1863.

Lincoln's reelection was in doubt following the 1864 spring and summer battles of the Wilderness, Spotsylvania, and Cold Harbor, where Union casualties were very high. During three months in the summer of 1864, for example, over 65,000 Union soldiers were killed, wounded, or missing in action—compared to the 108,000 Union casualties in the first three years of the war.[19] Support of the war in the face of such losses became an open question. As McPherson notes: "Financial markets were pessimistic. . . . A Union general home on sick leave found 'great discouragement over the North, great reluctance to recruiting, [and] strong disposition for peace.' Democrats began to denounce Grant as a 'butcher.'"[20] Later in 1864, when Richmond was under siege, Lee's army was nearly surrounded, and Sherman's march to the sea was under way, progress toward ultimate victory was in sight. The president was reelected, and support for the war was never again a major issue.

At the start of the war, Lincoln deferred to General Winfield Scott, hero of both the War of 1812 and the Mexican War. Quickly, he found Scott wanting and replaced him with McClellan. He also deferred initially to McClellan, with disappointing results. Deference was perhaps the natural result of the president acknowledging his own inadequate understanding of what it took to wage war and the experiences his generals had or appeared to have had. In short order, however, he learned—especially in the dark days of 1862—that he could not merely hand over the war to his generals. In fact, it was early that year, in January 1862, that he came to believe that the best approach to Union military success was by simultaneous advances throughout all the theaters of the war.[21] The results of 1862 only confirmed his belief: battles and campaigns had to be means toward achieving his administration's political ends. Further, battles and campaigns had political costs. Thus, Lincoln learned that neither policy nor national strategy could be separated from military strategy, operations, and tactics—all had to form a coherent whole.[22]

In attempting to find a general who was capable of executing his simultaneous advance strategy, Lincoln was sequentially let down by Henry W. Halleck, Don Carlos Buell, John Pope, Ambrose E. Burnside, Joseph Hooker, and William Rosencrans, but he never deferred again. Even after he discovered Ulysses S. Grant, a commander who was capable of executing that strategy and in whom he could place significant trust and responsibility, never to be disappointed, he kept his hand on the pulse of military strategy and operations.[23] He visited the front often, as he did military hospitals; he received reports from his own agents in military commands, like Charles Dana, who was placed in Grant's headquarters; and he corresponded with his commanders frequently by letter and telegraph. Monitoring execution became part of his repertoire of leadership behaviors.

The president's personal leadership behavior, the managerial and organizational innovations of his secretaries, his work with Congress, his discussion with senior military commanders and staff officers, and the mechanisms Lincoln put in place to ensure he benefited from a robust dialogue that included asking "hard questions about the assumptions behind strategy, whether war goals were appropriate and can be achieved, how much progress has been made, and more"[24]— all demonstrate two essential elements in the war-waging dimensions of conducting war: first, creating a cooperative civil-military effort in order to devise appropriate war aims, adequate policy, proper strategies, and correctly aimed campaigns; and, second, an equally cooperative and important effort to ensure that policy and strategy are executed and adapted as the war unfolds. Without both, his aim to preserve the Union would not have been achieved, and the lives and resources used in waging that war would have been wasted. Lincoln did not come to office fully understanding what it meant to conduct war, but the reality of being a war president taught him quickly that conducting a war involves more than fighting; it also involves waging war, and this second dimension of conducting war is an inherently civil-military responsibility.

Conducting war, Lincoln, his cabinet, and his generals found, is both a complex and a serious endeavor. Complexity emerges from several areas. Wartime success requires constant balancing and rebalancing war ends, strategies, and policies with the use of military forces on the battlefield and nonmilitary diplomatic and political actions. It is also complex because in war few things are static, opportunities come and go, the enemy actively attempts to foil plans, obstacles arise, and domestic and international situations affecting the various strategies required in war ebb and flow. Lincoln also found that the need to sustain the legitimacy of the war in the eyes of the public required having the right war aims and making progress toward those aims, another dimension of war's complexity. Finally, war's complexity is seen in the nature of making decisions and taking action.

While Lincoln may have been the final decider, he could neither figure out the Rubik's Cube of war nor supervise the execution of war alone. As Andrew J. Polsky reminds us: "No president leads alone in wartime, and Lincoln's effectiveness depended a great deal on others."[25]

Decision and action in war demand a constant civil-military dialogue and constant coordination between civil and military bureaucracies. Constructing a set of sufficiently coherent strategies is one thing; executing those strategies and adapting them as conditions change is quite another. In both, Lincoln required civil and military organizations and processes to help him decide and execute. He knew how to control the processes that surrounded him, and he knew how to lead. He emerged, as Doris Kearns Goodwin says, not only the commander in chief but also "the captain of [a] most unusual cabinet."[26]

Lincoln also learned, as succeeding presidents would, that war is far from the sterile chess game that some envision it as. In fact, it is no game at all. Life and death are inherently involved—not just of enemy combatants, but also of the American citizens-who-become-soldiers,[27] of the innocent, friendly and enemy, and sometimes of political communities. As the president said at Gettysburg: "It is rather for us to be here dedicated to the great task remaining before us—that from these honored dead we take increased devotion to that cause for which they gave the last full measure of devotion—that we here highly resolve that these dead shall not have died in vain—that this nation, under God, shall have a new birth of freedom—and that government of the people, by the people, for the people shall not perish from the earth."[28]

Poor war aims, strategies, and policies, badly thought-through campaigns and major operations, and inefficient and ineffective civil-military dialogue and execution can join to prolong a war unnecessarily, decreasing the probability of success, and, thereby, increasing the probability of risking the lives of the innocent and the life of the political community unnecessarily as well as wasting the lives of soldiers and national treasure on a scale much larger than that of the fighting itself. When a soldier errs, the cost in lives may be counted in the dozens. When a commanding general errs, that count may extend to the thousands or more—even tens of thousands, as in the case of several Civil War battles, or hundreds of thousands, as was the case in World War I. When senior political and military leaders get war aims, strategies, and policies wrong or decide on those that cannot be executed by the associated military and civil bureaucracies with sufficient effectiveness, the fiscal price and human costs—individual and communal—can be even more staggering.

In traditional just war theory, *jus in bello* is governed by principles that emerge from the tension between winning and fighting well, the two competing responsibilities of soldiers and their military leaders. These principles and the tension from which they flow govern moral behavior while fighting and describe the tactical aspect of *jus in bello*. They are a necessary part of just war theory, but alone they are not sufficient. Right conduct in war also has a strategic dimension, the war-waging responsibilities described in the Civil War case and the example from World War II in the previous chapter. In this dimension, traditional just war theory is deficient, for it holds that political leaders are responsible for the war itself and that military leaders are responsible for the conduct of war. Lincoln would have found this distinction not just unhelpful but also factually incorrect.

The moral issues associated with the strategic dimension of *jus in bello*, Lincoln, his cabinet, and his generals would find, result from a tension among three competing responsibilities associated with senior political and military leadership. As mentioned, these include the following: First, achieve coherence by setting war aims and making strategy, policy, and campaign decisions that increase the probability of achieving those war aims. Second, generate organizational capacity to translate those aims and decisions into action to achieve war aims at the least cost, in lives and resources, and least risk to the innocent and to one's political community, then adapt decisions and actions as the vagaries of war unfold. Finally, maintain legitimacy by doing all the foregoing while observing the war convention,[29] sustaining public support for the war, and ensuring proper subordination of the military to civilian leadership.

In sum, Lincoln came to understand conducting war in a broad and complete sense. His understanding reveals that a complete account of justice in the conduct of war must include both the war-fighting and the war-waging dimensions of war's conduct. He also came to realize that, because of the dynamic interrelationship among his five functions, conducting war required iterative decisions, a sustained civil-military dialogue, and continual coordination and cooperation among the civil and military bureaucracies.

These war lessons remain valid today. Many of the lessons Lincoln learned as he, his cabinet, and his generals waged the Civil War were initially ignored in America's post-9/11 wars. Some came to be relearned; others have still not been learned.[30] Lessons learned or not, the wars in Afghanistan and Iraq confirm that the war-waging functions that emerged during the Civil War and the tripartite tension inherent in waging war remain operant.

Beyond the Civil War: Waging War in Afghanistan and Iraq

On October 7, 2001, twenty-six days following the September 11 attacks on New York and Washington, DC, the United States invaded Afghanistan, where those attacks were planned and launched. When the Taliban rulers of Afghanistan refused to extradite Osama bin Laden and the rest of the al-Qaeda planners, the United States was forced to go to war. As President George W. Bush put it: "I felt the gravity of the decision. I knew the war would bring death and sorrow. Every life lost would devastate a family forever. . . . My anxiety about the sacrifice was mitigated by the urgency of the cause. Removing al Qaeda's safe haven in Afghanistan was essential to protecting the American people. . . . We were acting out of necessity and self-defense, not revenge."[31] In sum, the president concluded that going to war was justified, worth the cost in lives and treasure, and worth the risk to the innocent and to America. The country—in fact, the world—was in support.

At the start of the war, Bush deferred to his generals. Again in his words: "I did not try to manage the logistics or the tactical decisions. My instinct was to trust the judgment of the military leadership."[32] In relatively quick order, the Taliban was routed. By the fall of 2002, NATO had assumed partial responsibility for the International Security Assistance Force, but it would not assume full responsibility until four years later, in October 2006. In the interim, three strategic decisions began to erode the initial success, prolong the war, and set the conditions for the return of the Taliban.

The first decision was to allow execution to precede planning and preparation. In a speech delivered to a joint session of Congress on September 20, 2001, the president said that this would be a war to punish and bring to justice those who attacked the United States, a war "against a radical network of terrorists and every government that supports them . . . a war on terror . . . that will not end until every terrorist group of global reach has been found, stopped and defeated."[33] He corroborated the expansive nature of the war aims in his memoir, *Decision Points,* noting that they involved "removing al Qaeda's safe haven in Afghanistan," "destroy[ing] the al Qaeda network," "help[ing] the Afghan people liberate themselves," "bring[ing] these people [al-Qaeda] to justice," and changing the impression "that, in the words of Bin laden, Americans were 'paper tigers.'"[34] Thinking through the political, diplomatic, fiscal, organizational, and material resources necessary to achieve these war aims is not a trivial task.

Yet the speed at which the United States invaded Afghanistan meant not only that resources and other means were not fully aligned with aims but also that the aims themselves may not have been fully vetted and debated. Further, the execution plan was, to say the least, far from fully developed.[35] Without doubt, the scale of al-Qaeda's attack on the United States and the resultant death and destruction caught America and the world by surprise and justified an immediate response. The Bush administration was under tremendous pressure to respond and was justified in doing so. Haste, however, resulted in insufficient intellectual, strategic, organizational, and logistic preparation, and this haste affected the conduct of the war in Afghanistan from the very start and continues to do so to this very day. The items on Lincoln's list—policy, national strategy, military strategy, operations, and tactics—were far from sufficiently aligned as the first Americans landed in Afghanistan.

For example, Bob Woodward observed that, even as the initial battles raged, Secretary of Defense Donald Rumsfeld believed that the CIA was in charge of the offensive to remove the Taliban, while the CIA believed that it was a military operation.[36] In his memoir, *Known and Unknown,* Rumsfeld presented a different picture, one of a prearranged shift in overall command and control. "The CIA," he wrote, "would have the lead initially, since its personnel would be in Afghanistan first. Command would shift to [General Tommy Franks, commander of US Central Command] . . . as the campaign took on more of a military character."[37] This arrangement was to provide flexibility and cooperation without creating confused lines of command. Shifts in command within an agency, let alone between agencies and during active combat, are inherently complex, and there is little evidence that the details of this shift were sufficiently coordinated. Ultimately, the mix of CIA operatives, special operations forces, massive airpower, and Afghan militias proved to be sufficient to rout the Taliban.

This mix of forces, however, was hugely insufficient to remove al-Qaeda's safe haven in Afghanistan, destroy its network, bring its fighters to justice, or deal with a post-Taliban Afghanistan—war aims the president identified. Shortly after the Taliban was routed, the inadequacies of planning and policy became clearer. The deficiencies in numbers and types of troops, confused command and control organizations, overly compartmentalized intelligence and planning arrangements, and the piecemeal method of unit deployments all contributed to the Taliban's and al-Qaeda's escape into Pakistan, thus prolonging the war.[38]

The second decision was to allow NATO to take a lead nation approach to the rebuilding of Afghanistan. This approach resulted in Germany being responsible for training the Afghan national police, the United States for training the Afghan army, Great Britain for the counternarcotics mission, Italy for the reform of the justice system, and Japan for the disarmament and demobilization of the Afghan warlords and militias. In addition, the United States continued its combat operations against the remnants of al-Qaeda and the Taliban—independent from the NATO effort. Unity of purpose and cohesion of action were lost almost immediately and stayed diffuse for years. Further, many of the allied nations agreed to their tasks under the assumption that they would be operating in a posthostility environment, akin to the peacekeeping missions in Bosnia and Kosovo. They quickly found that this was not the case, so their efforts were, to say it kindly, seriously impaired.

Haste was at least partially responsible for not using the Roosevelt-Churchill-Marshall-Brooke model of carefully building organizations and processes that were necessary to wage a global war. Over the years of World War II, these organizations and processes improved, but they began to emerge very early from 1939 to 1941—prior to the Japanese attack on Pearl Harbor in December of the latter year. Lincoln, his cabinet, and his generals also required a period of learning. But, by 1863, the administration's decision-making and -execution methodologies were sufficiently mature, effective, and efficient.

It was 2006, however, five years after the initial invasion of Afghanistan, before Bush realized that the approach in Afghanistan had to change. "The multilateral approach to rebuilding . . . was failing," he wrote. "There was little coordination between countries, and no one devoted enough resources to the effort. . . . The multilateral mission proved a disappointment as well. . . . The result was a disorganized and ineffective force with troops fighting by different rules and many not fighting at all." Not only were too few troops allocated to the task, but also, as the president concluded: "Our government was not prepared for nation building."[39] Meanwhile, the Taliban began to return, casualties among both combatants and noncombatants mounted, the war dragged on, and public support became an issue.

Writing about this period, Ronald E. Neumann, the US ambassador to Afghanistan from 2005 to 2007, said: "The public has little understanding of any aspect of the [Afghan] conflict other than the military engagement, mostly at the tactical level, which makes for compelling stories but offers a limited view of the larger picture." "As I worked my way through the fourth war that I have experienced up close," the ambassador writes, "I was struck by how little either the public or senior policymakers understood the complex business of implementing policy. . . . Divorcing high-level policymaking from implementation leads us to ignore information from the ground level necessary to make policies work and prevents us from learning how to adjust policies when they do not. . . . [I]ncomprehension of the complexity of implementation makes finding the proper balance between policy and operations difficult."[40]

Dov Zakheim—who was one of the original members of a group of eight who advised George W. Bush on foreign and national security policy issues and who became, in 2002, the US Department of Defense civilian coordinator for defense activities in Afghanistan, a position that he held simultaneously with comptroller and chief financial officer at the Pentagon—reinforces Neumann's perspective. He notes: "In the case of Afghanistan, . . . through sins of both commission and omission, the Bush administration was often incapable of effectively implementing manifestly good policies, sound ideas, and wisely chosen goals." Zakheim describes a US government that did not engage, anywhere in any of its various departments and agencies, in extensive planning for a post-Taliban Afghanistan. He also claims that the assumption that the international community would pick up the pieces after the Taliban regime fell was simply false. He describes several years, especially in Afghanistan, where "there was no functional system of governance in Washington to support [those executing civil and military operations in the theater]": "The reason is . . . the absence of standard government procedures and institutions to implement [wartime] policy, [and] no one understood the importance of devising such procedures beforehand." Securing funding necessary to conduct the war, mobilizing the US military's reserves, and securing allied troop and monetary contributions, he continues, "turned out to be more complicated and frustrating than it might, or should, have been." Even determining the size of the ground forces the nation would need to fight in Afghanistan, in Iraq, and in the global war against al-Qaeda was a matter more of contention than consensus. With regard to funding, for example, the Office of Management and Budget, the Department of State, and the Department of Defense were more competitors and obstacles to each other than cooperative agencies in pursuit of a common wartime goal.[41]

Zakheim goes on to explain that the US government's "neglect of Afghanistan," a neglect that Neumann's *The Other War* documents as well, "allowed the Taliban to gradually seize control of key areas of the country, particularly in the country's southern and eastern provinces."[42] Zakheim and Neumann describe the inability to achieve coherence and generate organizational capacity—two of the three war-waging responsibilities. No surprise, then, that the result was a slow loss of legitimacy.

The third decision that began to erode initial success, thus setting the conditions for the return of the Taliban and prolonging the war in Afghanistan, was to invade Iraq. The invasion caused US attention to wander from Afghanistan, according to Bruce Riedel, a former CIA analyst, White House counterterrorist specialist, and Brookings Institution fellow. The result: the effort to rebuild Afghanistan stalled, and the Taliban regrouped in Pakistan and staged a comeback.[43] Peter Tomsen corroborates Riedel's conclusion in a recent article in *Foreign Affairs*, noting that the consequences of the decision to invade Iraq were felt almost immediately.[44]

The invasion of Iraq is relevant to understanding the broader scope of *jus in bello* independently of how it affected the war in Afghanistan.

Setting aside the justness of the decision to invade Iraq—for historians, strategists, lawyers, and moral philosophers continue to argue the wisdom, necessity, and morality of that decision—the invasion and its subsequent operations show that conducting a war involves both warfighting and war-waging activities.

On March 19, 2003, Bush ordered Operation Iraqi Freedom to begin. On April 9, Baghdad was close to falling into coalition hands, and, on May 1, the president gave his speech aboard the USS *Abraham Lincoln* under the "Mission Accomplished" banner. The initial invasion and immediate aftermath in Iraq looked eerily similar to what had been done in Afghanistan.

The Iraqi regime fell as quickly as did the Taliban in Afghanistan. Then a new reality emerged. The security vacuum in Iraq—fueled by years of oppression under the Saddam regime as well as insufficient numbers of coalition forces, the destruction of the Iraqi army, and the collapse of the police—resulted in looters carrying artifacts out of Iraq's national museum as well as pillaging many of the country's ministries and committing kidnappings and murders.

The US Central Command, responsible for US military actions throughout most of the Middle East, used three three-star military headquarters—one army corps, one marine expeditionary force, and a common, three-star headquarters—to plan, coordinate, and execute the campaign to remove the Saddam regime. All three of these headquarters were withdrawn about ninety days after the initial invasion. They were replaced by a single, different army corps headquarters that would be responsible for executing the postcombat phase of the Iraq invasion, though neither its commander, Lieutenant General Ricardo Sanchez, nor its staff participated in the planning or the preparation. In fact, Sanchez was interviewed by the secretary of defense only in April—one month after the invasion and less than two before he would assume his responsibilities in Iraq.[45]

One three-star headquarters is much less capable than three such headquarters. One—especially one led by a newly minted lieutenant general with an underfilled staff—would not be able to attend properly to the combination of active combat leadership requirements, the tasks associated with rebuilding the Iraqi military and police forces, the logistic tasks inherent in supporting an effort like that in Iraq at the time, and the administration of large detention operations that fell under its jurisdiction. Nor would one be able to attend adequately to all these tasks as well as to the demands of coordination with the political, diplomatic, and nongovernment agencies that were responsible for reconstruction and humanitarian assistance.

In retrospect, not recalling his interview with Sanchez or his role in the general's assignment, the secretary of defense wrote that the commanding general had been put "in a terrible position": "The establishment of a government, the long-term care of detainees, the training and equipping of [Iraqi] security forces, and, ultimately, the engagement of an increasingly deadly terrorist threat called for a senior military official with far more experience." Rumsfeld continues by saying that this decision was a "serious misassessment," acknowledging that the tasks assigned to Sanchez "required a large, fully staffed supporting headquarters" but that what he got was "less than half—37 percent—of the staff he required."[46] This "misassessment" was not corrected until June 2004, one year after the initial invasion. Reflecting on his experience, Sanchez agreed: "Without the four-star command in Iraq, CJTF 7 [Combined Joint Task Force 7, the corps headquarters that he led] had assumed the entire burden for the strategic political-military interface *and* for the tactical warfighting aspects of the mission. It was simply too much of a burden for an Army corps headquarters to bear."[47] The commanding general, however, was not the only one in a terrible position.

The Office of Reconstruction and Humanitarian Assistance (ORHA), for instance, had been created hastily in January 2003, just a little over two months prior to the invasion. This organization was charged with devising the plans for the rebuilding of Iraq and turning those plans into action. The civilian who would initially become responsible for the reconstruction of Iraq—Jay Garner, a retired US Army three star—was first contacted by the Department of Defense just a few months before the invasion. About thirty days prior to launching the invasion, Garner orchestrated a meeting that assembled, as Michael Gordon and General Bernard Trainor note, "most of the players in the government's postwar game, including the Pentagon, State Department, CENTCOM [US Central Command], the vice president's office, and [Lieutenant General David] McKiernan's command at Camp Doha [the Kuwaiti base of the three-star headquarters overall responsible for planning, preparing, coordinating, and executing ground operations in Iraq]." They continue: "[The meeting] was intended as an opportunity for each agency to pitch its ideas about how to proceed, but there was, as yet, no master strategy." In fact, one general who participated in the session concluded (as Gordon and Trainor put it): "The U.S. agencies were not ready, had no real understanding of what Iraq was like, and did not yet have a coherent plan. . . . There was no clear demarcation between what would be run by the civilians and what the generals would control. The funding for the multibillion-dollar undertaking in Iraq was still up in the air, and it was ludicrous to expect that it would all come from the U.N."[48] By May 2003, ORHA was disbanded. Garner and his staff returned to the United States. In their stead came Ambassador L. Paul "Jerry" Bremer and the Coalition Provisional Authority (CPA).

In April 2003—a month after the invasion of Iraq and only two after Garner held his initial meeting at Camp Doha—Bremer had been contacted about the possibility of assuming the responsibilities originally given to Garner. After an initial interview with Bush, the ambassador agreed. He later recalled: "Over the next two weeks, I had a frenzied series of meetings at the Pentagon, struggling to get 'read in' on the situation in Iraq before my departure. Between sessions, I scrambled to assemble a staff." Shortly before he left for Baghdad, he again met with the president, asking to be given "full authority to bring all the resources of the American government to bear on Iraq's reconstruction." The president agreed but, as Bremer put it, made one thing perfectly clear: "I was neither Rumsfeld's nor Powell's man. I was the president's man."[49] Many on that staff that he assembled were young professionals who had never worked outside the United States and would never leave Baghdad's secure "Green Zone." Many rotated in and out of their jobs in well under a year. Some rotations were as short as ninety days; many were more politically correct than professionally competent.[50] The ambassador would hold his job for about a year, until June 2004—the same tenure as Sanchez.

For a variety of reasons, progress that year was, at best, fitful. Saddam Hussein was captured, and Iraqi sovereignty was transferred to an interim government that set the conditions for drafting a constitution and holding elections. But the insurgency grew, as did al-Qaeda's involvement in it, fed in part by the increase of foreign fighters but also by the disbanding of the Iraqi army and the de-Ba'athification program—two Bremer-related policies that were at the time and remain controversial. Violence from an expanding Shia militia also contributed to insecurity and instability, as did the misdeeds committed by the Iraqi security forces, crimes committed by US soldiers in the Abu Ghraib prison, and overly aggressive tactics used by some ground forces. Neither the still-forming Iraqi army nor the police were proficient enough or numerous enough to help stem the rising violence. Simply put, the situation in Iraq deteriorated.[51]

In 2004, one well-known defense analyst put it this way: "It quickly became apparent that the . . . administration had paid far more attention to the planning and conduct of the war than to the planning and conduct of the 'peace.'" Moreover, he continues, one of the main obstacles was the "continuing division . . . over U.S. policy toward Iraq and the respective roles of the State and Defense Departments in formulating and implementing that policy."[52] Major General Spider Marks, who was a senior intelligence officer in Iraq at this time, said: "My position is that we lost momentum and that the insurgency was not inevitable. . . . We had momentum going in . . . but we did not have enough troops to conduct combat patrols." General Jack Keane, who was the vice chief of staff of the US Army at the time, said more bluntly that the US mission in Iraq was made all the more difficult by the administration's aversion to nation building and its determination not to study the lessons of its predecessors. He added that "military leaders, including the Joint Chiefs of Staff, the Vice Chiefs, and General Franks, share responsibility [with the political leaders at the time] for the problems in Iraq."[53]

Confusion, insufficient attention, and lack of civil-military cohesion followed the initial success in Iraq, just as it had in Afghanistan, and the price of this confusion—insufficiency as well as lack of cohesion and of organizational capacity—was paid in blood (and continues to be paid). As Afghanistan slid toward the Taliban, Iraq was coming apart.[54]

In the early summer of 2004, Bremer and Sanchez were replaced by Ambassador John Negroponte and General George W. Casey. Negroponte's US embassy and its staff would replace the ad hoc CPA. To replace the lone three-star army corps, Casey would create a large staff commensurate with his four-star rank (Multi-National Force, Iraq). Additionally, understanding the complexity and scope of his task, he brought in three three-star deputies: one to run combat operations (Multi-National Corps, Iraq), a second to help create the Iraqi military and police forces (Multi-National Security and Transition Command, Iraq), and a third to run the special operations in Iraq. The strategy, policies, and organizations that were put in place in 2004 would govern the war in Iraq almost until the American departure in 2011. But the violence went from bad to worse.

"The summer of 2006," Bush writes in *Decision Points,* "was the worst period of my presidency. I thought about the war constantly. While I was heartened by the determination of the Maliki government and the death of Zarqawi [then leader of al-Qaeda in Iraq], I was deeply concerned that the violence was overtaking all else. . . . For the first time, I worried we might not succeed." In sum, the strategy in Iraq—pursuing extremists and reducing the (already too small) military footprint as the coalition trained Iraqi military and police forces—as well as the policies and military operations supporting that strategy were failing. By the summer of 2006, Bush noted: "An average of 120 Iraqis a day were dying. The war had stretched to more than three years and we had lost more than 2,500 Americans."[55] In March 2003, when the invasion of Iraq began, 75 percent of Americans polled believed that the United States had *not* made a mistake sending troops to Iraq, and only 23 percent thought that sending troops was a mistake. By December 2006, the numbers were 45 and 53 percent, respectively. Support for the war was clearly slipping.[56]

"For two and a half years," Bush writes, "I had supported the strategy of withdrawing our forces as the Iraqis stepped forward—the 'we'll stand down as they stand up' policy. But in the months after the [2006] Samarra [mosque] bombing, I had started to question whether our approach matched the reality on the ground." Although there were successes in Iraq—for example, elections to choose an interim national assembly to draft a constitution, a ratified constitution, and an election of a prime minister and a permanent legislature—violence escalated nearly out of control, the legitimacy of the war was being questioned, and the president concluded that he required a new strategy with radically new resources and policies.[57]

The 2006 situation in Afghanistan was no better. As Bush put it:

> My CIA and military briefings included increasingly dire reports about Taliban influence. The problem was crystallized by a series of color-coded maps I saw in November 2006. The darker the shading, the more attacks had occurred in that part of Afghanistan. The 2004 map was lightly shaded. The 2005 map had darker areas in the southern and eastern parts of the country. By 2006, the entire southeastern quadrant was black. In just one year, the number of remotely detonated bombs had doubled. The number of armed attacks had tripled. The number of suicide bombings had more than quadrupled.[58]

When the United States invaded Afghanistan in November 2001, 89 percent of Americans polled believed that the United States had *not* made a mistake sending troops to Afghanistan, and only 9 percent thought that sending troops was a mistake. By August 2007, the numbers were 25 and 70 percent, respectively. Support for the Afghan war was slipping as well.[59] The US and NATO strategy—diplomatic, military, economic, and political—was failing, the Afghans had lost faith in their government, and sanctuaries in Pakistan contributed to this worsening situation.[60] Further, legitimacy in the eyes of the American public had begun to be an issue.

The wars in Afghanistan (still not over) and Iraq (facing an existential threat from the Islamic State in Iraq and Syria and the prospect of increased US involvement)[61] have cost the United States over sixty-eight hundred killed, over fifty-two thousand wounded, and an estimated $4.4 trillion.[62]

The point of reviewing Iraq and Afghanistan and recalling the Civil War is not to recount mistakes. No war is devoid of mistakes at any level, tactical through strategic, made by military and political leaders. Every war contains a record of the learning and adapting necessary to move from prewar beliefs and doctrines to what waging war and fighting actually require. Rather, the point is to provide a more detailed account of the war-waging responsibilities first presented in chapter 1.

Further, the Afghanistan and Iraq accounts point out how difficult it is to exercise these responsibilities sufficiently well and how badly the poor execution of them affects the conduct of war. Lives—of the innocent and of citizens-who-become-soldiers—are lost in every war; every war also involves risk to the political community, whether existential or some lesser degree.

What both the Afghan and the Iraq accounts highlight is that sufficient effectiveness in executing war-waging responsibilities reduces the risks and lessens the likelihood that the lives used in war will be used well, not wasted. The reverse is also true: ineffectiveness in waging war increases the loss of innocent life, the risk to the political community, and the likelihood that the lives used are wasted. In sum, all four examples—World War II, the American Civil War, and the US post-9/11 wars in Afghanistan and Iraq—demonstrate that the conduct of war includes both war-fighting and war-waging dimensions, that both dimensions are related to individual and communal life, and that effectiveness in waging war matters as much as effectiveness in fighting a war.

To be a complete account of justice in the conduct of war, therefore, *jus in bello* cannot be limited only to right conduct in battle. Such a narrow focus omits a crucial way in which senior political and military leaders can meet or fail to meet their wartime responsibilities. *Jus in bello* must include right conduct in waging war, just as it includes right conduct in fighting war.

War-Waging Responsibilities and the Moral Value of Soldiers

The discussion of World War II in the previous chapter and the brief review of the American Civil War and the initial look at the more recent wars in Afghanistan and Iraq in this chapter reveal that waging war involves at least the following senior political and military leader responsibilities:

1. Making the best initial decisions possible concerning war aims, strategies (domestic, diplomatic, military, and nonmilitary), policies, and campaigns.

2. Adapting initial decisions as the dynamics of war unfold.
3. Raising and allocating forces, other resources, and funds necessary to achieve those aims.
4. Engaging in adequate diplomacy.
5. Attending to the legitimacy of the war, that is, maintaining public support.
6. Making the military and nonmilitary government agencies work well enough to execute strategies and policies and attain war aims.
7. Establishing mechanisms that facilitate proper dialogue, decision making, action, and adaptation.

Depending on the effectiveness of these war-waging activities, a war can be shortened or prolonged. Prolonging war unnecessarily entails more deaths—combatant and noncombatant—and requires more of a nation's other resources. When these actions are not adequately attended to, the cost is paid in lives, just as surely as with failures on the battlefield.

Again, every war has its mistakes, tactical through strategic, and every war contains a record of the learning and adapting from prewar misconceptions to the realities of war. Some mistakes will, fortunately, not result in unnecessary loss of life. Others will. Still others are not really mistakes at all. Rather, they amount to failures of some senior political and military leaders to meet their war-waging responsibilities. These kinds of failures are neither an unfortunate consequence of war nor merely examples of human fallibility that are understandable. Rather, they are a kind of failure that just war theory must have the means to identify, criticize, and judge.

Soldiers and their leaders who observe the tactical *jus in bello* principles that traditional just war theory includes mitigate part of war's nastiness. Applying these principles in combat is part of a soldier's and a leader's moral responsibility in war. Sufficient capacity at the strategic, war-waging level can also mitigate part of war's nastiness. Applying the appropriate war-waging principles (presented in chapter 6) is part of a senior political or military leader's moral responsibility in war.

The standard for deciding on war aims, strategy, policy, and military as well as nonmilitary campaigns, then executing those decisions and adapting as the war unfolds, is not perfection; no government or set of civil-military leaders could ever meet it if it were. Every government will make mistakes initially. Every government's policy and strategy and every government's execution will be only partially effective and efficient. If its civil and military leaders can learn and adapt quickly enough, a government can make fewer mistakes than its enemy does, improve its efficiency and effectiveness, and, thus, increase the probability of success and decrease the probability of putting the political community at risk and wasting the lives of the innocent and the citizens-who-become-soldiers as well as other national resources.

If, however, a government's civil and military leaders do not learn and adapt but continue to conduct a war for unattainable aims, using known inefficient and ineffective strategies and policies or employing known inefficient and ineffective organizations and management processes, they should be morally blameworthy—even if not legally guilty—for the results of their actions, just as soldiers and their leaders ignoring the war convention would be on the battlefield. Life, even if a soldier's, is not a resource to be used without compunction. Those senior political and military leaders whose responsibility it is to wage war have a responsibility to act in ways ensuring that lives—not only of the innocent but also of the soldiers they employ—are respected, not squandered.

Walzer, illustrative of traditional just war theory, firmly establishes the important role that the lives of the innocent play in *jus in bello*. Conducting a war necessarily entails putting the lives of the innocent at risk, and the war-fighting *jus in bello* principles that he adduces are designed, and rightly so, to limit risk to the innocent. Luban's recent work on the limits of risk confirms the importance of protecting the innocent. Conducting a war also necessarily entails *using* the lives of other human beings—whether at the war-fighting or the war-waging level. *Jus in bello* must also address how these lives can be used. Walzer's emphasis on the lives of the innocent and on the effect that respecting the value of these lives has on the conduct of war is necessary, absolutely necessary, but it is insufficient. A soldier's life also retains moral value, and respecting the value of these lives also affects the conduct of war.

Confused and ill-thought-out war aims, strategic concepts, and operational policies have consequences in the conduct of war, as do personnel policies, logistics policies, management structures, the speed of learning, and decision-making and -execution processes. As Afghanistan and Iraq policies were being argued, decided, and implemented, innocents as well as American citizens-who-became-soldiers were dying each day. Citizens-who-become-soldiers understand that their lives change once they become soldiers. Soldiers become instruments, but not mere instruments. They can be killed in war justifiably; they are expected to risk their lives on behalf of the innocent, their fellow soldiers, and their political community. They remain, however, not only moral agents but also human beings and citizens.

The continued value of their lives during the conduct of war is manifested in four morally relevant relationships. The first is with the innocent—reflected in the requirement that soldiers afford due care to the innocent and take due risk in affording that care. Walzer and Luban treat this relationship adequately.[63]

The second morally relevant relationship is among soldiers themselves. This relationship is actually a set of networks of relationships. Soldiers rely and depend on one another—literally for their lives in some cases. This is a significant relationship of trust. Part of the moral injury that Nancy Sherman describes in *Afterwar* rests on actual or perceived violations of this trust: soldiers who "were not there" for their buddies or thought they "should have been there." One of the most famous examples of the relationship between two soldiers—who, in this case, both happen to be generals—comes from a letter that W. T. Sherman wrote to U. S. Grant: "I knew wherever I was that you thought of me and if I got in a tight place you could come—if alive."[64] The Sherman-Grant relationship is illustrative of how seriously soldiers take their bond of trust.

The third morally relevant relationship is that of soldiers with their military leaders. Walzer points out that soldiers are in one sense instruments with which leaders are supposed to win victories, but they are also men and women whose lives, because they are a leader's to use, are also in that leader's care.[65] There is no argument that an important aspect of one's right to life changes—even if it is not lost—when one becomes a soldier: one can be killed justifiably. The status of being able to be killed, however, is a conditional one—even when it is justified.[66]

It applies only when one is a soldier, only during a war or some other form of hostility, and only relative to the enemy being fought. A soldier cannot be killed justifiably by just anyone. *Murder* is still the appropriate term for the intentional killing of a soldier by one of his or her fellow soldiers or by a noncombatant.

This third morally relevant relationship reveals another aspect of trust: leaders, too, sometimes believe that they have violated the trust their soldiers place in them by letting them down, whether they actually have or not. The military chain of command also rests on the trust that junior leaders have in their seniors' integrity, and vice versa.

This soldier-to-leader relationship acknowledges that soldiers' lives retain their value in the eyes of their leaders and that their leaders should care a great deal about preserving their lives for more than merely utilitarian reasons. The enduring value of the lives of citizens-who-become-soldiers is revealed in an exchange between a commanding officer and his soldiers in Iraq during the summer of 2005.

US special operations forces were fighting a series of battles in the Euphrates River valley (the same area that the self-styled Islamic State now controls) in an attempt to stem the flow of foreign fighters utilizing the valley's infiltration routes, *ratlines* as they were called. Al-Qaeda had rooted itself throughout the valley, setting up way stations and safe houses in the rural desert compounds and riverside cities connecting Syria to Baghdad. "If the black Al Qaeda flags that insurgents draped over the sides of compound walls or flew from rooftops weren't evidence enough of how deeply entrenched Zarqawi [the leader of al-Qaeda in Iraq at the time] sympathizers were in the upper corridor [of the Euphrates]," writes General Stanley McChrystal, who commanded the special operations forces during these battles, "the violence that ensued when we contested these areas proved it." The al-Qaeda fighters hardened their safe houses, sometimes rigging walls with explosives, began wearing suicide vests constantly—even sleeping in them—and used makeshift pillboxes inside the houses. The fighting was bitter and close, with whole units of foreign fighters sometimes barricading themselves in basements and firing up through floors.[67]

Even after adapting their tactical methods to match the enemy's preparedness, the losses among McChrystal's forces grew, as did the stress of months of constant close-quarters combat. At one point, the general met with leaders and soldiers in a small compound in the valley. "Listen," he said, "this really hurts. But let me tell you what would make these [operations] hurt even more: if it is all in vain." He then went on to discuss the importance of their battles within the context of the larger strategy in Iraq, explaining how the nighttime raids in the Euphrates valley were not only linked but also vital to the overall strategy in Iraq.[68]

Dying in vain would not matter if the lives of citizens-now-soldiers had no value other than as instruments. Their lives could be used any way that their leaders saw fit—utility being the only limiting factor. What McChrystal's comments reveal, however, is that how those lives are used does matter. Officers and other leaders are responsible for ensuring that they are used for a purpose, that any sacrifices made are made to achieve higher aims, and that those lives are not merely wasted. This responsibility derives from the fact that soldiers, at least American soldiers, remain citizens and that the democracy for which they fight retains its obligation to provide adequate care for its citizens. Part of an officer's commission involves the responsibility for exercising this obligation. Walzer himself admits that "soldiers have every right to expect . . . [the exercise of this obligation] of him [the officer] and to blame him for every sort of omission, evasion, carelessness, and recklessness that endangers their lives."[69]

The last morally relevant relationship is between citizens-who-become-soldiers and the senior political and military leaders whose responsibility it is to wage war. This relationship and its relevance to *jus in bello* are all but absent from traditional just war theory. This fourth relationship is reflected in Lincoln's words at Gettysburg as well as in Bush's remarks on the evening of January 10, 2007, when he stepped in front of television cameras and said: "The situation in Iraq is unacceptable to the American people—and it is unacceptable to me. Our troops in Iraq have fought bravely. They have done everything we asked them to do. Where mistakes have been made, the responsibility rests with me. It is clear that we need to change our strategy in Iraq." Here, the president is clearly referring to what the government owes the citizens-who-become-soldiers so that their lives are used well: properly identified war aims, strategies, and policies as well as effective military and nonmilitary campaigns and the political and military bureaucracies that can translate plans into actions, all so that their sacrifices are not in vain. Separate from his remarks on television, Bush clearly described the necessity of dialogue between senior political and military leaders in his discussion not only of the decisions he made leading up to the 2007 changes in strategy, policy, and personnel but also of their execution.[70]

Traditional just war theory recognizes that political leaders should not plan, prepare, initiate, and wage an aggressive war, else the war would be unjustified. Accordingly, Walzer is careful to say that governments must use the lives of their citizens-who-become-soldiers only for "purposes worth dying for, outcomes for which soldiers' lives are not too high a price": "The idea of a just war requires the same assumption. A just war is one that it is morally urgent to win, and a soldier who dies in a just war does not die in vain. Critical values are at stake [i.e., the defense against aggression or other uses of force authorized by the legalist paradigm and its exceptions]. . . . The deaths that occur in [wars'] course . . . are morally comprehensible—which is not to say that they are not also the products of military stupidity and bureaucratic snafu: soldiers die senselessly even in wars that are not senseless." For Walzer, the legitimate ends of war—its goals—set limits for even a just war. "Once they are won, or once they are within political reach, the fighting should stop. Soldiers killed beyond that point die needlessly, and to force them to fight and possibly to die is a crime akin to that of aggression itself."[71] Nor can political leaders set in place policies that require war crimes. These are the three limits that *Just and Unjust Wars* places on the legitimate use of state power. A government's relationship to its citizens-who-become-soldiers, however, demands more.

In *Just and Unjust Wars,* Walzer did not address this relationship or its moral relevance with respect to the conduct of war because traditional *jus in bello* is only a matter of right conduct in the fighting of war. In *Spheres of Justice,* however, he provides a way in which to account for the relationship between citizens-who-become-soldiers and the senior political and military leaders whose responsibility it is to wage war and explains a fourth limit on the legitimate use of state power in the waging of war: that lives are to be used as wisely as possible.[72]

In democracies, Walzer argues, state power, which flows from citizens to political leaders and institutions, is necessary but limited.[73]

Democratic sovereignty does not entail domination over citizens. The moral relevance of Walzer's two most basic human rights of life and liberty is manifest in his account of *jus in bello* at the tactical, war-fighting level; those two rights also provide an account of senior political and military leaders' war-waging responsibilities and should be captured by *jus in bello*'s strategic dimension.

These rights, retained by citizens-who-become-soldiers relative to both their military and their political leaders, prevent service from becoming enslavement. The concept of slavery entails an absence of any kind of rights. The slave is not a person. He or she becomes an object, a piece of property that can be used as can any other object one owns. This is what makes slavery so morally objectionable. In becoming a soldier serving a democracy, whether conscripted or volunteer, a citizen does not become a slave, nor does the state become a tyrant. As with all other citizens, the power of the state is limited with regard to citizens-who-become-soldiers.

Certainly, as we have already seen, soldiers can be used in ways in which other citizens cannot. Justice places limits, however, on how the lives of soldiers can be used. That is, even in a just war, justice demands that a government use the lives of its citizens-who-become-soldiers as wisely as possible. Ineptitude in waging war—errors beyond understandable mistakes resulting from human fallibility—forces citizens to fight under conditions that increase the likelihood that their sacrifices will be in vain.

One way to understand the limits of how the lives of soldiers can be used is to employ Rawls's "veil of ignorance."[74] Walzer summarizes Rawls's system of justice as "the one that ideally rational men and women would choose if they were forced to choose impartially, knowing nothing of their own situation, barred from making particularist claims, confronting an abstract set of goods."[75] Not knowing his or her position in a society, set of natural assets and abilities, or level of intelligence, no citizen would choose a system that might require a total loss of rights should he or she become a soldier. Rather, the rational choice from behind this veil of ignorance would include limits as to how the government can use the lives of citizens-who-become-soldiers—even in war.[76] These limits may be ambiguous, like the line between due risk and due care or that between bravery and heroism, but limits exist nonetheless.

Rawls might argue, and Walzer agree, that clear limits, for example, are set by duration—the increased risk demanded of soldiers ends when a soldier is captured, wounded, or leaves service. A second clear limit is condition—risks acceptable during a war are greater than those acceptable in peacetime training. Scope is a third clear limit—a democratic government cannot limit a soldier's right to religious belief, for example, or to own personal property. But there is an important fourth limit.

Senior political and military leaders waging a war on behalf of a democratic government may not squander the lives of the citizens-who-become-soldiers without accruing moral blame. Rather, they must use these lives responsibly. Responsible use is a fourth limit on government power. When senior political and military leaders fail to meet their war-waging responsibilities and their failure is not merely a mistake or an error, they act beyond the limit of responsible use and are, therefore, morally blameworthy.

Conclusions: Filling the Gap

Identifying a gap in traditional just war theory and describing that gap constitute a good start. Describing how to fill the gap is much harder. Filling the gap requires an account of how senior political and military leaders—those who have war-waging responsibilities—must relate to one another and how the bureaucracies they lead must interact to ensure that their war-waging responsibilities are met. In the next chapter, I take up one possible answer, a theory that posits political leaders as principals, military leaders as agents, and the relationship between the two as one akin to an employer-employee relationship.

3

Principals and Agents

Any attempt to understand the war-waging responsibilities of senior political and military leaders must examine two important civil-military theories: the principal-agent theory and its antecedent, the objective control theory. The former is primarily expressed in Peter Feaver's *Armed Servants,* the latter in Samuel Huntington's *The Soldier and the State.*[1] Both approaches analyze the interaction between senior civil and military leaders and the bureaucracies they head. This is the intersection at which waging war occurs.

Both theories use a paradox to identify the core issue of the civil-military relationship in a democracy. On one hand is a functional imperative: to provide security, which is a military force's function; a nation's military must be large enough and have sufficient skills, leadership, and materiel to create and sustain the capacities the nation needs to be secure relative to the threats it faces or believes it faces. This imperative rises in importance during war. On the other hand is a social imperative: a nation's military cannot be so strong that it ends up destroying the very state it is designed to serve. That is, the political leadership of the nation must maintain control of its military, else the democratic political community itself may be at risk.

"The military institutions of any society," Huntington claims, "are shaped by two forces: a functional imperative stemming from the threats to the society's security and a social imperative arising from the forces, ideologies, and institutions dominant within the society."[2] Achieving a proper balance between the functional and the social imperatives is, for both objective control theory and its principal-agent

successor, the crux of the relationship between civil and military leaders as well as the bureaucracies they lead.

The Predecessor and the Successor

Huntington, writing in the late 1950s, suggests that the proper balance
is achieved through a complex set of power and attitudinal relationships among civilian and military groups. "Nations which develop a
properly balanced pattern of civil-military relations," he writes, "have
a great advantage in the search for security. They increase their likelihood of reaching right answers to the operating issues of military policy. Nations which fail to develop a balanced pattern of civil-military
relations squander their resources and run uncalculated risks." And
those risks result in either being ill prepared for war or waging a war
poorly.[3]

For Huntington, increasing the likelihood of reaching right
answers to the operating issues—that is, executing the war-waging
activities presented in the previous chapters: identifying strategic aims,
then crafting strategies and policies as well as conducting military campaigns that will lead to achieving those aims, and creating decision-
making bodies to adapt initial decisions to the unfolding realities of
war—is an important part of the functional imperative. Having and
using a military force, should use become necessary, without putting
the state itself at risk results from properly balancing both the functional and the social imperatives. *The Soldier and the State,* Huntington's seminal work, posits five ways in which to balance the functional
and social imperatives, thus creating a proper civil-military relationship. He ultimately rejects the first four and adopts the fifth.[4]

Military officers and political leaders form the core of the civil-
military relationship. The military officer corps, Huntington says, is
the active directing element of the military structure and is responsible
for the military security of the society. The political leaders of the state
are responsible for the allocation of resources among important values,
including military security.[5]

The first way in which to ensure a proper balance between the
functional and the social imperatives Huntington calls *subjective civilian control.* In this form, the civilian group that has gained control

of the state simply selects a sufficient number of officers who agree with the controlling group's ideology. Huntington says: "Except very recently in western society, civilian control has existed only in this subjective sense. Subjective control is, indeed, the only form of civilian control possible in the absence of a professional officer corps." The second alternative he considers is called *civilian control by government institution*. This alternative has the military forces under the control of the nation's chief executive (the crown, the president, or the prime minister) or the nation's representative body (a parliament, council of representatives, or congress). The third method is called *civilian control by social class*. Here, military forces are controlled by an aristocracy or some other subgroup, sect, or tribe of the nation at large. Fourth, Huntington poses *civilian control by constitutional form*. That is, civilian control is identified with democracies, while military control is associated with absolute or totalitarian governments. Huntington rejects these four forms of civil-military relationships as proper for the United States because each increases the military participation in politics, which, in turn, puts the social imperative at risk.[6]

The fifth alternative—the one that Huntington ultimately adopts— is *objective civilian control*, which maximizes military professionalism. The essence of objective civilian control is the recognition of autonomous military professionalism, whereas the essence of the forms of subjective civilian control is the denial of an independent military sphere. Huntington realizes that even in a democracy the military may acquire political power through the legitimate processes and institutions of democratic government and politics and use that power to undermine civilian control. He posits a form of objective control, however, that seeks to prevent that possibility by using a highly professional officer corps that will carry out the wishes of any group of political leaders regardless of its ideology. Crudely put, a degree of military autonomy is exchanged for an apolitical officer corps and military. Objective control strengthens the military's functional capacity while ensuring that it remains a tool of the state; the forms of subjective control decrease functional capacity because they civilianize and politicize the military and increase the military's involvement in politics, thus putting both the functional and the social imperatives at risk.[7]

Huntington then acknowledges that in the United States the constitutional separation of powers is a stumbling block to the ideal version of objective control because the military must report to both the legislative and the executive branches of government and, therefore, will be involved in the political struggles between those branches. In the end, however, he concludes that no actual civil-military relationship is ever ideal: "Within the framework of the separation of powers, institutional adjustments can be made which will reduce its deleterious effects. . . . A lesser measure of civilian control and lower standards of military professionalism are the continuing prices the American people will have to pay for the other benefits of their constitutional system."[8]

Since its publication in 1957, *The Soldier and the State* has had an ongoing, significant, and one might even say dominant influence on the way in which American military and political leaders view each other's roles.[9] Reflecting this continuing influence, General Barry McCaffrey, who has had experience with US civil-military relations as both a general and a cabinet member, suggested in 2009 the following guidelines for senior military officers: "First, senior military leaders must adamantly manifest nonpartisan behavior and attitudes while on active service. . . . [They] must be viewed by the public and senior civilian leaders as politically neutral and blind to partisan considerations. Second, senior military leaders must be utterly transparent and honest when dealing with their constitutional masters in the Congress; with the president and the president's officers; and, where appropriate by law and regulation, with the media. . . . Senior uniformed leaders must speak frankly and objectively where their professional judgments are asked for and not reflect a loyalty to hierarchy that leaves the policy process adrift."[10] Walzer, too, reflects Huntington's influence—even if not intentionally. Huntington's objective control theory, and the autonomy of the political and military spheres that it requires, lays the foundation for the hard line that Walzer draws between war itself and the conduct of war and for the strong role differentiation that he derives from that line.

As Peter Feaver's *Armed Servants,* written over forty years after *The Soldier and the State,* recognizes: "Huntington's theory . . . remains the dominant theoretical paradigm in civil-military relations, especially the study of American civil-military relations. . . . Huntington's model is widely recognized as the most elegant, ambitious, and important statement on civil-military relations theory to date." Feaver seeks to update, perhaps even replace, Huntington by drawing on relatively recent advances in the study of the political oversight of nonsecurity bureaucracies—principal-agent theory.[11]

Ultimately, however, the principal-agent framework used in *Armed Servants* will be found incapable of providing an adequate foundation for the war-waging responsibilities of senior political and military leaders. The principal-agent framework's overfocus on military compliance and on the economic-based relationship between civilian principals and military agents risks excluding other essential aspects of senior leader war-waging responsibilities as well as treating the lives of citizens-who-become-soldiers as if they have less value than they actually do.

The Principal-Agent Framework

The principal-agent framework is an approach developed by economists to analyze problems of agency, where one person has delegated authority to someone else to act on his behalf. Civilians invent the military, so to speak, then contract with it to protect society from enemies. In figuring out the details of this notional contract, civilians find it necessary to assure themselves that the military will behave as intended. The framework supposes that a specific type of employer-employee relationship exists between civilians and the military. Feaver explains that relationship in this way:

> The employer (principal) would like to hire a diligent worker (agent), and, once hired, would like to be certain that the employee is doing what he is supposed to do (working) and not doing something else (shirking). The employee, of course, would like to be hired and so has an incentive to appear more diligent during the interview than he really is; this fact complicates the employer's efforts to pick the sort of employee who will want to work hard. . . . Once hired, moreover, the employee has an incentive to do as little work as he can get away with, all the while sending information back to the employer that suggests he is performing at an acceptable level; this fact complicates the employer's efforts to keep tabs on the employee. . . .

The principal-agent approach, then, analyzes how the principal can shape the relationship so as to ensure that his employees are carrying out his wishes.[12]

In the case of the civil-military (i.e., employer-employee) relationship, Feaver says: "The military officer is promising to risk his life, or to order his comrades to risk their lives, to execute any policy decisions. The civilian actor is promising to answer to the electorate for the consequences of any policy decisions. The military officer is expected to obey even stupid orders, or resign in favor of someone who will. The civilian is claiming the right to be wrong." This kind of military officer–civilian leader relationship forms what Feaver calls *the subtextual* to the civil-military discourse for all policy making in the national security realm.[13]

This particular principal-agent theory defines the functional imperative in terms of *working*—that is, the employee doing what the employer wants and doing it the way the employer wants it done. Doing anything other than what the employer wants as the employer wants it done is *shirking*. Working, according to Feaver but quite unlike Huntington, does not necessarily mean that the outcomes of military action will please civilians. In fact, some of the things that civilian leadership wants done may in fact result in losing a war, for working and shirking are not synonymous with winning and losing on the battlefield. One side can work in the narrowly defined, principal-agent framework sense and still lose; likewise, one side can shirk and still win. In the principal-agent framework, "the military should advise against such policies [i.e., those they consider ill advised], but the military should not prevent those policies from being implemented."[14] What Feaver is insisting on is not a civil-military relationship that increases the probability of choosing wisely with respect to war aims, strategies, policies, or military campaigns—which was inherent in Huntington's understanding of the functional imperative. Rather, because of the very specific way in which the principal-agent framework understands the employer-employee relationship, the resultant military officer–political leader relationship is based primarily, perhaps even solely, on power, control, and obedience. The result is not a balance of the functional and social imperatives but, rather, a situation in which the social imperative dominates.

Further, according to the principal-agent framework that Feaver uses, employees are always likely to shirk, given the chance. Even if employee goals and desires coincide with those of the employers, the employers would not necessarily know that. As such, civilian employers must figure out how to best monitor and control their military employees so as to make sure that they do *what* the employers want and do it *how* they want it done. That is, civilian employers must identify cost-effective monitoring schemes that increase the likelihood of their military employees working and reduce the incidences of shirking.

In some ways, Feaver's discussion is unremarkable. Senior leaders of all large organizations—whether government bureaucracies, corporations, or military headquarters—are charged to get things done and, thus, must monitor their workforce and subordinate leaders. Goals without strategies to execute them are dreams, and execution—especially in large, complex, and geographically dispersed organizations—requires monitoring schemes. In this sense, all senior military leaders monitor their own organizations through a combination of personal inspections and staff and subordinate leader reports and assessments. Senior political leaders—executive and legislative—also monitor (or should monitor) the civilian and military actions within not only the Department of Defense but also the other departments, agencies, and organizations that make up the US government. Such monitoring always has been and always will be conducted.

Similarly unremarkable is Feaver's "right to be wrong" if this formulation can be taken merely as a strongly worded way in which to say that in democracies the final decision authority concerning war aims, strategies, policies, and campaigns lies with senior political leaders, not military leaders. Civilian principals have the right to direct military agents to do something that ultimately proves costly, foolhardy, and even disastrous. Military agents have an obligation to point out, honestly and clearly, the potential negative consequences of proposed courses of action. Feaver recognizes that senior military leaders should always present their views and assessments, argue over what they believe are imprudent strategies or policies, and make every attempt to mitigate risks inherent in the final decisions.[15] In the end, however, the choices for senior military leaders are few: execute the decisions of the senior political leaders as if they were their own and inform political leaders of any adaptations to initial directives based on unfolding realities on the battlefield, or resign.

In this unremarkable sense, Feaver's approach is merely descriptive of what is necessary to ensure the proper balance between the functional and social imperatives, thus making sure that a nation has a military that is strong and capable but also subordinate to civilian authority. In other ways, however, his approach goes well beyond this unremarkable sense, causing an imbalance between the functional and the social imperatives.

A civil-military relationship based on power and control is not the kind of relationship necessary to wage war. The object of the wartime civil-military relationship—to identify the set of war aims, strategies, policies, and military and nonmilitary campaigns that, when executed, have the highest probability of success and adapt these aims, strategies, policies, and campaigns as the reality of war unfolds—is left out of a framework that defines *work* as narrowly as does *Armed Servants*. An overemphasis on power and control—doing *what* the principals want and *how* they want it done—replaces, or at least significantly diminishes, the functional imperative as Huntington conceived of it.

Feaver describes the Vietnam War as "a case of military working even in the presence of sharp disagreements between civilians and the military." This description and the reasoning for it provide a good example of why Feaver's approach is radically incomplete. The principal-agent framework is not concerned with evaluations of whether the United States should have intervened, whether the intervention was executed well, or the outcome of the intervention. Rather, it is concerned "first and foremost with whether and why military agents acted as directed by civilian principals, whether the military complied with its civilian masters."[16]

Feaver concedes that the military did not press the war on reluctant civilian leaders; rather, the reverse was the case. While he describes several times during the Vietnam War at which the military could be rightly accused of shirking, he notes that there is some conventional wisdom saying that the military did not shirk enough during the war and was "overprofessional" in its attitude.[17] But, in the end, he calls attention to the fact that the Joint Chiefs of Staff did not resign en masse in 1967 and, thus, concludes that the military did not shirk as much as one might have expected and that Vietnam was in general an example of military subordination in which the military obeyed an order to fight. In terms of the agency framework, civilians monitored intrusively, and the military worked in the narrow principal-agent sense.[18] The civilian leaders may have kept the military under control and in that sense gotten what they wanted, but the Vietnam War was certainly not waged well and the nation surely not served well.

As to why the military subordinated itself to civilian leadership during Vietnam and to what result, Feaver presents three main reasons. First, the evidence suggests that soldiers' expectations of punishment, if they shirked, were high. In the 1960s, senior military leaders would have had clear memories of General Douglas MacArthur's insubordination to President Truman and subsequent removal from command in Korea. This memory was reinforced during a conversation between President Johnson and General Westmoreland in February 1966. The president reportedly told the general: "I have a lot riding on you. . . . I hope you don't pull a MacArthur on me." Second, the Johnson administration manipulated the services: "Interservice rivalry and the preoccupation of senior military officers with advancing their own service interests gave civilian principals the opportunity to offer service 'side payments' in the form of an expansion in the size of the Marine Corps or control over particularly desirable billets that inflated the value of working." Finally, civilian leaders used a form of subjective control and promoted senior military officers who concurred with the civilian viewpoint, or at least did not disagree so strongly.[19]

The Vietnam War lasted over two decades—from the 1954 advisory effort to the final withdrawal in 1975.[20] It resulted in 58,220 US deaths,[21] cost about $738 billion (in fiscal year 2011 dollars),[22] and did not attain the stated US war aims. These results, however, do not matter with regard to analyzing the war from the principal-agent perspective. Feaver is very clear: "The goal civilians pursued, the substance of 'working,' was to preserve South Vietnam without conquering North Vietnam. . . . This was quite clearly what civilian leaders wanted, and they refused to pay for anything more. Such a goal was inappropriate and perhaps unachievable, given . . . strategic realities. . . . But it was the policy the civilians asked for and, by and large, it was the policy the military delivered. So far as civil-military relations go, civilians have a right to be wrong. This time they were."[23] The narrow perspective in which principal-agent theory is interested is this: Vietnam was an example of a divergence of views between political and military leaders. Intrusive monitoring, threats of punishment, and manipulation were required to ensure that the military worked and did not shirk. The Johnson administration used each of these mechanisms, and the military worked in the narrow, principal-agent sense.

According to this narrow perspective, the Vietnam War is an example of a proper civil-military relationship. Feaver looks at other cases as well—the Cold War, the First Gulf War, Somalia, Haiti, Bosnia, and Kosovo—to show how the principal-agent framework applies in each.[24] But each case is evaluated by one criterion: whether the military worked or shirked; that is, whether political leaders retained power and control over the military. Feaver's fundamental issue is to establish how principals act in order to secure compliance with their agents.

The intent of *Armed Servants* is not, however, merely to analyze one aspect of the civil-military relationship, civil control over the military. Rather, it is to present agency theory as a worthy alternative to the reigning institutional paradigm of civil-military relations, Huntington's objective control model. Feaver seeks to replace that model with his, one that should be used to guide the interactions between senior civil and military leaders.[25] His intent is to present not just a descriptive theory but one that could become normative.

Just as Huntington's analysis concluded that the American democracy should not adopt the forms of subjective control, Feaver hopes to demonstrate that the principal-agent framework should be adopted in lieu of Huntington's objective control theory. Toward this end, he demonstrates that Huntington's model, which predicted that the military would work only under nonintrusive civilian monitoring, is inaccurate. He uses Cold War and post–Cold War cases to show that the military generally worked—in the narrow definition of *work*—even when the military disagreed with civilian decisions and even under intrusive civilian monitoring.[26]

Power, control, obedience, compliance, and the right to be wrong—the core of the principal-agent framework and the subtext for all civil-military policy discourse—are important and essential parts of the relationship between senior political leaders and their military subordinates. A variety of monitoring regimes, some intrusive and others not, are also necessary—as they are in every bureaucracy. In the sense of understanding how the civil and military bureaucracies interact and how principals get agents to comply with their directives, Feaver's approach is insightful.

If agency theory is to replace the reigning model and be useful normatively, however, it will have to explain more than it does now. While ensuring compliance is important, it is but a small component of the civil-military relationship necessary to wage war. For example, by themselves, power, control, obedience, and intrusive monitoring inhibit, rather than encourage, the very dialogue that even Feaver recognizes is necessary to wage war successfully.[27] The relationship between the senior civilian and military leaders who wage war is more complicated than the principal-agent formulation: members of the military (agents) promise to risk their lives, and civilian leaders (principals) promise to answer to the electorate for the consequences of any policy decisions.[28] These promises do not suffice with respect to war-waging responsibilities. Senior political and military leaders both have responsibility for the lives of citizens-who-become-soldiers who are used in war and for the lives of the innocent who are inherently at risk in war. Further, both are responsible to the American population, albeit in different ways, as to how US lives and resources are used. And both share the responsibility as architects of strategy and policy and as those who execute their bureaucracies and adapt to war as it unfolds. The significant relevant difference is that senior political leaders have final decision authority, whereas senior military leaders do not.

Feaver ends *Armed Servants* by saying: "Let civilian voters punish civilian leaders for wrong decisions. Let the military advise against foolish adventures, even advising strenuously when circumstances demand. But let the military execute those orders faithfully. The republic would be better served even by foolish working than by enlightened shirking."[29] Whatever truth this conclusion contains, from the war-waging perspective the republic would be best served by senior political leaders making war-waging decisions that are likely to lead to success. Compliance with orders is simply not enough; the substance of orders is also important. Justice in war demands more than compliance.

In *How Wars End,* Gideon Rose makes a similar observation concerning the civil-military interactions during the Iraq War:

> [Secretary of Defense Donald] Rumsfeld felt contempt . . . for the [Defense Department's] conventional wisdom, and calmly set about bending the military to his will. His first order of business was to eliminate the Joint Chiefs of Staff as an independent source of authority. Then he stocked the hierarchy with officers who would follow his lead. And finally he took personal charge of the war planning process, demanding endless drafts and relentlessly pushing [General Tommy] Franks to deliver something that conformed to his [Rumsfeld's] specifications. . . . So most officers simply shelved whatever disapproval they may have felt and gave their boss what he wanted.[30]

In principal-agent parlance, the military worked, but the result was far from what best served the nation.

Rumsfeld demonstrated power, established control, and received compliance, but as Thomas White, the civilian secretary of the army during this period, put it: "If you grind away at the military guys long enough, they will finally say, 'Screw it, I'll do the best I can with what I have.'"[31] In *Dark Victory,* Jeffrey Record corroborates Gideon Rose's appraisal: "Rumsfeld . . . believed the Clinton administration had given the professional military too much latitude . . . and he was determined to reassert the authority of the Office of the Secretary of Defense. . . . 'I want to reinstate civilian control of the military!' he roared during a meeting shortly after taking office."[32]

Rose's and Record's descriptions of the civil-military relationship and the decisions and actions that emerged from them accord with the principal-agent framework. The military worked because it did what the civilian leadership wanted, how it wanted it done, but the Iraq War lasted longer—in fact, at the time of this writing, it is still ongoing—and resulted in more death, innocent and soldier, than it needed to in part because of this kind of relationship. The cost of the Iraq War has been over five thousand Americans killed, tens of thousands of Americans wounded, even more Iraqi casualties (military, police, and civilian), and an estimated price tag of $1 trillion to the United States alone. A civil-military relationship based on power and control, one that seeks compliance over outcome, lacks the normative power that is likely to generate effective war-waging decisions and actions.

Feaver admits that he has paid relatively less attention to how, as principal-agent theory requires, civilian control might affect the ability of the military to carry out its functional role to defend and advance the national interest.[33] But that is just the point.

The Vietnam War and the Iraq War cases show that it is no more possible to understand war-waging responsibilities using power, control, obedience to a right to be wrong, and intrusive monitoring to achieve compliance without reference to outcomes than it is to understand a professional sport using the internal dynamics of a sports team and the team's relationship to management without reference to scoring. Agency theory cannot be a worthy alternative to Huntington and will have little normative appeal until it includes an analysis of the functional imperative. And it cannot account for senior political and military war-waging responsibilities until it includes the importance of outcomes in war.

Civilian control of the military remained intact throughout the Vietnam War, but the functional imperative—effectiveness—suffered; tens of thousands of lives were used to achieve no worthy purpose. Of course, winning the war but losing civil control would be a worse outcome. Huntington's central idea concerning the two imperatives, however, was not to take an either/or approach; rather, it was to get the balance right: have a military instrument capable of successfully protecting the nation while remaining subordinate to civil authority. The principal-agent framework, at least as far as it goes in *Armed Servants,* emphasizes the social imperative over the functional and in doing so diminishes, even masks, a significant portion of the war-waging responsibilities of senior political and military leaders. If, in some future study, Feaver takes up an analysis of the effect of agency theory on the functional imperative, he will have to explain not only how civilian control affects the military's responsibilities for tactical, war-fighting functions but also how it affects the strategic, war-waging functions that senior political and military leaders share.

Implications for *Jus in Bello* War-Waging Responsibilities

Perhaps one day principal-agent theory will take up the task of its effect on the functional imperative. In the meantime, the question relative to just war theory is whether, or to what extent, the framework presented in *Armed Servants* can illuminate an understanding of senior political and military leaders' *jus in bello* war-waging responsibilities. This question is a legitimate one even if Feaver himself does not ask it.

The principal-agent framework is helpful in understanding war-waging responsibilities in several ways. First, it addresses the second war-waging responsibility by explaining at least part of what is required to translate decisions concerning war aims, strategies, and policies into action. Monitoring regimes—intrusive, nonintrusive, or some combination of the two—are, agency theory points out, necessary to make sure execution stays aligned with decisions. Such monitoring will be necessary both for military and for nonmilitary bureaucracies because war aims cannot be achieved through military means alone.

Second, the principal-agent framework corroborates the necessity of robust civil-military dialogue as the means to identify war aims, strategies, and policies—even as, as will be seen below, the framework's own structure inhibits the very dialogue it finds necessary.

Finally, agency theory identifies the necessity of civil primacy. Democracies require that elected leaders, as opposed to military officers, have final decision authority and retain ultimate control of the military. The tripartite tension in the war-waging dimension of *jus in bello* recognizes this primacy.

These three contributions to understanding the war-waging responsibilities of senior political and military leaders, however, are accompanied by four areas that prevent the principal-agent theory from providing an adequate foundation for *jus in bello*'s war-waging responsibilities. First, the internal dynamics set in motion by power, control, obedience to a right to be wrong, and intrusive monitoring can obstruct the very dialogue necessary to wage war. Second, compliance monitoring inhibits adapting initial decisions to the changing realities inherent in war. Third, because the economic-based principal-agent framework leaves out other aspects of the relationship between citizens-who-become-soldiers and their government, soldiers' lives are treated as if they had less value than they actually have. Finally, the civilian right to be wrong is too absolutely stated to be a useful guide in the conduct of war. Each of these shortcomings is taken up in turn.

First, the internal dynamics set in motion by power, control, obedience to a right to be wrong, and intrusive monitoring can obstruct the very dialogue necessary to wage war. The kind of dialogue necessary to properly execute war-waging responsibilities is unlikely to emerge from people in a work relationship based solely, or even primarily, on power and control and where work is defined as doing what the civilian leadership wants done, how it wants it done. More likely to emerge from such a relationship is a toxic work environment.

Every work relationship has an economic dimension to it as well as power and control dimensions. But overemphasizing power, control, and economics and overly narrowing the definition of *work* can distort one's understanding of a proper work relationship. Such overemphasis as the primary basis for an employer's relationship with employees and subordinate leaders is more likely to establish a toxic work environment than one in which employees feel free to voice their opinions and contribute to the success of the enterprise.

Lyndon Johnson, known for his ability to establish power and control over those with whom he interacted, certainly did so with his military advisers. For example, in early November 1965, the Joint Chiefs of Staff requested a meeting with the president to discuss how the war was being fought. This was, in the words of one attendee, "to be the meeting to determine whether the U.S. military would continue its seemingly directionless Vietnam buildup to fight a protracted ground war or take bold measures designed to bring the war to an early, favorable conclusion." The president "did not offer his guests a seat" and after "only a few minutes . . . attacked them in the most vile and despicable terms, cursing them personally, ridiculing their advice, using the crudest and filthiest language."[34] The result, not just of this single incident but of an environment set by the president and his secretary of defense in which control was paramount, was not an open dialogue that produced strategies and policies with a reasonable probability of success. Rather, it was one that did not permit a candid assessment of the situation or an evaluation of possible American actions designed to influence it and one that created a relationship in which the president remained ignorant of the chiefs' opinions and the chiefs remained ill informed of the direction in which the administration's Vietnam policy was headed.[35] It was a classic toxic environment.

Rumsfeld's desire to assert civilian control and the authority of the office of the secretary of defense over the Joint Chiefs and the services was similarly toxic and had similar results. "Long before Operation Iraqi Freedom, even before 9/11," writes the defense analyst Jeffery Record, "civil-military tensions inside the Pentagon were running higher than perhaps at any time since the reign of Robert McNamara [Johnson's secretary of defense during the Vietnam War], who, like Rumsfeld, was an abrasive, assertive, exceptionally self-confident man who was not afraid to impose his views on the professional military."[36] President George W. Bush acknowledged Rumsfeld's strengths but admitted that at times even he was frustrated with Rumsfeld's abruptness toward military leaders and members of the presidential staff.[37] The emphasis on establishing the power of the office of the secretary of defense and its control over the military resulted in what Matthew Moten has characterized as a "broken dialogue." The broken dialogue ultimately affected planning for and execution of the Iraq War. "Rumsfeld's insistence on controlling every detail," Moten observes, "exacerbated their [the Joint Chiefs'] concerns." In the end, Rumsfeld's actions undermined the credibility of senior military officers and created a management style and an environment that cast subordinates as adversaries.[38]

Contrast Rumsfeld's approach with that of his replacement, Robert Gates, who gained a reputation for honest consultation and listening to military leaders, and, although not always accepting their advice, never denigrated it either publicly or privately. Ironically, Gates proved far more willing to discipline his subordinates than did Rumsfeld, firing a service secretary, relieving general officers, and accepting the retirement of combatant commanders. Such action, however, did nothing to diminish his good reputation with the uniformed military, and it raised the quality of the dialogue and in doing so improved the likelihood of quality decisions.[39]

Power and control are absolutely necessary elements in the relationship between senior political and military leaders who wage war. When this power and control are asserted too quickly in a dialogue, are overused, or become the primary basis for the civil-military relationship, however, the result is counterproductive to war-waging responsibilities.

Second, compliance monitoring inhibits adapting initial decisions to the changing realities inherent in war. Compliance monitoring makes sure that the agent does what the principal wants done in the way the principal wants it done. Such monitoring is absolutely necessary when running any larger corporate endeavor. Compliance monitoring is also necessary in waging war. Senior political and military leaders both use compliance regimes in executing their war-waging responsibilities, but waging war also requires other forms of monitoring methodologies.

Compliance regimes are a natural fit within a principal-agent framework where *work* is defined as agents doing *what* principals want done, *how* they want it done. They are also a natural fit for some aspects of waging war. In those areas where standards are fixed—for example, in determining the level of fiscal, personnel, contracting, and materiel accountability or in monitoring logistic delivery times—they are the perfect tool to use. They do not question the standards; they concern only compliance with the standards. Strategies, policies, and campaigns, however, are not areas where standards are fixed.

These areas are relative in three ways: relative to war aims, to the enemy, and to one's own capabilities. If strategies, policies, and campaigns are not helping achieve war aims, the question is not just whether military and nonmilitary departments are complying with them. Rather, the strategies, policies, and campaigns themselves need to be questioned. If they are having no effect or an insufficient effect on the enemy, continued compliance with them is rarely the proper action to take. Rather, the proper action is to question the strategies, policies, and campaigns themselves. Finally, a strategy, policy, or campaign may be conceptually perfect, that is, just what is needed to subdue the enemy and achieve war aims, in theory. Simultaneously, a theoretically perfect strategy, policy, or campaign may be impossible to execute because one's military forces or nonmilitary departments are incapable of actually doing what is called for. These cases require either change to military or nonmilitary capacity or modification to strategies, policies, or campaigns so that they can actually be executed. Simply put, senior political and military leaders waging war need more than compliance-monitoring regimes.

Chapter 5 will take up this topic more completely. At this point, suffice it to say that the principal-agent framework's use of compliance regimes is understandable given its definition of *work*. Alone, however, compliance regimes are insufficient to execute war-waging responsibilities, for they offer little room in which to evaluate the substance of the strategies or policies that are being complied with or to determine whether the strategies or policies are the right ones.

Third, because the economic-based principal-agent framework leaves out other aspects of the relationship between citizens-who-become-soldiers and their government, soldiers' lives are treated as if they had less value than they actually have. In its most stark form, an employer's job in the principal-agent framework is to direct, monitor, and punish. This approach is understandable given the framework's focus on explaining how, in the face of the two problems described below, principals get their agents to do what they want done, how they want it done.

The first problem is the adverse-selection problem: "that the employer cannot know for certain about the true preferences and capabilities of the applicant." The second is the moral hazard problem, which derives from the fact that, as we have seen, the employer wants to hire a diligent worker and the employee has an incentive to appear more diligent than he is before he is hired and to shirk after he is hired. In the principal-agent framework, these two problems play out throughout the civil-military relationship.[40]

On the one hand, these two problems innocently describe some of the behaviors inherent in any workforce. On the other hand, Feaver introduces a not-so-innocent analogy—that the civilians within the office of the secretary of defense and the service secretariats are to the military as police patrol officers are to a community. "Police patrols" employed by civilian-principals are a form of intrusive monitoring that is "designed to turn up evidence of agent wrongdoing."[41] From the innocent perspective, such monitoring is standard management practice: put in place audit mechanisms to ensure that systems and processes are running as intended and deter employees who might be tempted to subvert the system or process or to use it to their advantage. But, from the not-so-innocent perspective, police look for criminals and prevent crime, and, in this sense, the principal-agent framework introduces something more deleterious than routine management.

In any work environment, a percentage of employees engage in wrongdoing. Such knowledge requires employers to have proper policies accompanied by adequate monitoring and enforcement mechanisms.[42] Common best business practices, however, show that, if an employer wants to create a positive work environment and, thereby, increase the probability of success in the enterprise of the business, he does not base his employer-employee relationship on the assumption of wrongdoing.

If all Feaver meant by the analogy was that employers must be on the lookout for wrongdoing as they monitor the efficiency and effectiveness of their organizational systems, his observations would be benign. His claim is stronger, however. He says: "In the civil-military context, an important indicator of police patrol monitoring is the size of the civilian secretariat of the Office of the Secretary of Defense and the service secretariats. These are extensions of the executive branch principals, the patrol officers. . . . [L]arge numbers of civilian officials are evidence of a police patrol monitoring mechanism." Here, he clearly equates the size and purpose of the Defense Department's staff with "police patrols . . . [that are] designed to turn up evidence of agent wrongdoing."[43] The staff has many more purposes than that.

The senior political and military leaders responsible for waging war require an approach more in line with common best business practices. They need inspectors general, internal and external auditing organizations, and other ombudsman-like agencies to help them run the large organizations for which they are responsible. Each helps ensure that the systems of a leader's organization are running properly. Each helps ensure that subordinates have avenues through which to voice concern outside the regular chain of command. Further, one of the important roles of the inspector general is the protection of civilian and uniformed employees, making sure that they are treated well and provided the care and support that law and regulation mandate. There are separate criminal investigation agencies that attend to illegal behavior when such behaviors arise. By narrowing the analysis aperture to power, control, the narrow definition of *work,* and the direct-monitor-punish model, the principal-agent framework misses important dimensions of the phenomena it intends to explain.

Citizens-who-become-soldiers are the people whose lives senior political and military leaders use in war. Direct, monitor, and punish may be part of a leader-employer's responsibility, but these three factors cannot suffice. Respect for those whose lives will be used in war demands more. Citizens-who-become-soldiers remain human beings, and the value of their lives must be respected. Respect for their lives is the reason why Walzer and others take seriously the principle of due care and due risk. The tactical aspects of this respect are demonstrated, in part, through a military chain of command that first provides soldiers what they need in terms of training, equipment, supplies, life support, leadership, and just treatment and then ensures that, when they are employed in combat, operations are conducted within the bounds of *jus in bello*'s tactical principles. But there is a strategic aspect of due care as well.

Respect for the value of soldiers' lives is also manifested through the decisions and actions taken by the senior civilian and military leaders who are responsible for waging war. First, if all senior leaders do is direct, monitor, and punish—rather than interacting with their subordinates as human beings, seeking their input, eliciting their opinions, and explaining orders or directives—then they are disrespecting subordinates at an individual level. Disrespect can take on a second dimension, however. If subordinates are treated merely as items to be ordered, monitored, and punished and they do not do what they were told as they were told to do it, then senior leaders develop an attitude toward them that fails to take their lives into consideration in ways that a valuable human life deserves. The potential for institutional or systematic disrespect, therefore, emerges. Ultimately, the result may be overly dangerous strategies, foolish policies, or poorly conceived campaigns where citizens-who-become-soldiers are killed or injured needlessly.

The senior civilian and military leaders who are responsible for waging war have more than direct, monitor, and punish responsibilities. They have at least three morally relevant responsibilities that derive from respecting the lives of citizens-who-become-soldiers. The first of these is, of course, not to force citizens to fight in illegal or unjust wars—a *jus ad bellum* responsibility. Walzer makes this point and declares it a responsibility of political leaders. He also describes a second responsibility to prevent even just wars from turning into crusades—a *jus in bello* responsibility to stop the fighting once a just war has attained its aims or its aims are within political reach.[44] He is not exactly clear as to whose responsibility this is, but it is descriptive of the civil-military decision that ended the 1990–1991 Gulf War.

A small group of civilian and military leaders discussed the war's end with President George H. W. Bush. Colin Powell, then the chairman of the Joint Chiefs of Staff, wrote that, as he sensed that the end of the Gulf War was near, he called General Norman Schwarzkopf [then the commander of US Central Command responsible for military operations during the war] to get his sense of the situation. One adviser said that the United States does not want to be seen fighting beyond "the rational calculation"; similarly, another commented that America did not want to be seen as "killing for the sake of killing." When the president spoke to the nation, he said: "Kuwait is liberated. Iraq's army is defeated. Our military objectives are met. . . . I am pleased to announce that at midnight tonight [February 28, 1991], eastern standard time . . . all U.S. and coalition forces will suspend offensive combat operations."[45] Bush held the responsibility for making the final decision, but a wider set of civilian and military leaders shared the responsibility to ensure that his decision was a good one. What both the president and his advisers had in mind was doing all they could to use the lives of soldiers justly and wisely and avoid unnecessary risk to the innocent.

The third responsibility is to treat citizens-who-become-soldiers with the dignity and respect—individually and organizationally— that they deserve as human beings. American citizens-who-become- soldiers may have their individual right to life changed or infringed or abridged or may have an altered legal status vis-à-vis the enemy, but their legal status is not altered vis-à-vis their own government. At the higher level, senior civil and military leaders have responsibilities to their citizens-who-become-soldiers. They should not knowingly use their lives foolishly or in stupid ways. They may make mistakes and err in their judgments and directives. They cannot, however, do so knowingly or callously. "The institution of rights against the Government," Dworkin points out, "is not a gift of God, or an ancient ritual, or a national sport. It is a complex and troublesome practice that makes the Government's job of securing the general benefit more difficult and more expensive."[46]

Citizens-who-become-soldiers certainly learn quickly that military life involves its share of foolishness and stupidity. They also learn that their lives could well be put at risk as a result of some foolish, stupid, or dumb order. But, unless such orders are the exception, not the rule, military discipline, trust in the chain of command, and respect between civil and military institutions will break down—and very quickly. At the tactical level, discipline is maintained, contrary to conventional wisdom, because the rule is that orders are reasonable given the circumstances, likely to contribute to mission success, and likely to contribute to self-preservation. Within tactical units, soldiers often argue among themselves and with their leaders—sergeants and officers—as to what is smart in a particular case. Soldiers in well-led, disciplined units expect to be heard and listened to; they expect reasoned leadership and appropriate orders, not foolish, stupid, or dumb orders handed out by an authoritarian whose only rationale is to demonstrate that he is in charge and who treats them as objects, not persons. These are among the ways in which soldiers' rights are respected at the tactical level. Soldiers also expect that the various echelons in their chain of command—all the way up to their strategic leaders, the senior political and military leaders who identify war aims, strategies, and policies—see to it that they are respected in these ways. Because citizens become soldiers, their lives can be used. They should not, however, be wasted, treated callously, or used in vain—whether by leaders at the tactical level or by leaders at the strategic level.

Again, a direct, monitor, and punish approach is understandable within a principal-agent framework with a focus on explaining how principals get their agents to do what they want done, how they want it done. Alone, however, such an approach cannot provide an adequate foundation for the war-waging responsibilities of senior political and military leaders. The citizens-now-soldiers, those whose lives are literally on the line, deserve better, and justice in war demands better.

Finally, the civilian right to be wrong is too absolutely stated to be a useful guide in the conduct of war. The principal-agent framework claims that the right to be wrong is necessary in a democracy.[47] Such a claim is correct in the sense that civilian leaders in a democracy must retain responsibility for making the final war-waging decisions. Senior military leaders are, and must be, subordinate to this final decision authority. The democracy requires such, even when senior military leaders believe that war aims, strategies, policies, and campaigns are not the best from their perspective.

Because the principal-agent framework is designed only to explain one aspect of the relationship between senior political and military leaders—how the senior political leader principals get their military subordinate agents to do what they want done, how they want it done—it has only to assert the existence of the right to be wrong. But, just as soldiers remain moral agents in combat, senior military leaders remain moral agents in the war-waging boardroom. Simple obedience is not the standard for soldiers and their leaders on the battlefield, and it cannot be the standard for senior military leaders in the boardroom. Justice in the conduct of war, therefore, requires an understanding of Feaver's right to be wrong and of what is involved in civilians claiming the right to be wrong deeper than that civilians have it and the military does not.[48]

According to some surveys, a civil-military friction is developing. This friction comes from a growing number of midlevel officers who show some reluctance to accept a civilian leader's right to be wrong. These surveys describe the belief among some military personnel that it is their role to "insist rather than merely advise or advocate in private, on key decisions, particularly those involving the use of force." The implication drawn by advocates of the principal-agent framework is the existence of a new civil-military norm in which midgrade officers imply that, "while their leaders should not be openly insubordinate, they may, indeed sometimes should, resist civilian direction or even resign in protest of civilian policies." Such a norm, according to principal-agent theory, could lead to real trouble.[49]

The normative implication is clear: best not to deviate from the principal-agent right to be wrong norm because such deviation may place the social imperative at risk. A different conclusion might also be drawn, however. The views expressed by the midlevel officers may not challenge the principle of civilian control. Rather, the midlevel officers are expressing concern over the duties of their military seniors during the civil-military dialogue necessary to exercise, responsibly, their shared war-waging duties. Further, they point to an important moral question: Is there a limit to the obedience that senior military officers owe their political masters? This question strikes at the heart of the basic assumption of the principal-agent framework.

The *right* in *right to be wrong* cannot be a universal right, a right that any civilian, on any topic, and under any conditions can claim against any member of the military. Rather, it is limited to some civilians, on some topics, and at some times. This limited set of people can claim the right to be wrong against some members of the military. That is, senior military leaders ought to obey the final decisions of those senior political leaders who have the authority to declare war, direct other uses of military forces, and employ military forces in it—even in situations where military leaders disagree with the decisions.

Clarity in identifying who can claim this right is not a trivial matter. The president, for example, can use constitutional and legal grounds to claim it. The Constitution identifies the president as the commander in chief.[50] The secretary of defense can also claim the right to be wrong. By statute, the secretary of defense has authority, direction, and control over the Department of Defense, is the principal assistant to the president in all matters related to the department, and is in the chain of command and, thus, exercises command and control over all US military forces for both operational and administrative purposes.[51] Conceivably, when speaking on behalf of the president, the principals of the National Security Council may also be legitimate claimants to this right.[52] With respect to the executive branch, however, beyond this small circle claiming to have the right to be wrong becomes problematic.

The validity of subordinates and staff of principals making a claim to the right to be wrong would be situational. On the one hand, some principals communicate through their subordinates and staff as a matter of efficiency. On the other hand, staffs, and sometimes even senior deputies, are notorious for saying that they speak for a principal in cases where they do not. Similarly, there are situations where one might question whether even a vice president can speak for the president and, therefore, claim the right to be wrong. Vice Presidents Truman and Johnson, for example, were, relative to Presidents Roosevelt and Kennedy, in different positions than was Vice President Cheney relative to President Bush. A common behavior in large bureaucracies like those of the US federal government is for staff or deputies to wield power *as if* they had it. Such behavior is a bureaucratic means to extend one's influence and power, but it is not a legitimate claim to the right to be wrong.

The legislative branch may also have constitutional grounds to claim this right,[53] but this claim differs from that of the executive branch. No single member of Congress—unless events trigger the statutory presidential succession—would be able to claim the right because none has the authority to issue orders. Congress as a body, however, has authorities related to raising and funding military forces and operations as well as declaring war and authorizing the use of military forces. These authorities are extensive, important, and related to the war-waging responsibilities of identifying war aims, strategies, policies, and campaigns. In 1975, for example, Congress did not authorize the funding necessary to execute President Nixon's strategy in Vietnam. Thus, American military support was not employed to assist the South Vietnamese in resisting North Vietnam's 1975 final military offensive. This congressional action could be understood as the legislative branch's collective claim to the right to be wrong.

Currently, the principal-agent framework provides no detailed discussion about who may claim the right to be wrong. Rather, it says merely that civilians have a right to be wrong. The reality is that this right can be claimed by only a small subset of civilian political leaders in identifiable executive branch positions and by the legislature acting as a body. For practical reasons, this is an important circle to draw; no civilian outside this circle has a proper claim to the right to be wrong. Clarifying the scope of who can legitimately claim the right to be wrong suggests that it is better understood as a positional duty similar to Walzer's account of the responsibilities of officers. Positional duties and obligations apply, as Fishkin explains, "only to those who have consented, promised, or come to occupy a relevant role."[54]

Similarly, principal-agent theory says nothing about when the right to be wrong can be used responsibly. Certainly, an authorized senior civilian leader can use it after extensive consideration of the facts of a situation, the alternative courses of action, and their potential costs, risks, and consequences. Even if, in the end, that leader or the set of leaders making a final decision are mistaken or in error, the right can be said to have been used responsibly. Anyone can be wrong. No one is infallible. Even the most earnest decision makers and the most proficient bureaucracies err. This case is an example of responsibly claiming the right to be wrong and is, therefore, uncontroversial. It would be similarly uncontroversial to have heated debate prior to making a decision that is ultimately proven to be mistaken. Such debate, however heated, is expected as part of the well-developed decision-making process.

There are controversial cases, however. What if a senior civilian leader or set of leaders claims the right relative to a decision that the battlefield has already been proven to be mistaken and wasteful of the lives? Cases like this, where the decision in question is known—or reasonably can be known—in advance, to be foolish, stupid, dumb, and wasteful are different from mistakes of an earnest decision maker. There could be even more controversial senses than repetitive foolishness, stupidity, and wastefulness. For example, what if the final decision was to promulgate a policy that limited distribution of bullets to three per soldier per day as a means to reduce the cost of the war and limit civilian casualties, even during active and heavy combat? Certainly, the right could be claimed in either of these cases, but such a claim would be controversial since it would not be claimed responsibly.

Clearly, every senior leader, civilian and military, involved in the discussions of decisions concerning known foolishness, extreme stupidity, or avoidable waste would argue strenuously against the three-bullet rule or the repeat of some other previously failed approach. Further, no actual leader would likely ever direct anything like known stupidity, extreme foolishness, or avoidable wastefulness. What makes cases like these important, however, is that they illustrate limits to when the right to be wrong can be reasonably claimed. They illustrate that the right to be wrong is a strong right in the way in which Dworkin uses it in *Taking Rights Seriously*. "In most cases," Dworkin says, "when we say that someone has a 'right' to do something, we imply that it would be wrong to interfere with his doing it, or at least that some special grounds are needed for justifying any interference."[55] It would be wrong for military or civilian leaders to interfere with the responsible exercise of the right to be wrong as explained in the uncontroversial cases. But it appears that there are special grounds in the controversial cases—cases where the right is not claimed reasonably—that would justify interference with a civilian leader's right to be wrong as *Armed Servants*'s principal-agent framework understands that right.

Military leaders as well as subordinate civilian leaders must work to attain war aims and execute strategies, policies, and campaigns that emanate from proper authorities, even if they disagree with either the decision-making process or the outcome. A democracy must insist on this. Disagreement voiced prior to a decision being made does not constitute interference. Military leaders are not to execute illegal or immoral strategies or policies, ones requiring genocide, or torture, or the indiscriminate killing of noncombatants, for example. These kinds of decisions seem to involve special grounds that not only justify interference but also require it.

The extreme cases of known, repetitive, or extreme foolishness or stupidity and avoidable waste, however, suggest that some decisions may cross a line separating honest mistakes in matters of prudence, on the one hand, and immoral directives and decisions, on the other.

War-waging decisions inherently involve using lives. Respect for the value of those lives, whether of the innocent or of citizens-who-become-soldiers, places a responsibility on those making such decisions. The responsibility is to make the best decisions possible given the known and knowable facts, the realities, background, and context of a particular situation, and the competing perspectives that must be considered. This responsibility is a positional responsibility attendant on those who can legitimately claim the right to be wrong. Waging war is also about recovering from honest mistakes as quickly as reasonably possible. Citizens expect their senior political and military leaders to wage war as wisely and prudently as possible. If senior military leaders propose foolish strategies or campaigns, citizens expect that political leaders will not approve them. Similarly, if senior political leaders exercise their final decision authority irresponsibly, citizens do not expect military leaders simply to salute and obey. These expectations are founded on a government's responsibility to respect and value the lives of its citizens-who-become-soldiers. That these expectations were not met during the Vietnam War was part of the outrage that followed the publication of the Pentagon Papers.[56]

Interference is not understood as senior political or military leaders trying to prevent making a foolish decision relative to war aims, strategies, or policies. It would not be interference, for example, to convince a final decision authority that a previous decision that had been executed was proved to be ineffective or that the three-bullet policy is foolish in the extreme and would use lives irresponsibly.

Certainly, decisions can be mistaken, facts can be misunderstood, alternatives can be wrongly analyzed, consequences can be unforeseen, and risks can be not fully understood. Human beings and the organizations they create to assist in making decisions can always be mistaken. An enemy's plans are not usually known, and, even when they are, plans are not always followed. Battle creates unforeseen opportunities and vulnerabilities for both sides. Friction and uncertainty reign supreme in war. So mistakes are common, even mistakes with tragic human consequences. These realities are the reasons for the robust dialogue that precedes initial war-waging decisions and the equally robust arguments about subsequent war-waging adaptations.

Either because of chance or unforeseen enemy action, tragic consequences may occur even if one used the best decision-making processes and executed the most thoughtful strategies and policies in the best ways. Neither senior political nor senior military leaders can be absolutely sure of the efficacy of their own judgments, either at the start of a war or during the course of it. Both understand that they could be wrong. These leaders actually need each other, therefore, to argue and debate fully so as to prevent foolish, stupid, dumb, or wasteful decisions from being made. Further, American society expects such interaction between their senior political and military leaders; it expects extensive dialogue and argument to precede consequential decisions that affect the use of the lives of its sons and daughters, husbands and wives, mothers and fathers, brothers and sisters. The absence of a robust dialogue is what should be upsetting, as Gideon Rose observed about the 2003 Iraq invasion: "A dysfunctional national security decision making process allowed the operation to proceed without serious questioning of heroically optimistic assumptions or proper contingency planning."[57]

Contributing to debate, even heated ones that extend over months, is part of the war-waging responsibility of those senior leaders, political and military, who participate in the decision-making dialogue. En route to a final decision, both civilian and military leaders have a duty to provide their best advice, make their best case, challenge assumptions and predictions, and present evidence and counterevidence as the debate ebbs and flows. The same duty applies to adapting, modifying, or reversing decisions made and executed because of the ever-changing realities of war. Responsible claims to the right to be wrong require debate and argument prior to decisions, and this seems to be what the midlevel officers in the previously mentioned surveys may be suggesting. They expect their seniors, the military leaders who participate in strategy and policy discussion, to argue forcefully so as *not* to get into a position where disobedience or interference becomes the only option. Moreover, they expect their seniors to represent them and their soldiers—the ones who have to execute on the battlefield—and argue forcefully and completely before foolish, stupid, or potentially wasteful orders, directives, strategies, policies, or military operations are set in motion. If this is what the midlevel officer meant by *insist* or *resist*, then all this is normal; none of it constitutes interference with the right to be wrong.

Interference with the right to be wrong, however, is understood as senior political or military leaders interfering with the execution of final decisions—after they have been made. One form of interference in this sense is akin to saying, No; I (or we) will not do that. A second form of interference involves duplicitous behavior, saying that one will comply but either subverting the decision or doing what one wants whether it conforms to the decision or not.

The second form of interference is impermissible. Whether the duplicitous behavior involves leaks that limit or close down ongoing debates, thus foreclosing a decision before it even gets proper consideration, or slow-rolling execution so that the decision made does not get a fair evaluation, or issuing directives to one's organization that are contrary to the decision made—all are disingenuous and disloyal at best. Some, depending on the situation and the consequences involved, may qualify for moral blame. But the first form of interference may be justified under some circumstances.

Two conditions are necessary, however, before the first form of interference could be justified. First, the decision in question must be immoral, not merely imprudent or disagreeable. Second, the interference must not challenge the ultimate principle of civilian control over the military. Certainly, cases like this would be rare, for fulfilling both conditions would be difficult. It is not impossible to envision, however, a senior military leader who, after participating fully in a robust debate and doing all he or she could to prevent a particular decision from being made, concludes that he or she cannot in good conscience obey the resultant order—like the three-bullet policy. That leader could resign quietly without going public, for a public act could challenge—or be perceived to challenge—civil control. It is also not impossible to envision a senior civilian leader resigning under the same circumstances, and, because he or she is a civilian, his or her resignation would not challenge civil control. If just war theory is to hold that soldiers and their leaders on the battlefield remain moral agents, then it must also acknowledge the individual moral agency of senior political and military leaders in the boardroom.

The resignation of a senior official, even if not public, would interfere with the execution of a decision at the very minimum because of the temporary pause before execution that would likely result. No administration would move forward on a substantive war-waging decision if a secretary of defense or state, or a national security adviser, or a four-star general, or an ambassador serving in a war zone would resign over a moral issue he or she had with a specific decision—even if the resignation was quietly done. Rather, an administration would be more likely to delay the decision or its execution until it was satisfied that, when the resignation and its reasons become known, the administration's decision would stand public scrutiny. Such a delay qualifies as the first form of interference, interference after a decision has been made. Further, even the potential resignation of a senior officer could have a significant and positive effect on the responsible use of the right to be wrong. Allowing for justified interference when both the immoral and the nonthreatening to civilian control conditions are met would have the practical effect of decreasing early or unreasonable exercise of the right. Justified interference would, even if rarely used, demonstrate that the reasonable use of the right is as important as the right itself. Meeting both conditions would be difficult, but the difficulty does not affect the importance of acknowledging the possibility of justified interference.

The situation resulting from McNamara's testimony in August 1967 shows how difficult it is to meet both conditions. In his testimony, McNamara claimed that America was winning the war in Vietnam. The Joint Chiefs were stunned, according to Mark Perry's *Four Stars*. Perry explains: "McNamara's testimony broke the unofficial contract between civilian leaders and military officers that, by necessity, exists in every democratic society: members of the military pledge they will obey civilian authorities without question; in return, civilian leaders pledge that those orders will not lead to the useless sacrifice of military life." The Chiefs knew that it was impossible to win with the current US strategy and policies and that there was no plan for winning the war. "[The Chiefs] believed," writes Perry, "that to continue the war under current conditions would be immoral; it would lead to a useless sacrifice." General Earle Wheeler, the chairman of the Joint Chiefs, afterward told his colleagues that "he believed they should resign 'en masse' during a press conference to be held the next morning." Ultimately, although convinced of the righteousness of their conclusion, the Chiefs did not resign en masse, for they believed that doing so would be mutiny.[58] In effect, they knew that they had met the first condition but could not figure out how to meet the second. They also knew that they had no alternative to offer on which they could all agree.

Some form of justified interference appears to be necessary in order to preserve the moral agency of senior officials, military or civilian, and recognize that reasonable use of the right is as important as the right itself—even if the form of interference is as stringent and unlikely as that described above.

Principal-agent theory may be beginning to realize that reasonable use of the right to be wrong is important. "At the highest levels," Feaver and Kohn write, "civilians have to exercise their responsibility, appoint strong military leaders, listen to them, query them closely, advocate national defense policies, and nurture the effectiveness of U.S. military institutions. Military leaders must reciprocate with candid advice and loyal subordination."[59] Here, they seem to be acknowledging that responsible use of the right to be wrong requires some form of mutuality between senior political and military leaders greater than is found in a direct, monitor, and obey-or-be-punished framework. These leaders have correlative duties: military leaders pledge loyal subordination, and civilian leaders exercise their responsibility wisely.

Conclusions: Looking Elsewhere

Using the lives of citizens-who-become-soldiers places obligations on both tactical and strategic leaders that are not based solely on the economic-based principal-agent framework. These shortcomings do not act as a criticism of the principal-agent framework, for it never set out to provide the kind of framework *jus in bello*'s war-waging dimension needs. These shortcomings do, however, identify elements that must be included in whatever foundation for the war-waging dimension of *jus in bello* is finally adduced.

Neither the stark line that Walzer drew between the political leaders who are responsible for war itself and the military leaders who are responsible for the conduct of war nor the sharp subordination of military agent-employees to their civilian principal-employers adequately describes how war is actually conducted at the strategic level. Understanding senior political and military leader moral responsibilities in the conduct of war, their war-waging responsibilities, will require looking elsewhere. And a good place to start looking is the very nature of war.

4

Dialogue and the Nature of War

War is a political instrument that uses violence and force to achieve political purposes; by its very nature, therefore, it demands a collaborative, political-military effort.[1] At the highest levels, Clausewitz admits, fighting and policy are intellectually one. Asking for a "purely military opinion" at this level merely demonstrates, according to Clausewitz, that one does not understand the nature of war. "The conduct of war, in its great outlines, is therefore policy itself, which takes up the sword in place of the pen."[2] For political and military leaders at the highest levels there can be no neat bifurcation of duties as suggested by Huntington's objective control, Walzer's line between the war itself and its conduct, or the principal-agent framework. In waging war, senior civilian and military leaders together face exceptional difficulties.

The first difficulty concerns the stakes at risk. There are personal stakes—for example, the political life and legacy of a president or prime minister and the professional reputation of senior generals—that affect the relationship among leaders as well as the policy decisions that flow from that relationship. As important as these stakes may be, however, they are secondary. The ultimate stakes are these: the life of the political community, the lives of citizens-who-become-soldiers, the lives of the innocent, and the destruction associated with every war. Second, there are difficulties resulting from the unique and extreme differences between the personalities, backgrounds, and experiences of political and military leaders. Third, the issues of waging war are far more complex than those faced in peacetime. Each of these complexities alone demands a collaborative political-military effort, one that will often result in sometimes furious arguments and uneasy, even conflict-ridden relationships. Taken together, these complexities and others grow geometrically. Wars where political leaders merely dictate military actions almost always end in folly.[3]

In *Supreme Command,* Eliot Cohen starts from this understanding of the nature of war and identifies the war-waging responsibilities that are as much a part of conducting a war as are war-fighting responsibilities. Further, he is clear that these are coresponsibilities of senior political and military leaders—even as he asserts, unequivocally, that the final decision authority rests with civil leaders.

Political leaders, Cohen explains, should make no apologies for putting military leaders under pressure, even severe pressure, through repetitive interrogations, probing, and questioning. Similarly, military leaders should make no apologies for putting political leaders under pressure through repetitive discussion of plausibility, limits of force, likely consequences, and inherent risks. Both sets of leaders should make no apologies in making every effort to assure that war aims are aligned with strategies, policies, and campaigns as well as with the military and nonmilitary means available. In waging war, aims, strategies, policies, and campaign plans are inexorably linked to execution. A blunt give-and-take between political and military leaders, Cohen maintains, highlights this linkage, for a proper dialogue ensures that the aims, strategies, policies, and campaigns decided on can actually be carried out.

The give-and-take dialogue conducted by senior political and military leaders occurs at the start of a war—sometimes even before a war starts—and continues throughout. It ensures that aims, strategies, policies, and military operations adapt as war conditions ebb and flow. This kind of tense dialogue, Cohen demonstrates, is necessary, not to assert domination or to clarify who is in control, but to arrive at an outcome with the highest probability of success, one that is most likely to succeed amid conditions of ambiguity and conflicting options.[4] In sum, therefore, Cohen's discussion directly addresses the senior political and military leaders' first war-waging responsibility (achieving coherency by setting war aims and making strategy, policy, and campaign decisions that increase the probability of achieving those war aims) and part of the second (adapting decisions and actions as the vagaries of war unfold).

The Unequal Dialogue

Supreme Command uses four historical examples—the American Civil War, World Wars I and II, and the War for Israeli Independence—to show that the best assurance against using lives wastefully, putting the innocent or one's political community at risk unnecessarily, or any of the other risks inherent in the conduct of war is streams of decisions amid opposing advice and sharp disagreements that emerge in long, sustained, interlocked arguments. Political and military leaders improve the war-waging decisions they must make through incessant, close, difficult questioning of positions, assumptions, and suggested courses of action.[5]

This kind of dialogue is, according to Cohen, a "dark form of wisdom" necessary in war, for neither political nor military leaders can claim that they are most likely right when it comes to the complexity of waging war.[6] The truth is that everyone, senior political and military leaders alike, is more or less wrong—or can be.

Clausewitz addresses the complexity and difficulty of making war-waging decisions in *On War*, where he defines the *essence of genius* as referring to "a very highly developed mental aptitude for a particular occupation." The harmonious combination of characteristics that he describes in the chapter "On Military Genius," however, seems more appropriate to an ideal or theoretical construct than to any real person.[7] Hence, Cohen calls his penultimate chapter "Leadership without Genius,"[8] that is, the leadership that recognizes that those responsible for waging war cannot count on a genius being available at exactly the right time and place. Rather, the reality is that good war-waging decisions are most likely to emerge from a set of political and military leaders bluntly and continuously arguing with one another in an attempt to identify strategy, policy, campaign, and organizational solutions to the complex and dynamic problems they face. In the principal-agent framework, obedience is what matters most, not the content of orders and directives; in Cohen's account, content matters significantly.

Cohen describes a process, the *unequal dialogue*, that demands much more of the senior political and military leaders who wage war than to direct, monitor, and punish or to simply obey. While always insisting on a political leader's final decision authority, the outcome of the unequal dialogue is aimed at achieving prudence in waging war. Achieving prudence requires moral courage of the senior political and military participants. Cohen's approach requires these leaders to argue strenuously until they can find an alternative to something as morally repugnant as sending citizens-who-become-soldiers to a war that they know cannot be won in the way in which it is being waged—as they did in Vietnam for years. Cohen is not advocating what Peter Feaver calls *shirking*—not executing a final decision, or executing it as a slow roll. Rather, the complicated and tense unequal dialogue demands that senior political and military leaders hold each other accountable for outcomes, for the decisions and actions they take together that affect the life of the political community and the lives of the citizens-who-become-soldiers as well as the lives of the innocent—lives they use and put at risk in war. The kind of dialogue Cohen envisions is an "uneasy, even conflictual collaborative relationship in which the civilian usually (at least in democracies) has the upper hand."[9]

The war-waging decisions produced by the unequal dialogue are not best by any absolute standard; rather, the ultimate standard is only that they work, that they are better than those of the enemy, and that they achieve the declared war aims. Political leaders make mistakes, adhere to false strategies, promote misguided policies, misjudge opponents, indulge incompetents, ignore realities, and can be unlucky. This is why senior military leaders cannot simply salute and obey and why political leaders must tolerate troublesome and sometimes uncomfortable disagreement.[10] Military leaders can also make mistakes, hold to foolish strategies and outmoded concepts, promote ill-conceived operations, underestimate enemy strengths and intentions, overestimate their own capabilities, and be unlucky. This is why senior political leaders cannot just hand off execution to their military subordinates and why they must drive senior military leaders to near distraction with sometimes embarrassingly probing questions. The unequal dialogue is not easy, for either political or military leaders, but Cohen is very clear: such dialogue is necessary.

In a democracy, Cohen reminds us, the political leaders must have the final authority to decide on matters of strategy, policy, campaigns, and sometimes even tactics.[11] All four case studies in *Supreme Command* demonstrate adherence to this principle, even after intense debate. Those with final decision authority, however, require that the route taken to a final decision be a rough one, lined with civilian and military egos bruised by long, hard arguments. The political community that political leaders represent and that commissions military officers is owed no less, as are the lives of the citizens-who-become-soldiers and the lives of the innocent.

The unequal dialogue does not entail a right to be wrong, however. It insists only on civilian leaders retaining the final decision authority and on military leaders subordinating themselves to this authority. On the surface, it might appear that this final decision authority and the right to be wrong are the same, but Cohen introduces an important subtlety. That is, because of what is at stake in war—the lives of citizens-who-become-soldiers, the lives of the innocent, and, potentially, the life of the political community—those with final decision authority as well as those who are part of the dialogue leading up to a decision have an obligation to be as right as possible before they make a decision. Here, Cohen is talking about the correlative obligation of senior political and military leaders to achieve the best possible final decision, all things considered.

The subtle difference in the unequal dialogue framework ensures that political leaders neither cut the dialogue short because it is uncomfortable nor cut it short because it is not headed in the direction they want. It also helps ensure that military leaders do not cut the dialogue short by subordinating themselves to political leaders too early because their perspectives are creating tension or because the questioning they receive is too intense.

At some point Cohen acknowledges that the dialogue has to end, decisions made, and directions given. At that point his senior political leader has the authority to say, "Thanks. I understand all the arguments, potential consequences, and potential risks. I know that not all of you agree, but here's what I've decided and what I want all of you to do." Here the dialogue ends and subordination and execution begin.

The dialogue cannot be shut down before that point, however. Doing so would be wrong, especially if it were merely to quiet opposing views, establish control, or demonstrate dominance. When lives are at stake, the unequal dialogue framework reminds us that shutting down opposing views is more than simply rude behavior. In casting the dialogue as he does, Cohen does not deny the power inherent in a senior political leader's final decision authority. Rather, he is emphasizing the obligation that such a leader has to those whose lives he will use or put at risk when invoking that power. His emphasis suggests that having final decision authority and exercising that authority responsibly are equally important.

The inequality of the dialogue is not absolute, however. It is unequal because political leaders have positional and legal authority over military leaders, so Cohen finds no need to talk about a right to be wrong. The unequal dimension of the dialogue ensures both civil primacy and military subordination. In other ways, however, the dialogue is between relative equals. For example, senior political and military leaders are both functionally equal. Both have vital knowledge, experience, and perspective necessary to construct the best possible strategies, policies, and military operations. One set cannot succeed without the other. Both are necessary and, in this sense, equal. Both are also morally equal, for both have responsibilities for the political community's defense, for the lives of the citizens-who-become-soldiers, and for the lives of the innocent.

The unequal dialogue framework requires a relationship between political and military leaders that is not merely an economic relationship between employers and employees where the employer can impose his power and exploit the employee by claiming a right to be wrong. It is a relationship based on more than instrumental and economic values, power, control, and compliance. In order to work, the unequal dialogue requires that among those in the dialogue a degree of respect and trust exists as well as an equal amount of respect for the lives, individual and communal, that will be inevitably used and put at risk in execution.

Reflecting this respect, the purpose of the unequal dialogue is to arrive at a set of decisions that have the greatest probability of protecting the life of the political community and using well the lives of the innocent and of citizens-who-become-soldiers—not merely to establish who is dominant over whom. The unequal dialogue serves the purposes of protecting a political community, producing prudent action to achieve that purpose, protecting the lives of the innocent, and respecting the lives of the citizens-who-become-soldiers by using them well.

This set of purposes represents values of major significance; it demands, therefore, that the senior political and military leaders responsible for war-waging decisions conduct their business in ways corresponding to these purposes.[12]

Each of the cases that *Supreme Command* reviews demonstrates the subordination of military leaders to their political masters. Unlike the principal-agent approach, however, Cohen's approach understands *working* in a much broader sense. The unequal dialogue might define *working* as producing decisions about war aims, strategies, policies, and military and nonmilitary campaigns that have a reasonable probability of success. Content and outcome matter in the unequal dialogue framework in ways in which they do not in the principal-agent framework.

The difference between the two approaches is reflected in how each looks at the Vietnam War. In Cohen's account, both political and military leaders failed in Vietnam: "After the initial decisions to enter the war, the American civilian leadership held back from the kinds of bruising discussions with their military advisers that caused so much grief to Churchill's subordinates. . . . During the period of escalation of the commitment to Vietnam there was no comprehensive politico-military assessment of American strategy."[13] In *Dereliction of Duty*, H. R. McMaster agrees with Cohen's assessment as he describes Vietnam in 1965 as a war without direction. The result is that American soldiers, airmen, sailors, and marines went to war without strategy or direction.[14]

The Vietnam War Revisited

General Harold K. Johnson, the army chief of staff at the time, corroborates McMaster's and Cohen's positions. In March 1965, and from then on, Johnson openly wondered whether the American military even belonged in Indochina, a view that was exacerbated by General William Westmoreland's requests for escalating numbers of troops.[15] He was not alone in his wondering.

Owing to numerous visits of various high-ranking officials, both civilian and military, to Vietnam, assessments done within the office of the secretary of defense, the CIA, and the White House, and reports done by senior military leaders,[16] Cohen concludes: "[Secretary of

Defense Robert] McNamara certainly, and [President Lyndon] Johnson possibly, knew that the war was not going well from the beginning—as early as 1966. Yet their scrutiny of operations in Vietnam focused chiefly on the level of effort being made, not on its fundamental direction." The problem did not lie with the strength of will of the president or the secretary of defense or the dominance both exerted over the Joint Chiefs; nor did it lie with their desire for details about the war or their insistence on monitoring their military subordinates. Rather, it lay with their inability to understand what military force could actually achieve in Vietnam and what it took to run a war, as well as with their inability to conduct an adequate dialogue with their military leaders.[17]

No adequate dialogue like that required by Cohen's framework could occur when President Johnson openly distrusted his military advisers, sought to keep the Chiefs from opposing his Vietnam policy, concealed the finality of his decisions on policy from senior military leaders, and remained ignorant of the Joint Chiefs' actual opinions. Nor could an adequate dialogue take place when McNamara continually attempted to sever all communications between the president and the Chiefs and when Ambassador Maxwell Taylor circumvented them.[18] Finally, no adequate dialogue could occur when the president's disdain for his senior military leaders and their advice was evident. Nor could it occur given the president's desire to be left alone because he had "bigger things to do right here at home."[19] Given the preoccupation with body counts, the lack of understanding of the war, the president's intermittent interest in it, and the dysfunctional civil-military relationship, it is not surprising that the Vietnam War ended in failure, using tens of thousands of lives in the process. Although they remained in control of their military subordinates, senior political leaders did not execute their fundamental war-waging responsibilities.

Neither did the senior military leaders. In August 1964, for example, the Joint Chiefs of Staff served more as technicians for the planning that was actually conducted in the office of the secretary of defense "than as strategic thinkers and advisers in their own right."[20] Corroborating this view, Mark Perry notes: "On the eve of America's most important military challenge since World War II [i.e., Vietnam], the nation's highest-ranking officers represented the most diverse and divided group of policy-makers in the [Joint Chiefs of Staff's] history." He then goes on to describe how the US service chiefs themselves had conflicting understandings of the war and what it took to win—from graduated reprisals to punish North Vietnam, to massive bombing, to concerted air and ground operations stopping somewhere short of war.[21] But it was the Chiefs' infighting that undercut their influence most.[22] Even if the civil-military dynamics had been more support-ive, no adequate dialogue could occur when the Chiefs fought among themselves, unable to construct even a military way forward on which they could agree.

In the end, President Johnson chose a middle course (suggested by McGeorge Bundy) that was described as "going to war—kinda." Beginning in mid-1966, General Creighton Abrams, Westmoreland's deputy, began to question his boss's big unit, conventional strategy. In 1967, all the military chiefs agreed that it was too late to withdraw and that what the United States was doing would not achieve success, but they could not agree on a strategy or on a way to present their views to the administration.[23] In 1968, Clark Clifford replaced Robert McNa-mara as the secretary of defense. Clifford recalls a conversation with the Joint Chiefs in which they said that they did not know how long it would take to succeed in Vietnam or how many more troops might be needed. Further, they offered no alternative other than to continue attrition and, thus, wear out the Communists, even though they had no idea when that wearing-out point might be reached.[24]

In *Armed Servants,* Feaver claims that the civil-military relation-ship during the Vietnam War worked (in the narrow principal-agent sense) because, in the final analysis, the military obeyed even the orders they believed were dumb.[25] And, given his narrow definition of *work,* he is correct, for the outcome that the principal-agent framework seeks is only military compliance, even in the face of moral repugnance. Jus-tice in war demands more. War always involves using and risking lives. Using and risking those lives, however, in ways that increase the prob-ability they will be wasted is morally abhorrent, and those responsi-ble for the strategies and policies leading to such waste are morally blameworthy.

During the Vietnam War, a war in which a proper unequal dia-logue was virtually nonexistent, neither senior political nor senior military leaders exercised their war-waging responsibilities well. "Let's be clear about it," wrote General Bruce Palmer Jr. in 1984 (as a general officer, Palmer was a field force commander in Vietnam, a deputy to Westmoreland, and the army's vice chief of staff), "the United States failed to achieve its objectives in Vietnam." Palmer then lists the price for the years of ambiguous aims, poor strategy, ineffective policy, and unproductive campaigns that resulted from an inadequate dialogue between senior political and military leaders: more than fifty-eight thousand American lives, even more Vietnamese lives (combatant and noncombatant), destruction in North and South Vietnam, many billions of dollars, damage to US self-esteem and confidence, and damage to American prestige abroad. Palmer then poses the question, Was it all in vain?[26]

Palmer uses *vain* in a different sense than did General Stanley McChrystal in the Iraqi desert. McChrystal was exhorting his soldiers to fight on, to accomplish the objectives they were assigned, and in so doing give meaning to their sacrifices. His was a tactical perspective. Palmer's question is a strategic one, for the *it* in it refers to the war itself. His is a strategic question that can be understood in at least two ways. First, was waging the Vietnam War worth paying this price? Said another way, were the benefits of the war proportional to the costs? This version of the question concerns *jus ad bellum*.[27] The second way in which Palmer's question may be understood, however, demonstrates that it is very much an issue of *jus in bello*. In this version, the question is, Did the way in which political and military leaders waged the war waste the lives of citizens-who-became-soldiers and put at risk the lives of the innocent unnecessarily? This version of the question is a matter of prudence in the waging of war.

This is also the question that haunted General Johnson, who noted in retirement: "I remember the day I was ready to go over to the Oval Office and give my four stars to the President and tell him, 'You have refused to tell the country they cannot fight a war without mobilization; you have required me to send men into battle with little hope of their ultimate victory; and you have forced us in the military to violate almost every one of the principles of war in Vietnam. Therefore, I resign and will hold a press conference after I walk out of your door.' Then, added Johnson with a look of anguish, 'I made the typical mistake of believing I could do more . . . if I stayed in than if I got out. I am now going to my grave with that lapse of moral courage on my back.'"[28]

Preventing, Reversing, or Sustaining Imprudence

Prudence has to do with exercising sound judgment, being able to assess the facts of a specific situation and pick out the best actual course of action to follow, given real limitations and constraints. A prudent choice avoids both the extreme of being brash, taking too much risk, and that of being overly cautious, avoiding any risk. Finally, prudence also includes action, execution, and implementation.[29] Properly understood, prudence lies at the very heart of *jus in bello*'s war-waging responsibilities.

Some may find any application of prudence in war oxymoronic. After all, on the battlefield, the imprudent, in some sense, is a daily routine. In other senses, though, it is not so, for prudence in war includes considerations other than risk and danger. War requires that soldiers be willing to risk their lives but also that their commanders and civilian leaders not ask them to do so foolishly or pointlessly. Soldiers expect that they may have to risk their lives trying to take some important objective, rescue a fellow soldier, or protect an innocent noncombatant. They do not expect to have their life thrown away or wasted in missions without much hope of achieving something that would give their sacrifices meaning. Unit citations and individual medals are awarded for valor: doing what many would consider rash. For example, the paratroopers who jumped behind enemy lines prior to D-Day, knowing that at best they would be surrounded as they fought to seize and retain objectives assigned to them; the rangers who climbed the cliffs of Point de Hoc under withering fire on D-Day; and the soldiers who stood against all odds to blunt the German advance during the Battle of the Bulge are all still honored. These actions seem imprudent from one perspective but not from another. The purposes involved gave these risks and sacrifices meaning. The soldiers who took these risks and made these sacrifices knew they were involved in achieving a worthwhile end; their lives were used for a worthy purpose, not wasted or used in vain, as Palmer's question suggests lives were in Vietnam.

Prudence has a place in war. "Prudent risks" (whether tactical or strategic) are acceptable, and leaders who can identify and take them are necessary to win wars. "Gambles" are not, for, whether tactical or strategic, they represent excessive risk because they put individual lives and perhaps the life of the political community itself in unnecessary danger. Any reader of Eisenhower's *Crusade in Europe* is struck by the multiple, extended conversations and arguments among Eisenhower and his senior leaders focused on the risks inherent in the operations he commanded and the degree to which they might be mitigated.[30]

Eisenhower's account illustrates the fact that prudence is—or should be—an essential behavior of the war leader. One can see it clearly by comparing commanders. In the American Civil War, General George McClellan is often used as an example of an overly cautious leader, missing opportunities that the battlefield presented to him, while General Ulysses S. Grant is more widely seen as an aggressive, risk-taking commander—although some say overly aggressive at times. In World War II, British field marshal Bernard Montgomery is usually judged to be more cautious (except perhaps in the Arnhem campaign), whereas General George Patton is recognized as an aggressive risk taker—again sometimes overly so according to some. In the Korean War, General Douglas MacArthur's Inchon operation is usually understood as an example of bold but acceptable risk; his drive to the Yalu River, on the other hand, many see as rash.

Senior political and military leaders seek, or ought to seek, prudence with respect to war aims, strategies, policies, and campaigns. They should seek to decide and act within the proper balance between the extremes of rashness and excessive caution. Identifying such an Aristotelian mean depends on the specifics—the facts—of each case. Sometimes, the prudent action will lean more toward the rash, other times more toward the cautious. A prudent judgment, and the actions that flow from it, is more art than science. Hence, a broad understanding of history, knowledge of the applicable principles, an analytic mind that can discern the relevant facts of a particular case, a synthetic mind that can see coherence amid the fog of ambiguity, the ability to listen to the experiences and judgments of others and allow a decision to emerge from an extended discourse—all are essential war-leadership traits, whether military leadership at the war-fighting level or senior political and military leadership at the war-waging level.

Waging war, the unequal dialogue reminds us, is too complex for any one person or small set of people to understand. There is no actual Clausewitzian genius, and the traits described above rarely are resident in one individual.[31] To discover the prudent set of war aims, strategies, policies, and campaigns necessary to wage war, therefore, senior political and military leaders need each other; they must collaborate. This is the central point of the unequal dialogue framework. Together, they must set war aims, identify strategies and policies, manage alliances and bureaucracies, decide on the nature of acceptable risk, and shape operational choices—even where the final decision authority lies with the senior political leaders.[32] Together, they must ensure that war aims and military, diplomatic, economic, and fiscal strategies and policies are as well aligned as possible. Together, they must constantly assess and reassess progress toward achieving strategic aims and changes to the multiple realities of war, then adapt their own aims, strategies, policies, and military operations, constantly rebalancing means and ends. A proper unequal dialogue has two basic aims: avoid taking imprudent action (whether imprudent because it is overly cautious or imprudent because it is overly rash) and, if an imprudent action is taken (whether that action is taken in error or taken correctly but proved to be imprudent as the war unfolds), adapt quickly so that the imprudence is short-lived—all in order to achieve war aims at the least cost in lives, both of the innocent and of citizens-who-become-soldiers, and minimize risk to the political community.

Finding the prudent course, avoiding the rash and the overly cautious, adjusting that course as a war unfolds, and maintaining sufficient unity in a nation's commitment to success are hard enough even under ideal conditions. In many cases, it is not the side who gets it right in some absolute sense that succeeds in a war. Rather, it is the side that makes war-waging decisions that are the least wrong, can adapt the fastest, and can sustain its will to win. A continual, open, respectful, straightforward, often brutally harsh facts-of-the-case-based discourse—as prudence demands and the unequal dialogue requires—increases the probability of getting it least wrong and adapting as conditions change.[33] No doubt, bullying, belittling, backdooring, undermining, one-upsmanship, slow-rolling, power struggles, egos, turf battles, and other ever-present human and organizational dynamics—whether intentional or not, whether military or civilian— are all too common. Equally without doubt is that, the more such dynamics dominate the dialogue among those senior political and military leaders responsible to wage war, the lower the likelihood of adopting a prudent course of action, the lower the likelihood of success, and, correspondingly, the higher the probability of wasting resources and the lives of citizens-who-become-soldiers as well as risking the lives of the innocent and the life of the political community.

As difficult as it may be, the responsibilities associated with waging war demand nothing short of the highest-quality discourse among senior political and military leaders, even if that discourse is uncomfortably brutal at times. The tripartite tension inherent in waging war requires that senior political and military leaders constantly assess and reassess progress toward achieving strategic aims, changes in enemy activities, and modifications required of friendly forces, then rebalance means and ends by adapting aims, strategies, policies, and military operations. This is the requirement that the unequal dialogue framework captures.

The Story of Two Dialogues

The war in Iraq under the Bush administration provides a good example of the role that dialogue plays in waging war and the effect that the quality of the dialogue has on a war. The senior political and military leaders who waged the Iraq War used two very different kinds of dialogues. The first governed the period between 2003 and 2006, the second that between 2007 and 2008. The first dialogue was characterized by a mix of Huntington's objective control approach and the principal-agent framework. Following Huntington, the president initially deferred execution to military leaders, while the secretary of defense demanded obedience and compliance akin to the principal-agent approach. The first dialogue used an ad hoc approach of multiple conversations and manipulation. Often, responsibilities were mixed and confused. The second looked more like the unequal dialogue that Cohen describes. The difference between what resulted from these two different kinds of dialogues is striking.

The first dialogue governed the planning for the invasion of Iraq and the waging of the war for the first several years, 2003–2006. By the time of the invasion of Iraq in 2003, the Bush administration had been at war in Afghanistan for two years. There were three early indicators that the 2003–2006 dialogue was broken. The first surrounded the concerns about the invasion strategy—the flow of forces, supply lines, and the tenuous "northern approach" through Turkey—that General Eric Shinseki expressed to the president in a closed meeting on January 30, 2003. Kore Schake, who attended this meeting with the president, said: "It's the only time in my life where I felt like you could hear the hinge of history turn. The President clearly didn't know what to do. So he thanked Shinseki and moved on."[34] The general did not press his point, and the president avoided it.

The second involved Shinseki's doubts about preparedness for what might follow regime change in Iraq, doubts he expressed in testimony before the Senate Armed Services Committee on February 25, 2003. When asked by Senator Carl Levin about the potential size of the force necessary to occupy Iraq after the Saddam regime was toppled, Shinseki replied: "Something on the order of several hundred thousand soldiers are probably . . . [what] would be required." This assessment was counter to the Bush-Cheney team's narrative, and it upset both Secretary of Defense Donald Rumsfeld and his deputy, Paul Wolfowitz.[35] In his own testimony before the House Budget Committee on February 27, 2003, Wolfowitz said that Shinseki's estimate was "wildly off the mark." Further: "Neither Rumsfeld nor Wolfowitz ever asked Shinseki about his public estimate and what he meant by it, so it was reasonable for the general to assume his views were not welcomed."[36] Shortly after Shinseki's response to Levin's question, the Defense Department started the discussion about Shinseki's replacement. The discussion took place publicly and earlier than normal, making Shinseki a de facto lame duck as the army's chief of staff—another indication that "it was reasonable . . . to assume his views were not welcomed."

The third indication happened during the initial invasion. Army lieutenant general Scott Wallace—the commanding general of the army corps responsible, with a marine expeditionary force, for the ground campaign that would topple Saddam Hussein's regime—gave a joint interview to reporters of the *Washington Post* and the *New York*

Times. In it, he said that the Iraqi irregular and paramilitary forces were "a bit different from" the enemy that had been anticipated. This remark, welcomed by some on the National Security Council who "did not feel that they were getting the straight story from Rumsfeld," was interpreted by Rumsfeld and General Tommy Franks (the commander of Central Command and Wallace's overall boss) as disloyalty, a repudiation of the strategy in Iraq, and a sign of Wallace's own lack of aggressiveness.[37] As one reporter put it, what Wallace had said "was dangerously off-message": "Rumsfeld was furious. Wallace was told to shut up around reporters. It was vintage Rumsfeld: after insisting on a very small invasion force, he refused to allow his generals to admit their surprises and their constraints."[38]

The tenor of these three early indicators was clear: Comply. Questions, doubts, and deviations are not welcome.

This approach, hardly an unequal dialogue in Cohen's sense, slowly eroded the nation's ability to see the on-the-ground reality for what it was and adapt accordingly. From 2003 to 2006, even in the face of evidence that the overall strategy in Iraq—create security by showing progress toward a democracy, transition responsibility to the Iraqis as quickly as possible, and withdraw—was failing, no serious adjustments to the approach were made.

In 2003, for example, violence was rising even as Franks withdrew the three major headquarters that conducted the initial invasion to topple the Saddam regime and replaced them with one, less capable headquarters. The CIA briefed senior political leaders on a growing insurgency in November 2003, and L. Paul Bremer reported to Vice President Dick Cheney: "We do not have a military strategy for victory." Yet the approach did not change.[39]

Neither did the approach change in 2004. In April 2004, the US Marines—at the direction of the White House and against military recommendations—initiated an intense battle in Fallujah against a determined enemy only to have senior political leaders direct them to stop the battle midstream. (Later that year, US forces went back to a bigger hornet's nest in Fallujah.) In November 2004, Deputy Secretary of State Richard Armitage told the president, "We're not winning in Iraq." The president asked, "Are we losing?" Armitage replied, "Not yet."[40] The administration's approach to Iraq did not change after

Armitage's report; nor did it change after Wolfowitz reported that, while the major violence in Iraq was in four of Iraq's eighteen provinces, the other fourteen were growing less stable, not more. Rather than use Wolfowitz's report to adapt—"almost punctuating the lack of interest," as Bob Woodward observes in *State of Denial*—"Bush reverted to the old talking points in a public question-and-answer forum: 14 of the 18 provinces in Iraq appear to be relatively calm."[41] In December 2004, the US ambassador in Baghdad, John Negroponte, sent a nine-page memorandum to Bush saying that a quick handover to Iraqis—a key component of the US strategy in Iraq—was not possible and that efforts to rebuild Iraq were hampered by a resilient insurgency that was hardly defeated.[42] Some senior political and military leaders were talking, but few were listening. The result was little dialogue and less change.

The year 2005 also opened and closed without any significant adjustments to aims, strategies, policies, or campaigns. Early in 2005, Secretary of State Condoleezza Rice commissioned an assessment of Iraq. The result was depressing. The assessment called Iraq a failed state with an active insurgency and a disaffected Sunni population. It concluded that the United States did not have a comprehensive, unified policy and that not enough attention was being paid to the political side of counterinsurgency.[43] About the same time, Colonel Derek Harvey presented an even starker assessment to the US Defense Policy Board. The conclusions of his study rejected Rumsfeld's position at the time that the United States faced only die-hard fanatics and dead-enders, not an organized insurgency. Rather, Harvey described, in great detail, how the insurgency was well trained, well led, and linked by family, tribal, and professional ties and was exploiting the remnants of the collapsed Iraqi state. He briefed the staff and selected principals of the National Security Council, White House, and Joint Chiefs of Staff. His message was not well received, for his description ran counter not only to Rumsfeld's personal belief but also to the more positive assessments being reported by the senior political and military leaders at the time. A senior CIA analyst also produced an assessment that was skeptical of the claims of progress. His analysis was that Iraq was slipping toward a civil war, that elections would not produce security and stability by themselves, and that Iran had already established intelligence and operational networks in Iraq.[44] Both civilian and military bureau-cracies were producing adequate information, but the information was not welcomed. In May 2005, for example, Vice President Cheney said on CNN that he thought that Iraq was "in the last throes . . . of the insurgency." As Woodward put it: "It was a total denial of reality and of the trend."[45]

Three years after the invasion, on June 28, 2005, the president reit-erated his original strategy in a speech at Fort Bragg, North Carolina: "Our strategy can be summed up this way: As the Iraqis stand up, we will stand down." Meanwhile, Steven Hadley, the national secu-rity adviser, did not believe that handing off to the Iraqis was a strat-egy and hired Peter Feaver to write and staff a more comprehensive strategy.[46] In July 2005, Zalmay Khalilzad replaced John Negroponte as the US ambassador to Iraq. Once there, he formed the so-called Red Team to assess the current situation and approach. The team con-cluded that the current approach was badly off course and had almost no prospect of success, that the timetable for handing power over to the Iraqis simply set them up for failure, and that the focus was too heavily weighted toward withdrawal rather than success. It also reported that the insurgency was resilient and capable of regenerating itself and that the planned size of the Iraqi security forces would likely be too small. Khalilzad showed his team's assessment to both senior military and senior civilian leaders, to no avail.[47] In September, Feaver produced the thirty-five-page "Strategy for Victory," which Bush approved, but nothing actually changed in Washington or in Iraq. By November 2005, Representative Jack Murtha would claim that the approach to Iraq was "flawed policy wrapped in illusion," but even this criticism from a longtime supporter of America's military did not prompt fun-damental change.[48]

The opportunity to actually change approaches in Iraq in 2005 would pass. The successful December 2005 election of a prime minis-ter in Iraq was judged to be sufficient political progress, confirming the original democracy/transition/withdrawal strategy. Simply put, Rums-feld "wanted to do everything possible to tamp down the critics," and General George Casey, the senior general in Iraq, remained convinced that the plan was on track and that handover to Iraqi security forces followed by US force reductions would be possible in 2006.[49]

In fact, in early 2006, "Casey made the decision to off-ramp two brigades . . . in effect cutting the force by that amount."[50] This force reduction took place about the same time as the bombing of a major holy site for Shia Islam, the Al Askari mosque in Samarra, on February 22, 2006—the attack that triggered massive sectarian violence in Iraq. Although both military and political leaders believed that "the nature of the conflict had changed," little changed as to the basic strategic approach. Casey reports that his command did explore various courses of action but determined that the Al Askari attack did not trigger a civil war, that the violence continued to be confined to only three provinces: "We [therefore] laid out specific objectives and tasks . . . much as we had in our earlier campaign plan."[51] Both military and civilian leaders at the time complied with the original strategy: progressing along the milestones set for Iraq's move toward democracy, handing over responsibility to the Iraqis, and withdrawing.[52] By the end of 2006, Casey had shifted his position, coming to believe that additional troops were required, but as he admitted: "I waited too long to make the decision to cancel the drawdown."[53] In sum, he is saying that more troops may have been needed to execute the strategy but that the strategy itself was sound.

The 2003–2006 dialogue between political and military leaders was not producing anything close to a prudent way to wage the Iraq War. Though this period was marked by multiple, intense discussions on Iraq, many visits, secure video conferences, meetings, briefings, and assessments, the war was not being waged well. All these discussions added up to a facsimile of the kind of dialogue Cohen recommends, but not the real thing. In retrospect, the facsimile had more in common with discussion around compliance with the plan rather than a dialogue around adapting the plan to unfolding realities. Adapting requires an actual, reality-based dialogue. Compliance does not. It needs only the people in charge demanding greater effort in doing what they want done, how they want it done—as called for by the principal-agent framework.

Meanwhile, the soldiers and marines who carried the weight of fighting the war during this period did all they were asked to do and sometimes much more. From the principal-agent perspective, waging the Iraq War of 2003–2006 was an example of working, but the realities in Iraq were more violence, more instability, a larger insurgency, emboldened militias, growing involvement of foreign fighters, and US strategic aims not being achieved. Senior political and military war-waging responsibilities in the period 2003–2006—the setting of war aims; making strategy, policy, and campaign decisions that increase the probability of being right; translating those decisions into action to achieve war aims at the least cost, in lives and resources, and the least risk to one's political community; and adapting to changing realities as they unfolded—left much to be desired.

In fact, the period 2003–2006 emerges more as an example of sustained imprudence than of prudence and of a broken dialogue that was aimed more at compliance with the original strategy than adapting to the unfolding dynamics of war. Further, as had been the case in Vietnam, casualties mounted, a successful outcome seemed less and less likely, and American political support for the war eroded. The legitimacy of the Iraq War was called into question because of the lack of progress and the appearance that the war was unwinnable. By early 2007, there was open discussion in Congress and across America of forcing a withdrawal from Iraq because many believed that the war was a lost cause.[54] This was the reality that Secretary of Defense Robert Gates, Rumsfeld's replacement, faced.

To deal with this reality, Bush, Gates, and other senior political and military leaders employed a much different dialogue to execute their war-waging responsibilities. Gates remembered that Senator Levin put it clearly in his opening statement at Gates's confirmation hearing on December 6, 2006: In his memoir, Gates reported Levin as saying: "The situation in Iraq has been getting steadily worse, not better. . . . [W]e thoughtlessly disbanded the Iraqi army and also disqualified tens of thousands of low-level Baath Party members from future government employment. . . . [W]e have failed . . . to secure the country and defeat the insurgency. And we have failed to disarm the militias. . . . And we have failed to rebuild the economic infrastructure of the country." He continued: "Finally, the man I would have to work with as committee chairman said that the Department of Defense's effectiveness had been reduced by a civilian senior leadership that 'has too often not welcomed differing views, whether from our uniformed military leaders, the intelligence community, the State Department,

American allies, or members of Congress of both political parties.'"[55] No dialogue worthy of the name existed in 2003–2006. Consequently, the war-waging responsibilities shared by the senior political and military leaders of the time could not be executed properly.

A second, and markedly different, Iraq dialogue began in the summer of 2006 and came to maturity during Gates's tenure. Perhaps this new dialogue was triggered by the significant rise in sectarian violence following the Samarra mosque bombing, or by a memo to the White House from aides in Baghdad that said that the strategy of political progress, transition to Iraqi control, and withdrawal was failing because the assumptions on which it rested were no longer valid, or by growing pressure from the American public and the Congress. Perhaps what led to a different approach was a combination of the above factors and others that added to the president's own torment after visiting casualties and meeting grieving military families. For it was in August 2006 that the president, when meeting with relatives of slain soldiers, heard from one mother, "Don't let my son have died in vain." From another he heard, "He did his job. Now you do yours." For the president, "withdrawing troops before Iraq was secure would be admitting [America's] sons and daughters had indeed died in vain, and this was something he just could not let happen."[56] Or perhaps it was a conjunction of reports and assessments in the last half of 2006, all of which described an increasingly violent Iraq, suggested that the original strategy and policies were failing, and predicted a dire result if a different approach was not taken. By the late summer and early fall of 2006, the situation in Iraq was so bad that no one could claim the strategy was working. Identifying the exact cause of the change in the dialogue, or causes, or the precise point in time when it changed is not important. What is important is that a real dialogue did emerge.

One of the major differences was the perspective of President Bush. Initially, he mostly followed developments in Iraq but delegated the conduct of the war to his subordinates. Following the Huntington model, his approach was to trust and delegate to his generals and civilian subordinates. "You fight the war, and I'll provide political cover" was the way he described it.[57] He was to become a much more involved and assertive presence in the second dialogue. Another difference was an insistence on a ground-reality-based discussion and an inclusion of more disparate views of the realities in Iraq. Besides his own staff, secretaries, and military commanders, Bush sought the perspectives of more junior members of his staff, academics, think tanks, the specially formed Iraq Study Group, and retired generals. A third difference was the fact that all options were on the table. This would be a well-focused, robust, often contentious, even brutal set of discussions that did not occur in the first nondialogue governing the period 2003–2006. Whereas the first sought to downplay differences, the second would not.[58] A fourth difference was a new secretary of defense who identified his "highest priority" as "turning the situation around in Iraq."[59]

This second dialogue ultimately came down to two opposing courses of action:

Course of action 1. Maintain the status quo, that is, make progress in Iraq's move to democracy, transition to Iraqi control, and reduce forces in Iraq toward ultimate withdrawal.

Course of action 2. Shift to a counterinsurgency strategy and surge, increasing the size of US forces in Iraq.

Most of the president's military and civilian advisers as well as the Iraq Study Group recommended the status quo or some variation of it, but the president chose change. This decision flowed from at least two sources: first, from a very detailed understanding of the political and military situations in Iraq and within the United States; second, from an extensive, extended, and often contentious and iterative set of discussions including the president, his principal national security advisers, active and retired senior military leaders, congressional leaders, think tanks, and academics. Besides the internal review ordered by the president, there were other, independent reviews by military headquarters, think tanks, and government departments. All contributed, directly or indirectly, to the final recommendations made to the president. The final decision was the president's to make, but the route to that decision was a contentious and inclusive one.[60]

In the end, Bush changed not only the strategy but also his leadership team. In Iraq, General David Petraeus replaced George Casey, Ambassador Ryan Crocker replaced Zalmay Khalilzad, Admiral William "Fox" Fallon replaced General John Abizaid at Central Command, and Robert Gates became the secretary of defense, replacing Donald Rumsfeld. The result of the second dialogue was twofold. First, it produced unambiguous strategic, political-military unity of purpose: clear strategic direction as well as new strategies, new policies, and a new military campaign to achieve the aims the president set. Second, it established a set of civil and military leaders who were expected to align not only policies but also the bureaucracies they led to execute the new direction and adapt as the war unfolded.

Over the next two years, 2007–2008, the execution of this new direction dramatically reduced the overall violence levels in Iraq, saw the acceleration of Iraqi security force growth in size, capability, and confidence, permitted nascent Sunni reconciliation to spread and Shia militia influence to diminish, and created the opportunity for political solutions that were absent in 2005 and 2006. By mid-2008, US force reductions began, and a Status of Forces Agreement was being negotiated between the United States and Iraq. In 2009, US forces withdrew from Iraqi cities, a move that set the conditions for the ultimate withdrawal of all American forces from Iraq.[61] The second dialogue helped contribute to turning potential failure into potential success.

Conclusions: The Unequal Dialogue, Necessary but Insufficient

The ability of civil and military bureaucracies to translate the war-waging decisions that emerged from the second dialogue into action, then adapt as events unfolded, also contributed to turning potential failure into potential success. An unequal dialogue is necessary, but the account so far is insufficient for two reasons.

First, dialogue—however good it is and however likely it is to produce right decisions—must be followed by action. Decisions and plans have to be translated into coherent military and nonmilitary as well as domestic and diplomatic action. In the principal-agent framework, execution is a matter of monitoring regimes to ensure compliance, that is, civilian monitoring to ensure that the military does what the civilians want done, the way they want it done. But, at least as presented in *Armed Servants*, the content of execution—decisions, orders, and directives—matters little; compliance matters more. In the unequal dialogue framework, content is important, but a discussion of execution is mostly absent. A full account of war-waging responsibilities must, therefore, include both decision and execution.

Second, an unequal dialogue requires a proper civil-military relationship environment. What makes the dialogue work from the principal-agent perspective is fear, fear of being caught by intrusive monitoring mechanisms and then being punished. Such an account is inadequate, for in practice it is unlikely to produce the kind of dialogue required. Correctly so, the "unequal dialogue" framework identifies respect and candor between senior political and military leaders as necessary to make the dialogue work, but it leaves unattended the important role that senior political leaders play in setting the right climate for a proper dialogue.

In the abstract, addressing these deficiencies and putting in place adequate war-waging decision-making procedures, organizations, and systems may not seem that hard. In reality, however, it is very hard.

5

The Decision-Execution Regime

Waging war requires management and focused leadership attention. For a nation to increase its probability of success in war, it must do the following sufficiently well, that is, at least better than its enemies: identify proper war aims; structure civil and military strategies, policies, and campaigns that, when executed, will likely achieve those aims; create coordinative bodies that can make initial decisions as well as monitor the war as it unfolds and adapt accordingly; and sustain the legitimacy of the war in the eyes of the political community on whose behalf that war is waged. Further, it must execute these functions not only within its own political community but also within those of its allies. Senior political and military leaders must establish and make work, therefore, a near-continuous dialogue-execution regime. Without such a regime, the political and military bureaucracies will do what they always do—business as usual.

This is no surprise to anyone associated with bureaucracies. They are designed to do the same thing repetitively, maintain a routine, and keep an organization moving on an even keel. Business as usual is the business of a bureaucracy, and to run large enterprises bureaucracies are absolutely necessary. No large organizations—like the US Departments of Defense and State, the military services, and geographic combatant commanders and their subordinate headquarters—could operate without a bureaucracy. When such organizations face something new, however—especially if it is also something that is rapidly and continually changing, like war—bureaucracies do not do so well. War is always new, always different, always atypical, and always changing rapidly. It poses great difficulty to bureaucracies and their leaders. To wage a war, therefore, senior political and military leaders must both use and break their bureaucracies as well as those of their allies or coalition partners. And therein lie the leadership and management challenges of waging war.

Friction in War

"Everything in war is simple," says Clausewitz, "but the simplest thing is difficult." He was talking primarily about war fighting and the friction inherent in actions on the battlefield and in support of active campaigns. His comments, however, apply equally to war waging, the actions required of senior political and military leaders and the friction that occurs at the strategic level. "Friction is the force that makes the apparently easy so difficult."[1]

Accordingly, Clausewitz explains that friction is one of the factors distinguishing real war from war on paper. He speaks of friction as physical, using a machine analogy: the smoothly running military machine slowed down by the physical effects of weather, terrain, and military movements. He also addresses the ways in which psychological friction slows the military machine: fear, stress, and tiredness among soldiers and their leaders. The enemy, whose actions are deliberately taken to interfere with friendly operations, is another source of both physical and psychological friction. These and endless other obstacles, great and small, all combine to slow the military machine in action.[2]

If Clausewitz were writing today, he would have expanded his discussion of the sources of friction. *On War* was written prior to the development of the large staffs and huge bureaucracies created in the late nineteenth century and expanded further during the twentieth century. This expansion responded to the need to coordinate large armies executing widely dispersed campaigns and assure efficient delivery of supply, equipment, units, and replacements from rear to front. Clausewitz also wrote prior to the advanced, integrative communications networks that currently proliferate from the individual soldier to senior political and military leaders. Napoleonic campaigns—the grist of Clausewitz's study—were certainly conducted by large forces and over what were for that time period expansive distances, but they were nothing compared to the global operations of a world war or the simultaneous operations in Afghanistan, in Iraq, and against al-Qaeda, the Islamic State in Iraq and Syria, and their affiliates. Scale creates a friction all its own. Friction is exactly why the apparently easy—conducting a proper dialogue among senior political and military leaders; identifying war aims, strategies, campaigns, and policies that have a good chance of success; translating those into action; and adapting as realities unfold—is actually very hard.

Friction is rife amid war-waging activities, and it comes from multiple sources. A modern-day Clausewitz would write about organizational friction and bureaucratic friction. These kinds of friction contribute to slowing the military machine and distinguish real war from war on paper just as much as the physical and psychological friction about which Clausewitz wrote. Four sources of personal, organizational, and bureaucratic friction stand out: experience and background differences between senior political and military leaders, the scale of complexity associated with waging war, bureaucratic inertia within and among the multiple bureaucracies now necessary to wage war, and the limits of human beings. All four permeate nearly every aspect of war-waging decisions and execution.

Simply put, senior political and military leaders have quite different developmental experiences and backgrounds. The difference in perspectives emerges inherently from the different purposes, responsibilities, careers, experiences, and methods of the political and military worlds.[3] Flexibility and ambiguity—in both concept and execution—help build political consensus and, thus, lay the foundation for political success. This is the art that political leaders learn as they develop. The world in which military leaders develop their art is one in which, because of the nature of the battlefield, exact and unambiguous orders require flexibility in execution. The complexity of waging war is akin to a multidimensional Rubik's Cube that must be solved under conditions of extreme ambiguity, high-stakes pressure, and continual change. Senior political and military leaders must find solutions in the face of an enemy deliberately trying to undo whatever solutions they emplace. Moreover, strategy, policy, and campaign solutions must not only fit the enemy situation; they must also be acceptable domestically and internationally. Finally, they must be executable by the set of civil and military, national and alliance bureaucracies necessary to wage war.

Each bureaucracy—the State Department, the Defense Department, and Congress, to name just a few of the US institutions involved in waging war—has its own culture and processes. Making any one work is hard. Making them all work in sufficient concert is harder still. Making them work in coordination with those of allies or coalition partners raises the degree of difficulty even further. Waging war is, therefore, inherently complex and requires both political and military art. The fact is, however, that the senior political and military leaders whose responsibility it is to work with each other in this complex, high-pressure environment do not often work together prior to war.

Moreover, the Rubik's Cube of war waged by a democracy necessarily involves the legislative branch of government, either through predecision briefings and discussions, through testimony to special committees, or through individual or small group engagements of key congressional leaders.[4] Waging war in a democracy also involves engaging with the media. Forthright testimony to Congress, media engagements, and public speeches must contain accurate descriptions of successes and failures, progress and obstacles. These aspects of waging war in democracies add to the friction of the already complex, high-pressure, and dynamic Rubik's Cube that senior leaders must solve.

Finally, senior political and military leaders remain human beings. As such they are limited in energy and capacity, and they are subject to foibles and folly just as is anyone else. Some are people of strong intellect and character, and others are not; most are somewhere in between. Some have the courage and capacity to challenge peers and seniors in a dialogue over substantive issues and the strength to be so challenged; others avoid or shut down such discussions or use ad hominem attacks to establish dominance. Some run large organizations well and provide excellent leadership in the bureaucracies for which they are responsible; others are virtually inept. Some have the wisdom to understand the necessity for the kind of dialogue described in the previous chapter; others fear such a dialogue, considering it a challenge to their position.

Put all this together, and the degree of friction becomes self-evident. What is apparently easy becomes difficult. Personal, organizational, and bureaucratic friction is real, and it affects both the war-waging dialogue and the translation of the results of that dialogue into coherent action.

Difficulty does not obviate necessity, however. War is, by its very nature, a political-military activity that requires a continuous civil-military dialogue-execution regime, not a discrete dialogue in which military leaders provide episodic advice or input, then wait to be told what to do. Nor is it a discrete action in which political leaders provide orders and direction, then wait to see what happens as the military executes.

Multiple Sets of Dialogues

As well as the unequal dialogue framework captures the difficulty and complexity of the interactions between and among senior political and military leaders, the description it offers is, nevertheless, only the tip of the proverbial iceberg. In *Duty,* former defense secretary Robert Gates says as much. Unseen by most political scientists, historians, reporters, and ordinary citizens are the specific events, experiences, and discussions that influence important decisions. Presidents and other senior officials, Gates explains, must listen to a wide array of voices, some within official government channels and others outside those channels.[5] In both the Bush and the Obama administrations, he describes multiple types of dialogues in multiple forums and with a variety of leaders and thinkers—all feeding discussions among a smaller set of senior civilian and military leaders responsible for structuring options and recommendations for a presidential decision.

Gates writes of many private and small group discussions. Some were conducted to ingest details and increase understanding, others to smoke out disagreements with conventional wisdom and discover alternative reasoning. Some were conducted face-to-face in the theaters of war or in the capitals of allies and coalition partners, others on secure video conferences, on the telephone, or during sidebar discussions. Gates describes discussions with the president and vice president, the national security adviser and the national security staff, cabinet secretaries and their deputies, ambassadors, senior US military officials—the chairman of the Joint Chiefs and the chiefs of the military services, US field and geographic commanders—members of Congress and their staffs, senior officials within the Department of

Defense, reporters from various media, think tank personnel, and academics. He records discussions with representatives of similar sectors within other countries—allies, friends, and coalition partners. He also describes multiple, often simultaneously conducted reviews that fed into the recommendations staffs made to more senior leaders, some by the Departments of Defense and State, and some by the national security staff. Others were done by the Joint Chiefs staff as well as the staffs of field commanders or regional geographic commanders. Still others were done by independent think tanks or by individual academics.[6]

The unequal dialogue framework focuses primarily on the small set of senior civilian and political leaders in discussion with the president. In *Supreme Command,* Eliot Cohen hints at the continuing and expansive nature of the dialogue when he discusses Churchill and Clemenceau.[7] Gates's account, however, provides a much deeper look into the realities of multiple sets of dialogues—the discussions and arguments that precede the final unequal dialogue between senior political and military leaders leading to a decision. These preceding discussions are an important part of the final dialogue, for, if they are well conducted, they can help ensure that the final dialogue is as factually based as possible, is informed by alternative analytic perspectives, considers a range of feasible alternative courses of action, and reflects the risks and opportunities involved. An unequal dialogue without them does a disservice to the president and other senior leaders because decisions will have been made on the basis of inadequate information, analysis, options, and risk/opportunity assessments.

Together, Cohen's and Gates's accounts provide a clearer picture of what is involved in constructing war aims, strategies, policies, and military campaigns that have a reasonable probability of succeeding. Together, they also provide a clearer picture of what is necessary to conduct dialogues like these: a proper leadership climate, protected space, time, leader/managerial focus, and attention to outcomes.

Proper war-waging sets of dialogues need a sufficient leadership climate. Cohen's unequal dialogue calls for a collaborative, even if sometimes conflictual, relationship between senior political and military leaders, a relationship that takes for granted the fundamental subordination of soldiers to civil control.[8] Gates provides more detail as to what such a dialogue needs: senior civilian leaders to "set an atmosphere so people would be more inclined to speak up," "an environment where all points of view can be expressed and have a robust debate." This is an important point. As the ones with the dominant legal and constitutional position and with the responsibility for making final decisions, senior political leaders have the burden to set the right climate for dialogue. In fact, Gates believed that it was "a major task of the secretary of defense . . . to help manage [the relationship between military and civilian leaders] and ensure that the president listens to professional military advice that he may not want to hear, and that the senior officers offer their best and most candid advice and obey loyally, especially when they are overruled."[9]

Even this expanded description, however, does not quite capture the totality. Dialogue requires the participants to listen to each other with open minds. Each must press the other and be willing to be pressed. Political leaders must insist on reasoned advice as to war aims and policies and demand of their military subordinates well-thought-out strategic and operational options. Military officers must "tell blunt truths" and have candor as a core value,[10] but telling blunt truths to brick walls is useless and quickly seen to be the futile activity it is.

Gates sums it up this way: "I will involve you. I will listen to you. I expect your candor. . . . I want to know when you are in disagreement with each other or with me. I want to know if you think I'm about to make a mistake—or have made one. . . . I respect what each of you does and your expertise. I will need your help. . . . But, once decisions are made, we must speak with one voice."[11] Here, he recognizes the difference between having an opportunity to provide one's advice and being heard. General Eric Shinseki was, as we have seen, given the opportunity to provide his advice; he was hardly heard. When participants, whether civilian or military, are dismissive of the perspectives of others, the dialogue breaks down and is quickly replaced with a facsimile or worse—no dialogue at all.

A broken dialogue looks like the one that governed the waging of the Vietnam War and the one that was in place during much of the Afghanistan and Iraq Wars. In these cases, although military leaders were consulted and the final civilian decision authority never questioned, the nation was not well served, the lives of the citizens-who-became-soldiers were not well used, and the lives of the innocent were risked unnecessarily. Justice in the conduct of war rarely arises in such an environment.

War-waging dialogues require protected space. Transparency is important in democracies, but the arguments over what exactly is happening in the war, the discussion of alternatives, and the debate over the best course of action must take place privately.[12] Premature public discussion—whether leaked or overtly provided, whether by the military or civilians—sows distrust and suspicion among the participants in the dialogue, making the dialogue harder than it already is. Further, the leak is often a technique used to manipulate the outcome of a dialogue. Such manipulation—whether by a senior political or military leader or by a subordinate or a staffer—is actually the antithesis of authentic dialogue, a way to pretend to participate in a legitimate dialogue while actually using position, power, and information to get a desired outcome that may not emerge from the dialogue otherwise. These are not dialogues from which are likely to emerge the best course of action, all things considered. These are debates where one side seeks to win even if it advocates a less worthy alternative relative to strategic aims, costs, risks, and legitimacy.

There are times when public discussions are not only important but also necessary, especially in a democracy. Some of these discussions—with members of Congress, the media, or others—precede a final decision. These must be done with integrity and candor but also carefully so that they contribute to finding answers to war aims, strategies, policies, and campaigns with the highest probability of success rather than unraveling pending decisions. The 2006–2008 conversations over what was the right policy in Iraq showed how difficult public discussion can be. On the one hand, parts of the public conversations were necessary and contributed to better strategy and policy decisions. On the other hand, parts were just public manipulation of facts that politicized the dialogue for personal reasons.

What these discussions show is that a proper war-waging dialogue takes time. Casting the dialogue in the singular, as an unequal dialogue, does not reflect the reality of waging war: the dialogue actually consists of sets of repetitive, overlapping, and iterative dialogues from which practicable aims, strategies, policies, and military operations can emerge. Continuing sets of repetitive, overlapping, and iterative dialogues—some private and some public—reflect Churchill's belief that the conduct of World War II emerged not from any one grand plan or strategy but from a series of conflicting and changing views, misunderstandings, personal interests, and confusions. They also match Clemenceau's use of "a stream of decisions."[13] Thus, patience and persistence among senior political and military leaders become as necessary as pressing and listening to one another. A singular dialogue does not match the reality described by Churchill, Clemenceau, or Gates.

Nor does the reality of multiple, repetitive, overlapping, and iterative dialogues corroborate either of the superficial models that some employ: the "military leaders merely provide political leaders advice or options as input to a political decision" model or the "I know what I want done and how I want it done; you just do it" model. These models are not satisfactory because they increase the probability that the political community will not be protected, the lives of citizens-who-become-soldiers will not be used well, and the lives of the innocent will be risked unnecessarily. Further, these kinds of pseudodialogues risk the legitimacy of the war. Cutting the dialogue short, overly restricting the sets of dialogues that are necessary, or manipulating the dialogue—all are perversions of senior political and military war-waging responsibilities.

War is dynamic, as is politics. Analysis conducted and decisions made at the start of the war are neither static nor everlasting. As hard as it is to conduct the initial sets of dialogues and arrive at a satisfactory solution to war aims, strategies, policies, and at least the opening campaign, these initial decisions are only the beginning. The same give-and-take must be sustained throughout the war.[14] Change is the only constant in war. Those responsible for waging war must, therefore, commit themselves to constant adaptation, which requires sets of ongoing, reality-based dialogues. All this takes time.

War-waging dialogues also require leader and managerial focus. One of the many examples Gates records is a five-hour meeting in Afghanistan with Generals Stanley McChrystal (the overall commander in Afghanistan) and David Petraeus (McChrystal's US boss as the commander of US Central Command), Admirals Mike Mullen (the chairman of the Joint Chiefs of Staff) and James Stavridis (McChrystal's NATO boss as the supreme allied commander, Europe),

Michele Flournoy (Gates's undersecretary of defense for policy), Lieutenant General David Rodriguez (the McChrystal deputy responsible for ground operations in Afghanistan), and a few members of staff. This meeting was one of many leading to the assessment and recommendation that McChrystal was tasked to make within the first ninety days of assuming command in Afghanistan. Later, Gates recalls nine other very long (two- to three-hour) meetings just on McChrystal's 2009 Afghanistan assessment and strategy recommendations.[15] While this dialogue was being conducted, events continued to unfold in both Afghanistan and Iraq as well as in the wider war against al-Qaeda and its affiliates. Nothing stood still as one decision was being made, not on the battlefield or in the capitals of the countries waging war. War and politics demand equal dynamism in the decision-making processes associated with war waging. Losing focus in this kind of dynamic environment is easy; the need for sustained, focused attention on the part of the senior political and military leaders responsible for waging war is both apparent and hard.

Busyness tends to dissipate focus. As important as were the wars in Iraq and Afghanistan and against al-Qaeda, they were not the only security items that needed the attention of the president, the Defense Department, and the national security principals. For example, at one point, the three wars that the United States was waging unfolded against a backdrop of the Iranian nuclear program, Somali pirates, North Korean nuclear tests, and a variety of developments in Russia, China, Israel, and Pakistan—to name just a few. Further, there were domestic issues, chief among them the American economic crisis and the many consequential decisions that had to be made as a result. Further still, there were routine issues like congressional testimony, management decisions associated with running the Department of Defense, budget submissions, decisions concerning major acquisitions, personnel assignments, and assorted official representational duties with visiting foreign defense officials. Blandly, Gates sums it up this way: "In short, despite the tremendous power inherent in the job, the secretary of defense must deal with multiple competing interests both within and outside the Pentagon and work with many constituencies, without whose support he cannot be successful."[16]

All this makes the right kind of continuing civil-military dialogue absolutely necessary. For, without the directed focus and attention of senior civil and military leaders, not only would unity of effort start to unravel, but also each bureaucracy for which these leaders are responsible would do what it does best—not change and migrate to the default position, business as usual. The result is limited unity of effort and cohesiveness of action toward common war aims. This is the nature of any complex activity conducted by multiple bureaucracies. This is the nature of waging war.

Senior political and military leaders are pulled in so many directions that one of the ever-present temptations facing them is to short-cut the process, falling back on one version or another of Huntington's objective control theory, the normal theory of civil and military role differentiation: political leaders decide and direct; military leaders execute. Another temptation comes from the principal-agent framework: just do what I want done, the way I want it done. Yielding to these temptations, political leaders might want to say, "Just give me your best military advice so we can make a decision," or military leaders might want to say, "Just tell me what to do, and let me do it." Such temptations must be resisted. As Cohen says at the outset of *Supreme Command*: "For a politician to dictate military action is almost always folly." And for a military leader to sit back and allow strategy and policy to be formed in a vacuum is equal folly. Furthermore, in reality, there is no arbitrary line dividing civilian and military war-waging responsibilities. With respect to waging war, there is no neat way of carving off distinct spheres of either pure political or pure military action—except that senior political leaders have the final decision authority.[17] War simply requires the sustained, focused attention of the senior political and military leaders responsible for waging it.

Finally, a properly conducted dialogue focuses on output: on getting it right, that is, making decisions that increase the likelihood of attaining war aims and decrease the probability of putting the innocent and the political community at risk or using poorly the lives of citizens-who-become-soldiers. In war-waging dialogues, differences in opinion as to what is happening arise not only among the senior political and military leaders but also among the wider sets of other groups—domestic and foreign, military and civilian—that make up the network of agencies, organizations, and leaders associated with waging war. Differences of understanding lead to different assessments, options, and recommended courses of action. Sometimes these differences are profound, as Gates describes the differing position between Vice President Joe Biden and other members of the national security team over the Surge in Afghanistan.[18] In these cases, focusing on outcomes is much more important than winning the debate or achieving dominance over those who oppose one's view.

Outcomes—actual progress toward achieving success or not—are the very purposes of the dialogue. Further, they determine legitimacy, at least in the eyes of American citizens. Legitimacy and public support for a war flow from a people who believe that the war is right and, further, that their nation, or political community, can win and is making progress toward winning.[19] Legitimacy and public support do not flow from winning the debate or achieving dominance over those who oppose one's view only to then execute decisions that reduce the likelihood of progress toward achieving common war aims.

A properly conducted set of dialogues, extended, inclusive, and iterative, requires an adequate leadership climate, protected space, time, leader and managerial focus, and an attention to outcomes. Such dialogues, however, represent only half of senior civil and military leaders' war-waging responsibilities. The other half involves translating the results of the dialogues into action, then adapting as battlefield and political events unfold.[20] The execution portion of waging war involves using the civil and military bureaucracies to carry out a continuous cycle of activities: *execute* the strategy, policy, and campaign decisions that emerge from their initial dialogue, *monitor* changes that occur in war, both on the battlefield and in the political communities, *adapt* initial strategy and policy decisions as the realities of war determine which work and which do not, *execute* these new decisions, and *continue* through the cycle again. In reality, therefore, the initial dialogue never stops; it just becomes part of a dialogue-execution regime, hence Churchill's series of discussions and Clemenceau's streams of decisions.

Execution: Making Bureaucracies Work

The dialogues that Gates describes in *Duty* and that Cohen shows had been useful to those studied in *Supreme Command* are not compliance oriented, as Peter Feaver's *Armed Servants* suggests. Rather, they are performance oriented. That is, dialogues are first intended to find the gaps between actual reality as it is unfolding during a war (on the battlefield, amid the political community or communities, and in the capital or capitals) and the desired reality (success at achieving war aims). Second, they are intended to result in decision and action. Outcomes matter. Once these gaps are found, senior political and military leaders then must adapt—understand, to the degree possible, what is actually happening; decide whether new developments required adjustments to aims, strategies, policies, or campaigns and, if so, what those adjustments should be; then issue the requisite directives and execute—quickly because, if one's enemy executes better, one loses. Sometimes, the adaptation involves changes to strategies and policies, even war aims themselves. Other times, the adaptation involves changes in campaign direction, in military or political leadership, in the behaviors of coalition partners, or in resource levels. The function that senior political and military leaders perform in war is this: conducting a war, in both its fighting and its waging aspects, better than their opponents do.

The extensive, inclusive, collaborative, contentious, and continuous sets of dialogues help maintain a focus on exposing reality. They also help identify the gap between that reality and desired outcomes. Finally, the sets help in adapting aims, strategies, policies, and campaigns accordingly.[21] These war-waging responsibilities are as essential to the conduct of war as is fighting. In businesses, the cost of chronic underperformance is money, market share, and perhaps the job and reputation of the chief executive; in war, the cost is lives—whether those of the innocent or of citizens-who-become-soldiers—and, in some limited cases, the very existence of the political community. When waging war, dialogue and execution both matter.

The unequal dialogue mentions but does not place sufficient emphasis on execution.[22] Perhaps this reduced emphasis is a matter of just not discussing the obvious. In the case of war, however, the obvious cannot be assumed. Properly conducting the sets of dialogues and arriving at initial war aims, strategies, policies, and military operations constitute but half the job. The other half involves executing and adapting, no easy tasks, as Robert W. Komer demonstrates in *Bureaucracy*

Does Its Thing, a study of US bureaucracies during the Vietnam War, at least up to 1972, when Rand published his research.[23]

"Why," Komer asked in 1972, when the war was not yet over, "has a cumulative enormous U.S. contribution . . . had such limited impact for so long? Why, almost regardless of the ultimate outcome, has U.S. intervention entailed such disproportionate costs and tragic side effects? . . . Why did we do so poorly for so long?"[24] These are questions about execution, about the gap between actual and desired reality and how the bureaucracy acted, or failed to act, to close that gap. A resurrected Komer looking at the wake of America's post-9/11 wars might ask exactly the same things.

In fact, the substance behind Komer's questions reappears in the form of impressions Gates formed soon after he joined the Bush administration as the secretary of defense. "Even though the nation was waging two wars," he observes, "neither of which we were winning, life at the Pentagon was largely business as usual when I arrived. . . . It was clear why we had gotten into trouble in both Iraq and Afghanistan. . . . [W]hen the situation began to deteriorate, the president, his senior civilian advisers, and the senior military leaders had not recognized that most of the assumptions that underpinned early military planning had proven wrong, and no necessary adjustments had been made."[25] That is, if the system of performance-oriented dialogue with consequential adaptive decisions and actions had been in place at all, it had broken down.

In both the Vietnam case and the pre-Gates Afghanistan and Iraq cases, the dialogue between senior political and military leaders was at best a pseudodialogue. And it was not sufficiently connected to execution and outcomes—except in the compliance sense. Such compliance-based dialogues lower the probability both of arriving at aims, strategies, policies, and campaigns with reasonable likelihood of success and of successful adaptation and execution. Rather, they increase the likelihood of working harder to comply with the plan. They also increase the likelihood both of unnecessary risk to the innocent and to political communities and of wasting the lives of citizens-who-become-soldiers.

Some of the main conclusions in Komer's study were the following: that a complete search of Vietnam War documents finds that a relatively sophisticated understanding of the culture and environment in which the war took place was present, that there was among senior political and military leaders fairly detailed knowledge of the lack of progress and the reasons behind it, and that those same leaders also realized by the mid- to late 1960s that the war could not be won as it was then being fought.[26] The senior political and military leaders of that time simply could not, or would not, translate what they knew into action. These conclusions were similar to those Gates reached on reviewing the landscape surrounding the wars in Afghanistan and Iraq.

In both cases, the senior political and military leaders were unable to put what they knew into action in part because of the dysfunctional civil-military relationships among the principals and the bureaucracies they controlled. Moreover, what was known about the war did not match the image of the war they had created in their minds. The decisions they made were based more on their created unreality than on reality. A further obstacle was the result of their basic inability to manage and adapt the organizations they led. Others reached similar conclusions about Vietnam.[27] One of Komer's main conclusions was that our experience in Vietnam shows how difficult it is to translate lessons into improved performance because to do so requires a consistent, deliberate effort to offset the inevitable tendency of bureaucracies to keep doing the familiar and adapt only slowly and incrementally.[28]

Instead of waging and fighting a war in Vietnam that matched reality, the United States fought the war it knew how to fight. In the process, more than fifty-eight thousand citizens-who-became-soldiers lost their lives. Even more Vietnamese were killed. And these tallies do not include the destruction of property and terrain, North and South. Nor do they include the decades of negative effects on America's social and political fabric. Komer's study asked how such a moral travesty could occur.

In the end, Komer concluded that there is much to be learned from the way in which we went about waging the Vietnam War. Regardless of what policy called for, his study shows that US government institutions tended to go about their business using existing repertoires of behavior, that there was little evidence that top-level follow-through or adequate management machinery forced them into different patterns of response, and, as a result, that much of what was done turned out to be futile, wasted, and even irrelevant.[29] Here, Komer addresses the strategic dimension of the conduct of the war, specifically, the war-waging decisions and actions taken by senior political and military leaders, not the tactical responsibilities of those who fought.

Gates highlights these war-waging responsibilities that he shares with President Obama when he says: "Mr. President, you and I—more than any other civilians—bear the burden of responsibility for our men and women at war. . . . What we owe them [if their sacrifices are not to be in vain] is not only our support, but a clear strategy and achievable goals."[30] These words echo President Bush's remarks when, announcing the 2007 Surge in Iraq, he clearly referred to what the government owes the citizens-who-become-soldiers so that their lives are used well: properly identified war aims, strategies, policies, and military campaigns as well as political and military bureaucracies that work to translate decisions and plans into actions.[31]

Coherent translation of decisions and plans into action was certainly not the case outlined by Dov Zakheim in *A Vulcan's Tale* or in Ronald Newmann's *The Other War* concerning Afghanistan (summarized in chapter 2 above). Rather, both authors describe the inability to execute appropriately coordinated strategies and policies. Neither did Zakheim and Newmann describe adaptive organizational structures and processes created specifically to deal with the dynamic challenges of the Afghanistan and Iraq Wars—the kinds of adaptive behavior exhibited by the senior political and military leaders in the face of the Civil War (see chapter 2) or created during World War II (see chapter 1). Given the many unique dimensions of both the Afghanistan War and the Iraq War—the facts that both were going on simultaneously, both included elements of irregular warfare, and both involved the complexity of coalitions—coordinated execution would seem to have been a natural point of emphasis.

The opposite was true, however. The difficulties in execution and adaptation that Komer depicts are of the kind that frustrated Gates, who describes the Department of Defense as "structured to plan and prepare for a war but not to fight one."[32]

Planning and preparing are steady state activities conducted over time; change in this environment is slow and incremental. These are important tasks and the kind that bureaucracies do well; that is why they are necessary. Fighting a war, however, requires continual adaptation to a number of rapidly changing situations, political and military.[33] These kinds of tasks require either changes to the bureaucracy itself, like the massive changes General George Marshall made to the War Department, or extrabureaucratic organizational and managerial action, like the new management structures Lincoln and his cabinet created during the Civil War or the new organizations created by the Americans and the British during World War II.

Mature, extensive bureaucracies are very hard to change. So making the civil and military bureaucracies work in war usually entails new structures and processes specifically designed for performance-oriented, dialogue-execution regime. Time and again, Gates lamented in *Duty*, he had to tackle that "damnable peacetime mind-set inside the Pentagon." He goes on to describe the huge difference between getting a decision tomorrow (which is often necessary in war) and getting a decision next week (which is usually acceptable only in peacetime). "[The Department of Defense]," he reports, "has been at war for over six years. Yet we still use the processes that were barely adequate for peacetime operations and impose a heavy cost in wartime."[34] The structures and processes necessary for a performance-oriented, dialogue-execution regime may last only as long as the war, but, ad hoc or not, they are a necessary element if war is to be waged successfully.

A performance-oriented, dialogue-execution regime is the kind of regime that President Lincoln and his civil and military subordinates created to wage the Civil War. It is also the kind President Roosevelt, his team, and the Allies created to wage World War II. It is the kind that President Johnson and his civil and military leaders failed to create during the Vietnam War. And it is the kind that at best has been achieved only sporadically in the wars following the September 11, 2001, attack on the United States.

Responsibility, Dialogue, and Execution

Simply put, senior political and military leaders need this kind of regime to fulfill their war-waging responsibilities. A performance-oriented, dialogue-execution regime increases the probability of identifying the right set of war aims, strategies, policies, and military campaigns—ones that have a higher probability of success. This kind of regime also increases the probability of correctly adapting the initial set of decisions. Using such a regime does not guarantee infallibility. Rather, the guarantee is more limited; it is merely an increase in the probability of prudent action and of using well the lives of citizens-who-become-soldiers, protecting the political community, and limiting risk to the innocent. Such a regime also increases the likelihood of creating and sustaining the legitimacy of a war. Without such a regime, the probability increases that war aims, strategies, and policies may be conceptually correct or politically desirable but unsuccessful because they are disconnected from reality and delegitimizing because they fail.

A performance-oriented, dialogue-execution regime requires a set of leaders committed to executing decisions that emerge from a proper set of dialogues, whether they agree completely with those decisions or not. It also needs leaders who are committed to executing decisions long enough to see whether they are working and can evaluate the outcomes of execution as honestly and objectively as possible so that they can adapt, that is, take the next set of decisions and actions that fit reality as it unfolds. Throughout, such a regime also needs civil and military leaders who can actually run the bureaucracies for which they are responsible—or are willing to change them.

Some of the performance-oriented, dialogue-execution regime leadership requirements appeared to be present during the 2009 decision to increase force levels and change strategies in Afghanistan, others not.

"In my entire career," Gates writes, "I cannot think of any single issue or problem that absorbed so much of the president's and the principals' time and effort in such a compressed period. There was no angle or substantive point that was not thoroughly examined." In the end, the president decided on a "mission that the public and the politicians could easily understand": "*Deny* the Taliban momentum and control, *facilitate* reintegration [of Taliban fighters], *build* government capacity selectively, *grow* the Afghan security forces, *transfer* security responsibilities, and *defeat* al Qaeda."[35] So far, so good.

Following this decision, the discussions focused on how to resource this strategy; several alternatives were discussed thoroughly. The strategy and resource debates were hotly contended. "The aggressive, suspicious, and sometimes condescending and insulting questioning of our military leaders," Gates writes, "made them overly defensive. . . .

A more collegial process, one that tried to identify points of agreement rather than sharpen differences, would have had a more harmonious conclusion and done less damage to the relationship between the military and the commander in chief." The dialogue turned into a debate and caused a significant rift between some senior political and military leaders. As Gates put it: "[Those] who had opposed the [resulting] decision would gather every negative bit of information about developments in Afghanistan and use them to try to convince the president that they had been right and the military wrong. That began before the first surge soldier set foot in Afghanistan." In this case, the performance-oriented, dialogue-execution regime unraveled quickly. Gates summed it up this way:

> The president made a tough decision on the surge in Afghanistan in November 2009, and he had, for all practical purposes, made me, Mullen, Petraeus, and McChrystal swear a blood oath that we would support his decision. Unfortunately, Biden and his staff, the White House staff, and the NSS [national security staff] apparently had not taken the same oath of support. From the moment the president left West Point [where he announced his strategy and resource decisions], they worked to show he had been wrong, that the Pentagon was not following his direction, and that the war on the ground was going from bad to worse.[36]

Without leaders committed to executing decisions long enough to see whether they work, the likelihood of coherent action is minimal, and the reality-based grist for the next set of decisions and adaptations that have to be made becomes distorted. Under these conditions, a proper performance-oriented, dialogue-execution regime has little chance of succeeding. If the kind of leadership behavior that Gates described existed in a corporation, the bottom line would be affected, the corporation possibly even going bankrupt. In war, the cost is much higher. Senior leaders behaving as Gates reports when the lives of citizens-now-soldiers and the innocent are at stake are not just poor leaders or managers; their behavior is morally reprehensible. Any president's decisions deserve a chance to work, and he is owed loyal support to make them work—by both his military and his civilian subordinates. If his decisions are proved incorrect or ineffective, then the dialogue should start again, and adaptations should be made.

In addition to adequate leadership, a proper performance-oriented, dialogue-execution regime also requires leaders to manage the work of their bureaucracy to produce what is needed to execute those decisions. Since bureaucracies do not easily adapt to new or rapid change—the very realities of war—senior political and military leaders responsible for waging war must manage their organizations more carefully than they would have to in normal times. Often, they must go beyond more careful management and create new, extrabureaucratic processes, forums, or organizations to accommodate the dynamism of war.

Failure in execution reduces the probability of success; no worthwhile strategy can be planned without taking into account the organization's ability to execute it. This is true for corporate leaders, and it is true for the senior political and military leaders who wage war. The processes of identifying war aims, strategies, policies, and military operations, then executing and adapting, are tightly linked to one another, not compartmentalized between and among leaders and their staffs.[37] With respect to waging a war, if, rather than learning and adapting, senior political and military leaders continue to use strategies and policies or organizations and management processes known to be inefficient, they should be held morally blameworthy—even if not legally guilty—for the results of their actions, just as soldiers and their leaders ignoring the war convention would be on the battlefield.

In *War and Politics,* the American strategist Bernard Brodie puts it this way: "Unless [a war] is in pursuit of a reasonable political objective, any nation resorting to war is simply perpetuating wanton destruction of life and goods on a vast scale." Wanton destruction and waste also result if the ends are reasonable but the decisions concerning strategies, policies, resources, military operations, and the execution of these decisions do not contribute to attaining those reasonable ends. Brodie concludes by paraphrasing an often-used maxim: "War is not only too important to be left to the generals but too important and far too complex to be handled adequately by any one profession."[38]

A performance-oriented, dialogue-execution regime increases the probability of identifying reasonable war aims as well as military and nonmilitary strategies, policies, and campaigns. It also increases the likelihood of properly adapting to the dynamic realities of war. Therefore, it improves the odds that the war will be waged prudently with progress made toward the reasonable aims decided on.

"Success Matters," a 2006 study by Jason Reifler, Christopher Gelpi, and Peter Feaver, analyzed public support for the Iraq War. It showed that the body bag count alone is an insufficient indicator of the legitimacy of and the public support for a war. Its core conclusion is that the American public's tolerance for the human costs of war is primarily shaped by the intersection of two crucial attitudes: "beliefs about the rightness or wrongness of the war, and beliefs about a war's likely success." While the two attitudes affect one another, the study demonstrated that "beliefs about the likelihood of success matter most in determining the public's willingness to tolerate U.S. military deaths in combat."[39]

Cast in the quantitative language of political science, "Success Matters" ties war-waging proficiency to legitimacy. The belief in the rightness of a war—whether a war is justified—is a consideration of *jus ad bellum*. The probability of wartime success, however, is at the heart of the strategic dimension of *jus in bello*—prudence in waging war. The probability of success increases when a properly conducted performance-oriented, dialogue-execution regime is used. "Success Matters" demonstrates that American citizens, and perhaps especially the citizens-who-become-soldiers and their families, will support a war that is progressing toward an ultimately successful outcome that matters.[40] Purpose, progress, and ultimate success give meaning to the sacrifices inherent in any war, thus giving legitimacy to a war.

Put another way, citizens consider illegitimate a war that appears to waste the lives of citizens-who-become-soldiers by placing them in situations of significant risk but for no worthy cause and with little chance of success. Thus, "Success Matters" ties the legitimacy of a war to its probability of success, which, in turn, is a function of the first two elements of the tripartite tension inherent in waging war: achieve coherency and generate organizational capacity.

The tripartite tension inherent in the war-waging dimension of *jus in bello*—(1) achieving coherence by setting war aims and making strategy, policy, and campaign decisions that increase the probability of achieving those aims, (2) generating organizational capacity by translating those aims and decisions into action to achieve war aims at the least cost, in lives and resources, and the least risk to the innocent and to one's political community, then adapting decisions and actions as the vagaries of war unfold, and (3) maintaining legitimacy by doing all the foregoing while observing the war convention, sustaining public support of the war effort, and ensuring proper subordination of the military to civilian leadership—is a dynamic relationship. War's essential uncertainty and constant change cause the dynamism inherent in the tripartite tension, and a properly conducted performance-oriented, dialogue-execution regime increases the likelihood that the elements of this tension remain in sufficient balance.

A properly conducted performance-oriented, dialogue-execution regime is far from the example of role differentiation that Walzer and others use to separate political leaders who are responsible for the war itself and military leaders who are responsible for the conduct of war. Actual war, waged by democracies at least, requires that senior political leaders retain final decision responsibility. En route to that final decision as well as in execution and adaptation, however, the responsibilities of senior political and military leaders are much more integrated and shared than Walzer and others admit.

Clarifying and describing those responsibilities must become part of just war theory's account of *jus in bello*. Unlike in the four case studies used in *Supreme Command*, nations are not always fortunate to have wise senior political and military leaders. In the analysis of the Vietnam War period, Brodie reminds us that "a wiser president would have ignored [poor military] advice; more strategically minded generals would have given better advice."[41] A nation cannot, unfortunately, count on wise presidents and strategically minded generals both being present at the appropriate time. Human failings, even stupidity in high places, and bumbling bureaucracies are at least as common as wisdom, genius, and managerial excellence. Realizing this, Cohen titled his penultimate chapter "Leadership without Genius" and commended the unequal dialogue as a substitute for the absence of genius. Such a realization is exactly right, but the unequal dialogue provides only a partial substitute. Nations that acknowledge the absence of genius, that understand the low probability of wise presidents and strategic generals emerging at just the right time, and that recognize the existence of human and organizational failings must demand a properly conducted performance-oriented, dialogue-execution regime. Further, to complete its account of *jus in bello,* just war theory must make a similar demand.

Conclusions: Looking for Guiding Principles

In "Building Trust," Richard Kohn describes two wartime secretaries of defense whose behavior in office resulted in poorly decided war aims, strategies, policies, and military operations and equally poor execution and adaptation. Secretaries Robert McNamara and Donald Rumsfeld were, he says, both people of "enormous drive, energy, and ambition: competitive . . . domineering, arrogant, dismissive, manipulative, hard-working, bullying, contemptuous, intimidating, ruthless, humiliating, and aggressive." Both created dysfunctional relationships between the topmost civilians and the most senior military officers, relationships that resulted in the lack of candor, consultation, coordination, and collaboration that, in turn, resulted in disastrous wartime policy and decision making.[42]

Kohn would agree that, in peacetime, such leadership would be unfortunate; in wartime, it is morally reprehensible, for the lives of citizens-who-become-soldiers and of the innocent are among the costs of executing the "disastrous policy" that emanates from dysfunctional relationships, dialogues, and execution.[43] Though senior political and military leaders act far from the battlefield, the quality of their work selecting war aims and then identifying, executing, and adapting strategies, policies, and campaigns to achieve those aims—that is, their war-waging responsibilities—are linked directly to justice in the conduct of war.

Accounting for *jus in bello* war-waging responsibilities starts to fill the gap in current just war theory. The final step is to identify principles that guide, or should guide, the senior political and military leaders who have these responsibilities.

6

Jus in Bello's War-Waging Principles

The principles of *jus in bello*'s tactical dimension describe right conduct in the midst of battle; applying them correctly helps assure that justice is done in fighting a war.[1] The principles of *jus in bello*'s strategic dimension describe right conduct in the waging of war; applying them correctly helps assure that justice is done in waging a war. In the end, *jus in bello*'s war-waging principles leave senior political and military leaders in a position akin to soldiers and military leaders on the battlefield: "The cruelest decisions [are left] to be made by the men [and women] on the spot."[2]

Like the *jus in bello* war-fighting principles of Walzer's war convention, the war-waging principles are designed to balance protection of individual and communal life with the legitimate conduct of war. At the tactical level, this balance occurs between winning and fighting well. At the strategic level, it occurs amid the tripartite tension inherent in the war-waging dimension of *jus in bello*: (1) achieving coherence by setting war aims and making strategy, policy, and campaign decisions that increase the probability of achieving those aims, (2) generating organizational capacity by translating those aims and decisions into action to achieve war aims at the least cost, in lives and resources, and at least risk to the innocent and to one's political community, then adapting decisions and actions as the vagaries of war unfold, and (3) maintaining legitimacy by doing all the foregoing while observing the war convention, sustaining public support of the war effort, and ensuring proper subordination of the military to civilian leadership.

War-Waging Principles

The five principles presented below emerge from the analysis and examples of the previous chapters. Together, they form a framework that, if followed, increases the probability that war-waging decisions and actions will use the lives of citizens-who-become-soldiers well and decreases the likelihood that the lives of the innocent and the life of the political community are risked unnecessarily. They describe what senior political and military leaders owe the citizens-who-become-soldiers that they lead, the political community that they serve, and the innocent whose lives they put at risk. Put another way, senior political and military leaders who follow the principles described below are acting justly with respect to the exercise of their *jus in bello* strategic, war-waging responsibilities.

1. The Principle of Continuous Dialogue

This principle recognizes the necessity for a robust civil-military dialogue prior to the initial decisions concerning war aims, strategies, policies, and military campaigns. It also recognizes the need for continuing a dialogue throughout the conduct and ending of war in order to adapt initial aims, strategies, policies, and campaigns to the dynamic nature of war. Because of the continuous nature of this dialogue, which is linked to both making and executing war-waging decisions and actions, senior political and military leaders must use the dialogue as a continuous decision-execution regime, not as a series of episodic, discrete events. The president and the secretary of defense are primarily responsible for setting the right conditions for this dialogue to take place, but the senior political and military leaders who participate in this regime are coresponsible for its conduct and content.

The *jus ad bellum* aspect of just war theory properly links war aims to the justification for going to war. For example, the aims of a war justified on grounds of self-defense cannot go beyond the defeat and reasonable punishment of the aggressor. The principles of *jus ad bellum* also limit war aims, strategies, policies, and military operations to the purposes of any specific war or intervention, thus preventing a specific use of military force from turning into an expansive crusade. *Jus in bello* entails limits as well.

War aims must be achievable. Strategies, policies, and campaigns must actually be executable and contribute to achieving the aims. Ideal aims, strategies, policies, and campaigns do not matter. What matters is much more practical: aims, strategies, policies, and military operations that have a reasonable probability of success relative to one's enemies. *Best* in this practical, all-things-considered sense emerges from a proper civil-military dialogue. Aims, strategies, policies, and campaigns decided without sufficient discussion about what actually is required to execute them, whether the time expectations are reasonable, and whether these requirements are available, affordable, and acceptable may commit a nation to the impossible, resulting in prolonged war, wasted lives, and wasted resources, or end in failure.

A robust, continuous dialogue, a decision-execution regime, is necessary not only before but also during and after a war. The reality is that war is so complex, unpredictable, and fast changing—especially in an era of 24/7 global media and social media—that decisions and actions have a limited shelf life in terms of utility. The First Gulf War of 1990–1991 provides a clear example of the requirement for robust, continuous dialogue before and during a war.

Iraq invaded Kuwait on August 2, 1990. Five days later, the first US troops arrived in Saudi Arabia to defend it from the possibility of Iraqi attack. On November 29, 1990, the United Nations issued a resolution setting a deadline for Iraq to withdraw its forces from Kuwait or face military action. The US Congress authorized force on January 12, 1991. The air campaign against Iraqi forces began on January 17 and the ground campaign on February 24, 1991. The United Nations accepted the terms of a cease-fire agreement on March 3, and the first US troops began arriving home on March 17, 1991.[3]

The US civil-military dialogue began on August 1, 1990, when President George H. W. Bush was notified of Iraq's pending invasion of Kuwait. War aims, strategies, policies, and military operations emerged gradually from this dialogue even as the first American troops deployed to Saudi Arabia. The discussions and debates among senior political and military leaders, between the administration and Congress, with regional partners and allies, and in the press were fast and furious. First to emerge was a set of principles used to guide final decisions as to war aims, strategies, policies, and military operations. That the United

States would not let Iraq's aggression stand was a relatively straightforward decision. But what exactly to do, with whom, how, and when were all matters of extensive and inclusive discussion—within the United States, with international organizations, and among allies and coalition partners. From this dialogue came war aims—those acceptable not only to the United States but also to the United Nations, allies, and coalition partners.[4] Several strategies emerged: diplomatic, political, and military. Throughout, there was a constant set of conversations, briefs, debates, consultations, and rolling decisions. The key US participants included the president, the national security adviser, the secretaries of defense and state, the chairman of the Joint Chiefs of Staff, the director of the CIA, and the commander of the US Central Command. Others were brought in as needed.[5] This dialogue continued right up to the final decision as to when and how to end the war.[6] The war was short, but this was unexpected. At the start, many, in and out of the government, were forecasting dark scenarios and warning of a range of potential casualty figures—from a high of twenty thousand or more to the more conservative military estimate of about two thousand.[7]

The civil-military dialogue associated with the 1990–1991 Gulf War was not a discrete event. It was continuous. Nor was it characterized by senior military leaders providing episodic military advice as input to senior political leaders to use in separate, decision-making discussions. Rather, it is best understood as a regime, a structured set of dialogues over time in which senior military leaders—primarily the chairman of the Joint Chiefs and the commander of US Central Command—were an essential part, not merely occasional attendees who provided input. Once hostilities began, few major adjustments were needed because the war ended more quickly than anticipated, but the speed of the war did require adaptations—even in this short, seemingly straightforward war differences of opinion arose.

One of the first concerned how long to wait before launching the air and ground offensive operations to expel Iraqi forces from Kuwait. Others concerned how long to allow sanctions to work, how long the coalition could hold together, how to assess potential risks and put in place mitigation measures, how to develop and sustain support in Congress and among the American people—all were argued by the senior political and military leaders. They also argued about the military strategy: Could airpower alone attain the war aims, how should an air and ground campaign be structured, when should each start, what to do if Saddam began withdrawing his forces before the ground offensive operation began, and how to keep the war from spreading throughout the region? They also debated when and how to end the war—how much of the Iraqi army should be destroyed and whether the offensive should transition to unseat Saddam.[8] At times, senior political leaders challenged military perspectives; at other times, the tables turned. The point is that both sets of leaders were responsible for the quality and content of the dialogue. Both were responsible for ensuring that the president's decisions were the best, all things considered, and that the decisions made could actually be executed and had a reasonable chance of achieving the aims set.

Exercising war-waging responsibilities involves leaders who can adapt to the dynamism of war, and, the longer the war lasts, the more such leadership is required. Adaptive leadership differs from authority, and the difference matters. Authority in a role—whether that of corporate CEO, military general, or secretary of defense—has a specific scope that defines the expectations of those who granted that authority.[9]

Tactical, war-fighting problems generally have solutions that can be implemented using current know-how, and have persons in authority that can apply that know-how. If, for example, the lieutenant does not know how to solve a problem, then one of his sergeants or his captain is likely to have faced a similar-enough problem many times. The lieutenant can count on that know-how and authority. If not, the lieutenant colonel or the sergeant major, or other seniors in the organization in which the lieutenant serves, almost certainly will have an answer. Generals and senior colonels and command sergeants major who circulate throughout the battlefield during combat often have discussions with subordinate leaders over particular tactical problems with which their subordinates are having difficulty. Such is the nature of tactical problems and battlefield leadership.

In organizational theory parlance, these are called *technical problems*.[10] Authority is important in solving technical problems. They may be very complex and critically important, but they have known solutions that can be implemented with current know-how. They can be resolved through the application of authoritative expertise and the organization's current structures, procedures, and ways of doing things.[11] Examples of the many kinds of technical problems that arise on the battlefield include conducting an attack or a defense, laying in an ambush, executing a security or reconnaissance plan, and executing a resupply or casualty recovery operation. Any one of these could be complex and important, but all can be resolved through existing capacities, and, appropriately, their solutions can be directed by a person in authority.

At the strategic, war-waging level, the problems are different, and authority plays a different role. War-waging problems are generally a mix of technical and adaptive problems. Adaptive problems cannot be solved through technical means. They commonly require a team of experts to come together to understand the problem at hand and help identify potential solutions. They also usually entail work that is outside the norm of the organization's routine.[12] Making progress on them requires going beyond any authoritative expertise and generating new capacity within the organization.[13] Many strategic-level problems contain a significant adaptive element because the problems themselves are not clear-cut and are often so complex that neither a single person nor a single bureaucratic perspective can understand them completely and because both identifying and solving the problems require learning on the go.[14]

Understanding an adaptive problem, or the adaptive component of a mixed problem, emerges from the context; so does implementing a solution. Since the context of an adaptive problem is continually changing, the solution changes continually as well. Examples of mixed technical and adaptive wartime problems are these: defeat the Confederate States in such a way as to preserve the Union; conduct a global war against the Axis powers and establish a more stable peace following their defeat; disrupt, dismantle, and defeat al-Qaeda and its affiliates; and defeat the Islamic State in Iraq, Syria, and beyond. Each of these problems may have subcomponents that can be solved through existing organizations, processes, and structures. Each, however, also has significant elements for which no authoritative expertise exists and that cannot be fully understood, let alone solved, at the start. Seeking technical solutions, using normal procedures, and relying on authority are simply inappropriate when facing adaptive problems. Understanding the problem requires getting into it, for the nature of the problem itself is dynamic, as is the set of activities that may result in a solution.

In fact, at the strategic level, often there are no actual solutions. Rather, there are resolutions that work for a while, but, because strategic problems generally unfold and change over time, the resolution must be continually revisited. As Ambassador Ryan Crocker once said about the problems that the senior leadership team faced in Baghdad in 2007–2008: "All we can do is manage problems; we can't solve them."[15] Such is the nature of strategic-level problems. Senior political and military leaders find themselves learning and experimenting their way to understanding and resolving the problems they face; that is why they need each other and the continuous dialogue-execution regime.

Adaptive problems like those that senior political and military leaders face in waging war are problems where no one authority is capable of identifying a resolution, let alone implementing it. There is no authoritative expertise. In cases like these, leadership shifts away from answer-giving authority, like that associated with technical problems. Rather, leaders facing adaptive problems must work to construct a relationship or sets of relationships and create forums in which to raise and discuss tough questions, hear divergent opinions, and argue about and assess possible solutions. Success in resolving them involves implementing some possible solutions as if they were experiments, then learning from and adapting to what actually works. In sum, leaders facing adaptive problems must use relationships and collaborative forums like that of a dialogue-execution regime as tools needed to work toward a solution, rather than finding someone in authority to provide an answer.[16]

"Dependency on authority appropriate to technical solutions," Heifetz says, "becomes inappropriate in adaptive ones."[17] This is why, when facing adaptive, war-waging problems, senior political or military leaders who simply direct what they want done and how they want it done increase the probability of being wrong. They are applying technical solutions to adaptive problems, applying an approach that may work at the tactical level but does not work at the strategic level. In fact, leading organizational theorists hold that the most common cause of failure in leadership is produced by treating adaptive problems as if they were technical problems.[18]

Adaptive leadership, the kind of leadership that waging war

requires, is, therefore, not about doing what your boss wants done how he or she wants it done, which is what compliance regimes demand. Rather, it is about challenging some of the boss's assumptions and decisions as the unexpected occurs. By practicing adaptive leadership, those involved in the decision-execution regime must tell each other what all need to hear regarding resolving the problems they face.[19] Only this kind of leadership can help senior political and military leaders make progress on the difficult war-waging issues they face together.

Unlike with technical problems, there is no clear and time-proven framework or checklist that will result in solutions to adaptive, war-waging problems. Those responsible for waging war need a plan, but they also need freedom to deviate from that plan as new events, situations, opportunities, and vulnerabilities arise. Continual evaluation and deviation constitute the hallmark of adaptive problems as well as of a proper performance-oriented, decision-execution regime necessary to wage war. When conditions change, as they do constantly in war, senior political and military leaders are rarely able to control the outcome completely. Rather, the reality of war is that, in any given situation, several possible outcomes are equally likely. Solutions to adaptive problems do not form a straight line. Adaptive leadership requires flexibility and openness even in defining success.[20] Waging war—one form of adaptive work—requires senior political and military leaders to work together in a cooperative leadership space, which includes, but is separate from, each participant's individual, role-defined scope of authority.

The president and the secretary of defense have the primary responsibility for setting the climate required for adaptive leadership and the dialogue-execution regime necessary to practice it. This is the proper role of authority with respect to adaptive problems; authority convenes the experts and sets the climate necessary in which the dialogue-execution regime takes place. Acknowledging this responsibility at a particularly difficult and frustrating time in the dialogue over changing US strategy in Afghanistan, President Barack Obama said to Secretary of Defense Robert Gates: "I've tried to set an environment where all points of view can be expressed and have a robust debate. I'm prepared to devote any amount of time to it." Gates too recognized that it was his responsibility to set an atmosphere so people would be more inclined to speak up.[21]

On the one hand, only the president and the secretary of defense have the authority necessary to convene the experts and establish the climate and the regime necessary for a war-waging dialogue. On the other hand, all involved in the process have the responsibility to participate as adaptive leaders in the dialogue-execution regime necessary to wage war. In this kind of regime, none are just role-specific technical experts. Any one of the participants may take leadership roles at one time or another, each can and should challenge the others, but none other than the president and the secretary of defense have the authority to convene, focus, and guide the set of leaders necessary to make war-waging decisions and take war-waging actions.

No president wants to be wrong when it comes to committing the nation to war. Too much is at stake. Nor does a president want to be wrong when it comes to waging a war once committed. Again, the stakes are too high. In fact, President George W. Bush said that sending Americans to war is the most profound decision a president can make.[22] In war, presidents do not seek a right to be wrong; rather, they become acutely aware of their obligation to decide and act as rightly as possible. Recognizing this obligation, the president and the secretary of defense use—or should use—their positional authority to gather the necessary participants in a proper war-waging dialogue-execution regime and focus those participants on the adaptive problems they face together, a regime that keeps them from being too wrong.

The president and the secretary of defense have the responsibility, therefore, to ensure that the set of senior political and military leaders focus on the right problems and make progress toward their resolution, have the information and analysis necessary when they need it, have the right forums and at the right frequency to discuss, argue, and attain sufficient unity with respect to their decisions, execute those decisions coherently, and adapt given what realities emerge. When this regime goes astray—as all such regimes inevitably will because of complexity, pressure, and personality—they have the responsibility to put things back on track, refocus the discussion, or manage the participants. That is, they have the responsibility for the integrity, efficiency, and effectiveness of the process, in addition to the outcomes of that process.

The other senior political and military leaders also have responsibilities in this process. They are coresponsible for the quality of the dialogue and the resultant initial decisions, just as they are for the ongoing dialogue-execution regime needed during a war and the resultant adaptations. Neither senior political nor senior military leaders have access to an answer book. All are imperfect judges of which strategies and policies are likely to work. Rare will be the case where either senior political or senior military officers would have waged war before, although some may have fought in wars. All are, therefore, imperfect predictors of the consequences of decisions and action—at home, abroad, or on the battlefield. None can foresee enemy reactions or decisions.

Whatever limited guarantee that can be found in waging war emerges from the set of leaders executing a proper dialogue-execution regime. That is, that limited guarantee comes from a regime that attempts to maximize both the political and the military expertise—both of which are necessary in waging war and neither of which is sufficient. This is simply the nature of waging war.

The principal-agent framework correctly pointed out that if the senior civilian leader exercises his final decision authority wrongly, the voters as principal punish the politician as agent by voting him or her out of office.[23] The vote-'em-out approach is one way in which to remove inept or ineffective leadership, but waiting until this point certainly seems to be an extreme that should be avoided in the first place. A proper dialogue-execution regime helps avoid it. Further, citizens expect senior political and military leaders to do what they can before the extreme obtains. Doing so is part of the responsibilities of their offices. The final decision authorities are held responsible by the citizens, but senior political and military leaders are also responsible both to the final decision authority and to the people. Their responsibility demands that they do what they can to avoid the extreme of deciding wrongly, when such a decision can be avoided, and modify initial decisions quickly once they have been proved wrong or ineffective.

A dialogue-execution regime that augmented each participant's limited experiences and perspectives, strove to find solutions with the highest probability of success, and acknowledged subordination but also encouraged open participation is the kind that governed war-waging decisions made by President Roosevelt and his senior civilian and military leaders during World War II. It certainly was stressful and imperfect, but the structure and style of this dialogue, as well as the participants in it, permitted just the kind of discussions and debates that are necessary to achieve the limited guarantee. This is exactly the opposite of the type of regime used by the Johnson administration during the Vietnam War—an example of an avoidable travesty in the exercise of war-waging responsibilities. Here, the structure and style of the dialogue—if it can be considered a dialogue at all—as well as the duplicitous behavior of at least some of the participants resulted in using lives in a war that could not be won as it was being waged and putting the innocent at risk unnecessarily.

The issue concerning war-waging responsibilities is not whether President Johnson had the authority to make the decisions he made. He did. Rather, the issue is how he and his senior political and military leaders exercised the adaptive leadership inherent in their war-waging responsibility. So the question becomes which of the participants in this dialogue were morally blameless and which morally blameworthy. Understanding the kind of dialogue-execution regime that is required to exercise war-waging responsibilities provides a framework to help answer this question.

To get the rough, give-and-take argument over analysis, alternatives, risks, and consequences required by the dialogue-execution regime, much of the dialogue must be conducted in protected space. Leaks harm the process, for they often foreclose options before foreclosure is necessary, harden positions too quickly, and add stress among participants whose common leadership challenge is already stressful enough. At best, leaks—even though they are the stuff of any capital city—detract from proper dialogue and execution. At worst, they prevent it all together. Similar results occur when participants in the dialogue take the discussion to the public prematurely, before the group has time to complete its work.

One prime example where a combination of leaks and public discussion nearly derailed a proper dialogue and made execution more difficult occurred during the complex set of discussions on Afghanistan in 2009. The *Washington Post* published an interview with General David Petraeus in which he dismissed an option still being discussed among the principals. A couple of weeks later, another *Washington Post* article was based on a leaked copy of General Stanley McChrystal's initial commander's assessment of the situation in Afghanistan. It ended by quoting the following assessment: "Failure to provide adequate resources . . . risks a larger conflict, greater casualties, higher overall costs, and . . . critical loss of political support. Any of these risks, in turn, are likely to result in mission failure." This article was followed by a television interview (taped months before but aired in sequence with the *Post*'s articles) in which McChrystal discussed elements of his assessment and its conclusions. The general also gave a speech in London in which, during the question-and-answer period, he dismissed out of hand the option that the vice president was supporting, which was still being debated. Gates was sure (correctly so, I believe) that none of this was an intentional attempt to derail the ongoing discussion but understood that the net result was not good. A wall was, he felt, going up between the military and the White House that was at the very least not helpful in making war-waging decisions and possibly bad for the country, even dangerous.[24]

Although Gates did not believe that either Petraeus or McChrystal purposely intended to limit the options under consideration, he recognized his own responsibility for the integrity and efficacy of the dialogue and admonished his military subordinates. He reminded both generals about the necessity to provide their best analysis and judgment in the ongoing dialogue—candidly, yes, but privately. Even as he did so, however, civilian members of the dialogue were, as he put it, "spilling their guts regularly—and disparagingly—to reporters about senior military leaders . . . and the decision making process."[25] Whether these senior political leaders were also admonished is unknown, but they should have been.

These and other instances created, at least for a time, the kind of poisonous, suspicious, and sometimes condescending atmosphere that, again at the very least, is not conducive to making good war-waging decisions and, furthermore, is completely avoidable. Simply put, those civilian or military subordinates who obstruct a high-quality dialogue, who do not press for the best decision, who participate with less than full candor, or who execute halfheartedly are not exercising their war-waging, *jus in bello* responsibilities.

To work properly, the president and the secretary of defense must be responsible for establishing the conditions for and the conduct of the dialogue overall, but both the civilian and the military leaders who participate in this dialogue are coresponsible for maintaining the dialogue's protected space and its substantive quality. "Dysfunctional relationships," Richard Kohn says, "between the topmost civilians and the most senior military officers—particularly lack of candor, consultation, coordination, and collaboration—can be disastrous for policy and decision making. . . . Poor communications can cause the United States to undertake unnecessary wars, prosecute them unwisely, and pile up hundreds or thousands of dead and wounded Americans, not to speak of many times that number of enemies and innocent civilians."[26]

Speaking of the 2009 dialogue on Afghanistan, Gates says simply: "On reflection, I believe all of us at the senior-most level did not serve the president well in this process."[27] This reflection is a multifaceted illustration. In it, the president is seen as responsible for making the final decision. He is also seen as one who is served by a dialogue-execution regime in which certain senior political and military leaders are coresponsible for its conduct and outcome.

2. The Principle of Final Decision Authority

This principle recognizes the essentiality of military subordination to civil authority in democracies. At the same time, it recognizes that the proper subordination and the responsible exercise of final decision authority both require the specific kind of continuous civil-military dialogue-execution regime described in the previous principle.

The final decision authority of the president and his senior civilian leaders extends not only to *jus ad bellum* matters—issues associated with the decision to go to war—but also to war-waging *jus in bello* matters. War aims, strategies, and policies, as well as decisions about major operations and campaigns, are not purely military matters; they are political-military matters over which the senior political leaders have final decision authority. Exercising this authority, however, is not arbitrary. Like all political power in a democracy, the power to make final decisions is limited. The US Constitution limits this authority, legally and institutionally, by splitting war-waging responsibility between the executive and the legislative branches. There are moral limits as well.

Exercising this war-waging final decision authority irresponsibly—in ways that lower the probability that decisions and actions will be effective, unnecessarily prolonging a war, thereby wasting the lives of citizens-who-become-soldiers and the resources of the political community and increasing risk to the political community or the lives of the innocent—is morally blameworthy, even if not illegal. These factors, therefore, help define the concept of the responsible use of a political leader's final decision authority.

The responsible exercise of final decision authority requires the kind of dialogue-execution regime described in the previous principle and the preceding chapters. Such a regime increases the likelihood of identifying war aims, strategies, policies, and campaigns with the highest probability of success. It also increases the likelihood of adapting correctly as a war unfolds and ends. Senior civil and military subordinates are properly subordinate when they ensure that a high-quality dialogue precedes the exercise of final decision authority. Those who have the final decision authority must demand that the dialogue leading to their decision is as complete, honest, and reality based as possible. Disagreement in the war-waging dialogue is not a sign of disrespect or disloyalty.

Civilian control of the military is completely consistent with the often rough-and-tumble dialogue-execution regime that waging war requires. It is also consistent with senior civil or military subordinates who, after a decision is made and executed, reengage in the dialogue if the results of that decision and action are found to run counter to what was intended.

Civil or military subordinates who obstruct the dialogue, however, or do not participate in it fully or carry out decisions completely and faithfully are disloyal not only to the final decision authority but also to the political community, to the citizens-now-soldiers who end up executing the faulty decisions that emanate from an improperly conducted dialogue-execution regime, and to the innocents whose lives are put at risk unnecessarily.

3. The Principle of Managerial Competence

This principle recognizes the necessity to use, bypass, or change, if necessary, civil and military bureaucracies to ensure that government structures and processes work to achieve war aims, execute strategies and policies, and support military operations. It also recognizes that the senior political and military leaders are responsible for managerial competence within their scope of authority and that executing this responsibility is part of an ongoing, civil-military dialogue-execution regime.

Once a final decision is made, the work of senior military and political leaders is not over; they must make their respective bureaucracies work to support that decision. Making a bureaucracy work, especially making it work doing what it does not want to do—that is, anything new or fast—is especially hard. In war, however, this is exactly the task.

Senior political and military leaders are not only coresponsible for a proper dialogue; they are also coresponsible for executing and supporting strategies, policies, and military campaigns. In execution, senior leaders have limited options: they execute using existing bureaucracies and their in-place processes, they put in place ad hoc organizations and processes designed to bypass exiting bureaucracies, or they create new organizations and systems needed to respond to previously unrecognized requirements.

Senior leaders who cannot use their bureaucracy well enough in one or more of these three ways are simply not living up to their war-waging responsibilities. Those who can hold soldiers and commanders in combat responsible for proper tactical execution under high-risk conditions but do not hold themselves accountable for executing their war-waging managerial responsibilities under much less risky conditions are at best duplicitous and at worst morally bankrupt.

Making a bureaucracy work requires focused leadership and management. Anyone who has tried to run a large bureaucracy knows that it is not easy. But neither is advancing in the face of enemy fire, or patrolling on roads where an enemy often employs improvised explosive devices (IEDs) or other forms of surprise attacks, or conducting raids or attacks against well-prepared enemy locations.

Among the many leadership and managerial tasks necessary to make a bureaucracy work, attention to at least three—compliance regimes, performance gap–adaptation regimes, and bypass or change regimes—is most important when it comes to war-waging responsibilities. Those three tasks rise in importance because each reflects the adaptive leadership that waging war requires of senior political and military leaders. Each of the three is linked to moving a bureaucracy out of its comfort zone—that is, out of what Gates called *business as usual* and what Robert Komer recognized as a bureaucracy's *default position.*

Compliance regimes are those that involve setting and implementing monitoring mechanisms to enforce compliance to standards. Conversations relative to compliance regimes are about whether individual or organizational behaviors meet standards and, if they do not, what behavioral changes are necessary to meet those standards. There is no discussion about the standards themselves; they are fixed. The discussion is about only performance to fixed standards.

Such regimes are necessary, for example, to ensure that contracting, acquisition, equipment accountability, and personnel actions are performed according to law and regulation. Compliance regimes are examples of technical problems that waging war includes. They use authorities, known experts, who can provide solutions within preexisting frameworks.

Performance gap–adaptation regimes are not like that. These regimes are required because war poses mostly adaptive, not technical, problems to the senior political and military leaders who wage it. A performance gap–adaptation regime involves (1) setting aims, identifying the means (e.g., strategies, policies, leaders, campaigns, and resources) necessary to attain those aims, then (2) monitoring the gap between desired and actual results, and finally (3) adapting ends and means as necessary. Monitoring in this case is not tied to compliance; rather, it is linked to adaptation.

Conversations relative to performance gap–adaptation regimes are designed to identify the gap between an organization's ends (what it wants to achieve) and the reality that organization is actually facing. These regimes are intended to help an organization identify how to adapt the ways and means being employed to achieve its ends, thus closing the desire/reality gap. They are also intended to stimulate a discussion about whether the ends are actually achievable. In a performance gap–adaptation conversation, the only fixed point is reality. Adaptation—of ends, ways, means, or all three—is based on the fixed point of reality. Reality may require changing ends (war aims), ways (strategies, policies, or military campaigns and operations), or means

(political or military leaders, force size and composition, funding, organizational procedures, or fiscal or materiel resources) or some combination thereof. A performance gap–adaptation regime is necessary in
the dynamic environment associated with any adaptive leadership challenge, like war, where initial assessments, decisions, and actions need
constant reassessment. Corporate executives need a performance gap–
adaptation regime; so do senior political and military leaders who wage
war.[28]

Using a compliance discussion where a performance gap–adaptation discussion is needed will inhibit an organization's success. For
example, if war aims, strategies, or policies become fixed standards,
the resultant conversation will be compliance oriented. The conversation will include not the viability of ends, ways, or means, but only a
discussion of whether behaviors meet standards. Over time, a compliance regime discussion can produce an unreality. Perhaps this is what
led President Bush to say: "For two and a half years, I had supported
the strategy of withdrawing our forces as the Iraqis stepped forward.
But in the months after the [February 2006] Samarra bombing, I had
started to question whether our approach matched the reality on the
ground."[29]

Following his intuition, the president initiated a performance gap–
adaptation discussion calling several experts from outside the government to Camp David for a two-day, top-level review. "Nobody within
the administration was prepared to directly challenge [Donald] Rumsfeld or [George] Casey in front of the President"—a clear indication
that no adaptive leadership was being exercised and that compliance
reigned. As the president began a new review, Casey seemed to have no
doubts. With Prime Minister Nouri al-Maliki and his cabinet in office
and Abu Musab al-Zarqawi (the leader of al-Qaeda in Iraq at the time)
dead, the general was convinced that the strategy was on track—and
that it was time to begin the withdrawal of the next few brigades of
American troops.[30] He was executing the plan, which is another clear
indication that the approach to monitoring the war in Iraq from 2004
to 2007 resembled more a compliance regime than a performance gap–
adaptation regime. That began to change with Bush's Camp David
review and completely changed by the time the president selected a
new strategy, new leadership, and new resource policies in 2007.

The third important leadership and managerial task necessary to make a bureaucracy work is a bypass or change regime. This kind of regime involves identifying parts of a bureaucracy that do not perform as necessary, then either creating a way to bypass the underperforming portion of the bureaucracy or changing the bureaucracy. For example, seeing that the bureaucracy's standard way of processing equipment for and delivering it to the Iraqi security forces was woefully lethargic and, thus, an obstacle to success, Gates directed that an ad hoc task force be created within the office of the secretary of defense. This reform did not replace or change the existing bureaucracy. Rather, for actions associated with providing the Iraqi security forces' equipment, the task force bypassed elements of the bureaucracy. This temporary reform left the bureaucracy in place for handling standard military sales but significantly improved US support to the Iraqi army and police forces.

Conversations relative to bypassing or changing regimes are about the difference between the speed at which bureaucracies normally work and the speed necessary to support dynamic war efforts. The former is generally too slow for the latter. For example, the routine Pentagon process for buying new equipment is a multiyear, sometimes decades-long one. Because of the numbers of casualties caused by IEDs in Iraq, soldiers needed better protection much faster than the routine procedure would allow. Two bypass mechanisms were put in place, one by Rumsfeld and the other by Gates. The first delivered better countermeasures, the second better vehicles. Neither of these fast-delivered innovations would have been possible using routine systems.

General Marshall's reorganization of the US Army and its bureaucracies at the start of World War II is an example of a change process. Another involves the creation of the entirely new staff organizations and processes needed to coordinate the decisions and actions of both the American and the British defense and military organizations during World War II. The reorganization that President Lincoln's secretary of war effected during the Civil War is a third example. Only some of these changes continued after the war in question ended; those that were no longer useful or necessary simply went away.

These three management processes, among others, are all necessary to wage war, but no one is sufficient. They are required within civil and military bureaucracies as well as among them. The point is that, in addition to identifying adequate war aims, strategies, and policies and directing that military campaigns or major operations take place, senior political and military leaders must translate initial decisions into action, then adapt as the dynamics of war create new realities. They must have enough managerial expertise to know when a compliance regime is applicable, when a performance gap–adaptation regime is needed, and how to establish and run both. They must also have the capacity—usually developed from experience—to use, bypass, or change the large organizations and bureaucracies for which they are responsible. And they must figure out how to coordinate the set of organizations and bureaucracies necessary to wage war sufficiently enough to create a coherent effort toward achieving war aims.

Simply put, senior political leaders must be more than politically reliable, and senior military leaders must be more than good war fighters. To execute their *jus in bello* war-waging responsibilities, they must be competent leaders and managers, individually and collectively.

4. The Principle of War Legitimacy

This principle recognizes that even justified wars can lose their legitimacy. Legitimacy concerns maintaining the support of the population as one conducts a war, that support being, in turn, a function of the righteousness of the war (a *jus ad bellum* issue) and progress toward probable success (a *jus in bello* issue). Legitimacy is tied directly to the competence of senior political and military leaders in executing their war-waging responsibilities.

When a war is perceived as just, its aims are seen as achievable, and progress is being made toward achieving those aims, the casualties resulting from that war are viewed as worth the cost, and the war is viewed as legitimate. The US public makes reasoned and reasonable judgments about war. It formed its attitudes regarding support for the war in Iraq, for example, by weighing the costs and benefits. Casualties stand as a cost of war, but they are a cost the public is willing to pay if it thinks that the initial decision to launch the war was correct and that the United States will prevail.[31] In sum, senior political and military leaders who cannot execute their war-waging responsibilities well enough erode the very legitimacy of the war in the eyes of their country's citizens.

Fighting a war poorly is one way to erode legitimacy; waging war poorly is another. In the Vietnam War, the American military was rarely, if ever, defeated on the battlefield. It fought well. The way the United States waged the war, however—its war aims, its strategies, policies, campaigns, and major operations—ultimately eroded legitimacy and popular support. The costs were seen by the American people as not worth it. The war-waging activities of this period were more an example of sustained imprudence than proficiency, more like incompetent than expert leadership and management.

Over time, incompetence or sustained imprudence tells the American people that a war is not being won and possibly cannot be won and, thus, that continuing the war is not worth the cost in terms of lives or treasure. War-waging capacity and legitimacy are connected. Such appears to be the case with respect to the war in Afghanistan. In 2001, for example, only 9 percent of polled Americans thought that it was a mistake; in 2013, that number was 44 percent. Opinions as to the righteousness of this war are also interesting. In 2002, 89 percent of those polled believed that the United States did not make a mistake by invading Afghanistan; by 2012, 62 percent still believed that the initial decision was right. Polling as to progress and the probability of success, however, tells a different story. During this same period, 45–62 percent believed that the war was going badly, and an increasing percentage believed that the United States should pull out as planned or faster.[32] The way in which the Afghan War has been waged affected its legitimacy in the eyes of the American people.

Not all war-waging errors lead to defeat or loss of legitimacy. World War II, for example, started off poorly. Victory in World War I had bred complacency and inhibited imaginative ideas and experiments in doctrine, organization, and materiel. A revulsion against war in general and disillusionment with World War I in particular, together with faith in the oceans as bulwarks of protection, prompted retreat into national isolation. The post–World War I period was one of rapid and significant decline in American military capacity. Because of the Great Depression, congressional appropriations dwindled, manpower declined, and procurement languished. As the historian Martin Blumenson noted:

"Even after World War II began in Europe, the American public had remained lethargic toward military issues."[33] The result was an incapable military force at the dawn of World War II.

Equally incapable were the war-waging systems necessary to raise, train, organize, equip, deploy, employ, and sustain a large military force fighting around the world. In November 1942, American troops made their debut in the European Theater in North Africa. The first main battle there, that of the Kasserine Pass, was a disaster, but, by May 1943, enemy resistance had ceased, and the campaign for North Africa was over. The American military forces had learned, and learned quickly, what succeeded on the battlefield. They had become a better war-fighting organization. As one historian observed: "No soldier in Africa had changed more—grown more—than [General Dwight] Eisenhower."[34]

America's war-waging capacity also grew. In a matter of months, the defeat at the Kasserine Pass was quickly turned into a successful campaign. Thus, an initial defeat did not result in a questioning of the legitimacy of the war. Had defeat followed defeat, however, over time progress and perhaps even ultimate success in the war may have become an issue. Senior political and military leaders' war-waging competence—the capacity to do what it takes to select achievable aims; identify strategies, policies, and campaigns to attain those aims; translate decisions into orchestrated military and nonmilitary action; and adapt as a war unfolds—plays an important role in building, maintaining, or eroding legitimacy. Senior leaders who fail to develop sufficient leadership and managerial abilities with respect to their war-waging responsibilities gamble with legitimacy. The war's legitimacy may survive, but such a gamble is not one that should be taken.

5. The Principle of Resignation

This principle recognizes that the resignation of senior political or military leaders is necessary and permissible under certain conditions. Such leaders remain moral agents, not mere instruments of a government. This principle is limited, however, by the necessity to retain military subordination to civil authority in a democracy.

The problem of resignation is twofold. On the one hand, resignation is necessary. It acknowledges that everyone, including senior political and military leaders, remains a moral agent responsible for his or her conscience. It is also a useful recuperative mechanism that helps large organizations know when there are significant problems with what they are doing or how they are doing it. Finally, it is useful in a performance-oriented, dialogue-execution regime, for it provides a way to ensure that no participants can merely be steamrolled into agreement. On the other hand, it has a significant potential downside, especially applicable to the senior military leaders in a democracy: it can be or be perceived to be a direct challenge to civil authority, civil primacy, and civil control of the military. The principle of resignation attempts to allow for the positive and necessary aspects of resignation while avoiding or mitigating its downside.

In the right circumstances, resignation often provides a healthy and necessary organizational recuperative mechanism, as Albert O. Hirschman argues in *Exit, Voice, and Loyalty.* Hirschman describes *exit,* the option to leave, in three ways. If there is a decline in the price, availability, or quality of a product, consumers exit by going elsewhere to buy or invest. If the decline is in management proficiency, a corporate executive may exit by leaving the firm. And, if the decline is in deteriorating government performance, then the exit involves an official leaving his or her position. *Voice,* according to Hirschman, is the option for a consumer, an executive, a government official, or some watchdog organization to complain about or attempt to improve things by pointing out the decline and need for change.[35] Within many organizations, both options are available, even though one option or the other may be preferable in a given situation or organizational culture. Exit and voice are ways that can help firms, organizations, and governments (at least nontotalitarian governments) know that what they are doing is not working and be prompted to do something about it.

Hirschman recognizes, however, that while feedback through exit or voice is in the long-run interest of organization managers, their short-run interest is to entrench themselves and enhance their freedom to act as they wish, unmolested as far as possible by either desertions or complaints.[36] In other words, some managers and leaders do not want feedback; they want silence and compliance—even in the face of evidence that what they are doing, or how they are doing it, is not working. These managers and organizations simply shut down both exit and voice to impose discipline and compliance. Such is the case with autocratic managers, for whom compliance and obedience are more important than success or progress and the threat of punishment replaces leadership; it is also the case in totalitarian governments, under which neither citizens nor leaders can leave or complain.

Denial is a second common organizational response. The customers, members, or leaders of an organization simply deny the report of decline. This response is common among those who have invested a great deal and, thus, have a considerable stake in the product, the service, the plan, or the organization in general. In the case of senior leaders, this investment may have been a lifetime of service including difficult sacrifices that, in turn, generated significant loyalty. In fact, Hirschman points out, the more loyal a person is to an organization, and the more he or she has invested in the organization or a specific product, service, or activity within the organization, the greater the ability to deny reports of decline. The loyalist—especially one who has been a senior leader—has great difficulty coming to the belief that his or her organization could decline or deteriorate in the ways in which some are pointing out.[37]

Co-opting is a third common organizational response to criticism. In this case, the organization domesticates the dissenters. The doubter is kept on and given an explicit role as devil's advocate or as a member of the so-called Red Team. In this way, the dissenter's conscience may be assuaged, but his or her effectiveness is reduced to a point where it is virtually discountable. Co-opting forces the dissenter to give up, a priori, his or her strongest weapon: the threat to resign under protest.[38]

Whether managers and organizations choose to shut down, deny, or co-opt criticism, the result is the same: the government—or whatever other type of organization that might use them—is denied needed recuperative mechanisms. When one or more of these approaches are employed, organizations are simply robbed of the ability to recognize and restore deteriorating quality in product or performance.[39]

General Harold K. Johnson, the army's chief of staff from 1964 to 1968, provides a good example. He considered exiting but rejected the idea. Doing so, he may have robbed the United States in ways to which Hirschman refers. "When the president elected not to follow the advice of the Joint Chiefs of Staff, they had little choice but to go along or resign," says the historian and biographer Lewis Sorley. He goes on to quote Johnson: "We had made our recommendations. . . . Our advice had been rejected and other courses of action were chosen, so we simply were good soldiers and did what we were told to do."[40]

Voice had failed, so, at one point in his tenure, Johnson concluded that he had to resign—that is, exit. As we have seen, he later said: "I remember the day I was ready to go over to the Oval Office and give my four stars to the president and tell him, 'You have refused to .tell the country they cannot fight a war without mobilization; you have required me to send men into battle with little hope of their ultimate victory; and you have forced us in the military to violate almost every one of the principles of war in Vietnam. Therefore, I resign and will hold a press conference after I walk out of your door.'" Had Johnson simply resigned because he could not reconcile the legal orders he was given with his understanding that the lives of soldiers were simply being wasted—that his legal orders were, therefore, immoral—he would not go to his grave, in his words, "with that lapse of moral courage on [his] back."[41] Had he held a press conference, however, he would have changed an individual act of moral courage and fidelity to moral agency to a challenge to one of the bedrock principles of a democracy: civilian control of the military.

When fighting, neither soldiers nor their military leaders are mere instruments. Rather, they remain moral agents. The principles governing *jus in bello*'s tactical, war-fighting dimension mandate that they retain their moral agency even in combat. "Soldiers," Walzer reminds all, "can never be transformed into mere instruments of war. . . . Trained to obey 'without hesitation,' they remain nevertheless capable of hesitating. . . . It is a mistake to treat soldiers as if they were automatons who make no judgments at all."[42] Senior political and military leaders, too, remain moral agents. As such, they remain responsible for the decisions and actions they take. The "I'm only following orders" argument does not hold much water for a soldier, a general, or a civilian leader—neither does the "they'll only get somebody else" argument.

Leaving a position of significant responsibility is difficult. Denial is very strong, as is co-opting. "[Any] final policy decision," Hirschman shows, "can always be made to look as some middle course between the two opposing points of view . . . ; hence [all] are made to feel that 'if it had not been for me, an even more sinister decision would have been taken.'" The desire to remain close to power is also very strong. Hirschman suggests a variant of the famous dictum, "Power corrupts, and absolute power corrupts absolutely": "Power corrupts; and even a little influence in a country with huge power corrupts hugely."[43] Finally, the organization itself may have formal or informal norms that treat either exit or voice as disloyalty, even treason or mutiny. These kinds of norms are very powerful and pose significant difficulty to those considering resignation or major criticism. Such difficulty is natural; the decision to resign should be hard, and that course of action should be taken only as a last resort and in extraordinary circumstances.

Difficulty, however, does not set aside a senior leader's responsibility to his or her own conscience or to the larger institution and the nation that he or she serves. Nor does it change his or her responsibility to the innocent and those citizens-who-become-soldiers destined to execute war-waging decisions. Loyalty sometimes requires criticism; this is the premise of Hirschman's argument. To operate properly, and especially in war, the nation to which a senior leader is loyal needs to know when its war aims, strategies, policies, and military operations are failing. Without this feedback—whether expressed through voice, as should take priority in the case of senior officers, or exit, the choice of last resort—the nation's chances of recuperating from deteriorated performance are reduced.

With respect to senior military leaders, however, resignation or criticism must be exercised in a way that does not challenge military subordination to civil authority—that is, "candidly and privately," as Gates put it.[44] Exit or voice options for senior civilian leaders are a bit different. Because their resignation or dissent does not threaten civil control of the military, it can be more public—the cases of Senator Eugene McCarthy during the Vietnam War and the congressional leaders and presidential candidates who publicly debated the merits of military involvement in Iraq and Afghanistan during their campaigns provide good examples.

Mass resignations of senior military officials, like that considered by the Joint Chiefs during the Johnson administration, or public resignations, like Johnson's would have been, are problematic because of the threat they pose to civilian authority. Public criticism of senior political leaders still in office—like that to which Rumsfeld was subjected by several retired general officers—is similarly problematic because it, too, challenges, directly or indirectly, civil control of the military. Resignation simply because advice is ignored is also problematic, but for different reasons. Here, petulance seems more at play than morality or the desire to provide the nation an opportunity to recuperate from deteriorated performance.

General Maxwell Taylor provides an interesting example of public criticism of policy without challenge to civil authority. After he retired as chief of staff of the US Army in 1959, he wrote *The Uncertain Trumpet,* in which he criticized the US policy of massive retaliation. He called this policy "the Great Fallacy," that is, the false belief that "the use or threatened use of atomic weapons of mass destruction would be sufficient to assure the security of the United States and its friends."[45] He argued against basing US national security on this fallacy and for a strategy of flexible response whereby the United States would be just as capable of deterring limited war as it would be of preventing World War III.

Taylor's book was a challenge to the logic of massive retaliation, whether such a policy made sense given the strategic realities of the early Cold War period. It did not challenge the authority and responsibility of senior political leaders to make this kind of policy choice. Nor did it challenge civilian control of the military. Rather, it was the kind of voice that Hirschman describes as a necessary recuperative mechanism. Taylor's voice was a private matter while he was on active duty, expressed with candor, but kept within the appropriate protected space necessary for a proper civil-military dialogue. American civilian leaders ultimately adopted a more flexible response strategy, and in 1962 Taylor was recalled to active duty to become President Kennedy's choice for chairman of the Joint Chiefs of Staff.[46]

Voice seems to have a recognized place with respect to senior political and military leaders but less so exit. Richard Kohn, for example, rejects resignation even if kept private. He writes: "Resignation—even the very hint of it, much less the threat or the act—is a direct assault on civilian authority. Civilian officials rightly interpret it as such. It inherently violates civilian control." Kohn believes that all lawful orders,

even if immoral, are to be followed. He points out: "Even military officers at the very top of the chain of command . . . cannot know all of the
larger national and international considerations involved, a calculation
that belongs properly to the political leadership, elected and appointed.
Nor is there historical evidence that military judgment has been superior to that of the politicians."[47] In this, he is exactly right. The scope
of the president's responsibility is larger than the scope of a general's.
That is why resignation over mere disagreement or the feeling of being
ignored, disrespected, or treated badly is wrong. A decision to resign
cannot be taken this lightly.

Those are not the grounds that Johnson cites, however. What
distinguishes his frustration with military advice not being taken or
the chiefs being cut out of many decisions—situations that did not
prompt him to consider resignation—from his moral anguish is this:
the strategies and policies in Vietnam had deteriorated to the point of
wasting the lives of citizens-who-became-soldiers in a war that could
not have been won, at least not in the way it was being fought. His
was not the problem of not knowing "all of the larger national and
international considerations involved," as Kohn puts it. Rather, his
was the problem of what he did know: that the lives of citizens-who-
became-soldiers were being wasted. His was a moral problem that
involved recognizing first that the value of human life is such that,
while under certain circumstances it can be used, it cannot be wasted
and, second, that he, his fellow chiefs, the president, and other senior
political leaders are coresponsible for the lives they use. The issue was
not potential lives that might be wasted; it was actual lives that were
being wasted. It was not whether he believed that he must obey dis-
tasteful, seemingly foolish, or sometime disastrous orders. He knew
that he must; after all, he fought the futile defense of the Philippine
Islands following the 1941 Japanese invasion, was captured, and sur-
vived the Bataan Death March, Japanese hell ships, and the neglect,
brutality, illness, and starvation of extended captivity. His issue was
one of moral agency.

Neither good order and discipline nor military subordination to
civil authority is at risk when moral agency is exercised properly. If
soldiers and leaders are to remain moral agents on the battlefield, they
must be moral agents in the boardroom as well. Further, Hirschman

might add, the correct exercise of moral agency in some circumstances might result in better organizational performance.

Johnson had no responsibility for the consciences of others, but he did have a responsibility for his own. He was also responsible to the innocent whose lives war always puts at risk, to the citizens-who-become-soldiers that he led, and to the nation that he served. An absolute prohibition of resignation is unwarranted because it denies the individual moral agency and denies the institution an important recuperative mechanism.

Sources and Purposes of *Jus in Bello*'s War-Waging Principles

The source of just war theory's tactical war-fighting principles is clear: usage. They are revealed, Walzer claims, in the ways in which men and women—some who are citizens, some who are soldiers, and others who are leaders—argue about war. They are embedded in the explanations, justifications, and judgments that ordinary people, as well as those responsible for the action in question, use. When moral philosophers analyze these arguments, justifications, and judgments, they seek out coherence, laying bare the principles that the arguments, justifications, and judgments exemplify. Walzer is claiming that those who use the arguments, present the explanations or justifications, and make judgments are making statements as "to their own principles," even though the principles may be worded and arranged more informally than they are when codified in just war theory.[48] He codifies the war-fighting principles from the analyses, arguments, justifications, and judgments of the historical illustrations presented in *Just and Unjust Wars*.

War-fighting principles—the combatant/noncombatant distinction, the principle of noncombatant immunity, the principle of double effect and double intent, the principle of proportionality, and the principle of due care and due risk—circumscribe what is morally permissible in combat.[49] Decisions are left to soldiers and their leaders who are on the spot, but principles exist to be used in clarifying expectations and guiding those decisions—prior to combat in training and education, during combat in decision and execution, and after combat in judging what was done. Application in a specific case often becomes an issue, even if the principles themselves are not. Whether one or more of the principles were applied in a particular, often-confused and stress-filled situation is correctly identified as the cruelest decision left to the men and women on the spot.

Jus in bello's tactical, war-fighting principles serve multiple purposes. More than guides for soldiers and their leaders in combat, they also act as a framework to explain and justify war-fighting decisions and actions. They also provide the framework within which one can identify whether and under what conditions moral blame is warranted. If asked, soldiers and leaders appeal to the war-fighting principles—even if unconsciously and indirectly—by saying that an act in question was *militarily necessary,* that they used *only the necessary force,* that they *tried to care for* the innocent, that they *never intended to harm noncombatants,* and that *the death of the innocent was unavoidable.* An investigation, if one is conducted, may find that they were correct, or not. The principles provide a way to judge moral blameworthiness after explanations and justifications are given, even if the act in question broke no law.

For Walzer, rights lay the foundation for the principles governing *jus in bello*'s war-fighting dimension; they also play an important role in understanding war-fighting responsibilities.[50] "Individual rights (to life and liberty)," Walzer says, "underlie the most important judgments that we make about war," even though taking another's life in war is, under specific circumstances, justified. Walzer's understanding of the right to life is neither absolute nor merely the result of arbitrary conventions or utility, for then justifying taking another's life in war would be too easy. So he characterizes these rights as "somehow entailed by our sense of what it means to be a human being" and claims that civilian noncombatants retain their right to life; soldiers do not.[51] "Simply by fighting," Walzer claims, "[soldiers] have lost their title to life and liberty. . . . Everyone else retains his rights."[52] The war convention rests on "a certain view of noncombatants," one holding "that they are men and women with rights and that they cannot be used for some military purpose, even if it is a legitimate purpose." Walzer understands that war necessarily places civilians in danger; that is another aspect of its hellishness. The principles of the war convention restrict the hellishness of war by demanding that soldiers and their officers minimize the danger they impose on civilians—hence the principle of due care and due risk.[53]

Jus in bello's war-waging principles also arise from usage. They have similar purposes, and they too are founded on a respect for the value of human life, individual and communal. They are different, however, in two respects. First, they apply to senior political and military leaders whose decisions and actions affect the conduct of war but who are far from the battlefield. Second, with the exception of the principle of resignation, they apply to processes, not particular decisions and actions. This difference results from the nature of the war-waging problems that senior political and military leaders face: adaptive problems that cannot be understood, let alone solved, by a single authority. Rather, the adaptive problems involved in waging war require a set of civilian and military leaders to create collaborative processes and forums in which the understanding and resolving of adaptive problems can emerge.

Usage—the actual discussions and arguments surrounding war-waging activities as well as the explanations and justifications used and the judgments pronounced—is revealing. Norms and principles are often not revealed in the acts themselves. Rather, they are found in explanations and justifications adduced by those who acted; they are also embodied in the expectations that underlie questions concerning actions taken.

The public discussion surrounding what happened in the Abu Ghraib prison in 2003 and 2004 and why it happened, the discussion in late fall of 2006 surrounding whether Bush's administration should stay the course in Iraq or take a new direction, and the 2009 discussion surrounding Obama's decision three years later whether his administration should change course in Afghanistan are all examples of explanations and justifications providing a window into principles.[54] As was the case with Walzer's war-fighting principles, usage reveals a moral depth beyond a discussion of a particular act, incident, or decision.

The Abu Ghraib discussion assumed that the conduct of war involved more than war fighting. Those involved in the discussion assumed that the senior political and military leaders had responsibilities that affected the actions some took on the battlefield. The public expectation was that senior leaders understand the practical consequences of their decisions before making them. The discussion and investigation concerned not only the individual acts of soldiers and leaders on the ground but also war-waging policy issues concerning the status of enemy combatants, the adequacy of training and personnel selection, and the effect that national policies may or may not have had on the local actions that took place in the prison.[55]

The public discussions surrounding Bush's and Obama's strategy decisions often concerned the degree to which consultation and collaboration among senior political and military leaders had preceded the final decision—a reflection of the principle of continuous dialogue. They also concerned the realities in Iraq and Afghanistan and the degree to which the Bush and the Obama administrations' strategies and policies should change because of the ways in which the wars had unfolded—illustrating the principles of continuous dialogue and adaptation. Next, throughout both discussions, regardless of the position taken on the pending decision, all assumed that the president had final decision authority. Further, all assumed that both senior political and senior military leaders shared the responsibility to help the president make the best decision and that the military and nonmilitary agencies and departments involved would be capable of executing whatever decision was made—manifestations of the principles of final decision authority and managerial competence. Finally, whether they believed the resultant decision to be reckless or responsible, both discussions recognized that the lives of citizens-now-soldiers and the legitimacy of the war were at stake—an example of the principle of war legitimacy. In other words, the public discussion of these two important presidential decisions pointed to principles that guide, or should guide, those who have the final say in decisions, those who participate in the decision-making process, and those who execute war-waging decisions.

War-waging principles, like their war-fighting cousins, serve multiple purposes. The five war-waging principles provide a framework that senior leaders can use to explain and justify their decisions and actions or that citizens or their representatives can use to question, judge, and, when appropriate, assign moral blame. The principles also provide the framework for public discourse—whether in the media, during congressional testimony, or in some other public forum.

As the public discussion over Bush's 2006 decision concerning the Surge in Iraq and the 2009 discussion surrounding Obama's decision over Afghanistan showed, both those in the decision-making discourse and those commenting on it appealed to one or more of the war-waging principles by saying that the decision or act in question was the result of "extensive civil-military consultation," that the "final decision was made by a proper authority," that "we're making progress," "that as things change we're changing with them," and that "we're doing everything possible in execution." In neither of these cases did a senior political leader say anything like, "I thought this up all by myself and ordered the military to do it, like it or not," nor did a military leader say, "Yes, I was told to do that. I don't agree with it, so I'm not doing it." Nor will one ever hear a senior leader talk about a decision that he or she knows, at the time it is made, is unexecutable. The war-waging principles of *jus in bello* codify practice, just as do *jus in bello*'s war-fighting principles.

Finally, the set of war-waging principles is useful in the training, education, and selection of political and military leaders who wage war. These principles, the associated responsibilities, and the tripartite tension from which both are derived begin to describe the requirements for war-waging leadership.

The value of human life, of the innocent, of citizens-who-become-soldiers, and of the political community forms the foundation of war-waging principles and responsibilities and the tripartite tension inherent in waging war. The senior political and military leaders who wage war—those whose responsibility it is to identify proper war aims, strategies, and policies and to direct military and nonmilitary campaigns and major operations—ultimately use or put at risk lives. Respecting the individual lives that are entrusted to one's care takes on a greater importance when *care* is replaced by *use*. Respecting the value of human life, even as it is used, demands of those responsible that the lives are used well, not wasted. Respecting the value of human life, even as it is put at risk, demands of those responsible that the risk is prudent. Further, waging war risks the life of the political community, sometimes existentially. But, even if the risk is not existential, how a war is waged can, and often does, have a profound effect on the life of the political community.

War-waging responsibilities are positional responsibilities, tied to some role or position, not natural duties, which are moral requirements that apply more generally to all.[56] Positional responsibilities, like those of senior political and military leaders who wage war, are attributed only to those individuals filling the position to which the responsibility is tied. That is, senior political and military leaders have certain performances expected or required of them within the scheme in question—that is, when waging war.[57]

Senior political and military leaders are in their positions voluntarily; they sought, or at least accepted, those positions. They entered them with their eyes open, sufficiently informed as to what duties and responsibilities they involved; their promise to fulfill the responsibilities of their offices obligated them.[58] When they fail to execute those responsibilities in waging war, they are not just politically liable, that is, putting their reelections or military careers at risk. They are also morally liable because of the lives, individual and communal, that they used poorly or put at risk unnecessarily.

Where Walzer uses his principles to describe right conduct in the midst of battle—the tactical level of war's conduct—the war-waging-principles describe right conduct at the strategic level of war's conduct. The principles of Walzer's war convention apply to the battlefield; the war-waging principles apply in the boardroom. The war-waging principles complete the description of justice in the conduct of war.

Conclusions: *Jus in Bello,* a Complete Account

The war-waging principles described in this chapter expand the practical morality that Walzer intended to describe in *Just and Unjust Wars,* thus providing a more complete understanding of the moral dimension of war. The combatant/noncombatant distinction; principles of proportionality, double effect, and double intent; and the principle of due care/due risk contain a suitable moral framework intended to guide moral action in combat and amid the tension of winning and fighting well.[59] Similarly, those same principles provide the men and women who face the hard choices involved in waging war with a set of guides and a way of explaining and justifying what they are doing or have done to those whose lives they use or put at risk. They also provide a framework to explain what they are doing on behalf of the political community in whose name they act. Both sets of principles—war fighting and war waging—provide the citizenry at large a way to judge what is done on their behalf, whether in combat or in capitals. Citizens, and their representatives, can use both sets of principles to understand and support a war or expose the hypocrisy or blameworthiness of those fighting or those waging war. The principles exist, and their recognition matters.

Recognition of both war-fighting and war-waging principles matters, first, because they are the moral standard to which the United States holds its political and military leaders and its military forces. At the war-fighting level, one need recall only the outrage over US soldier behavior in the Abu Ghraib prison in Iraq or the My Lai massacre in Vietnam—to name two prominent examples. At the war-waging level, one need be reminded only of the "disproportionate, powerful impact on American presidents, politics, and policy" that the Vietnam War has had: "No president can any longer reach critical decisions about committing troops to battle . . . without weighing the consequences of the American defeat in Vietnam. That war still casts an unforgiving shadow over Oval Office deliberations. Unwanted, uninvited, but inescapable, Vietnam refuses to be forgotten."[60]

Second, recognition matters because these principles are used to make both war-fighting and war-waging judgments. With respect to war fighting, the judgments concern which acts committed in war are legitimate and which are not, which can be justified and which cannot. With respect to waging war, they concern whether the decisions concerning aims, strategies, policies, resources, and campaigns have been made and executed well or not. They also concern whether the lives of citizens-who-become-soldiers are used well or wasted as well as whether the lives of the innocent and the life of the political community have been risked unnecessarily.

Both sets of principles allow argument about decisions and actions taken during war, about justifying some conduct and condemning other, and about judging the soldiers and leaders—tactical and strategic, civilian or military—who were involved.[61] Those doing the arguing, justifying, and judging are sometimes soldiers themselves. Or they may be senior civilian policy makers in Congress or the executive branch or senior military leaders, active and retired. At other times, they may be society at large, whether through the media or through direct communications via protests or demonstrations. In sum, both war-fighting and war-waging principles are part of the language and logic of war's moral dimension—a language and logic as important as any other dimension of war.

Finally, recognition matters because war-fighting and war-waging principles can become part of the training, education, and development of soldiers and their military leaders, tactical and strategic, and of the education of potential senior political leaders. These principles require that soldiers be taught that they are never mere instruments or killing machines but always remain moral agents—even in combat. Leaders—officers and sergeants—set the behavior climate within their organizations. Just as the climate a leader sets can result in high discipline or low, can produce a well-trained organization or not, it can tolerate moral abuse or prevent it.

Similarly, these principles require that senior political and military leaders are never mere instruments or solely political actors; they also remain moral agents, even in the boardroom. Senior political leaders set the climate for the proper war-waging decision-execution regime. This climate can either increase or decrease the probability of making decisions and taking actions that reflect right action in the waging of war. It can also increase or decrease the probability of adapting to the ever-changing realities of war or, alternatively, being stuck to a cycle of sustained imprudence. Thus, once again, the climate that senior political leaders set helps determine whether lives are used well or wasted, whether the innocent are placed under necessary risk or unnecessary, and whether the life of the political community is put at risk or strengthened.

In some ways, neither the war-fighting nor the war-waging principles and the positional responsibilities that derive from them are new. They are part of the historical record of every war. War as a political act and the consequential essentiality of both the civil and the military perspectives are long recognized in theories of war, within the military profession, within political science, and among national security theorists and practitioners. But neither the war-waging responsibilities nor the principles that should guide senior political and military leaders have been sufficiently recognized by moral philosophers in just war theory. This deficiency, as this book has argued, results from a fundamental misunderstanding of the conduct of war.

172 JUST WAR RECONSIDERED

Conducting a war involves both fighting it and waging it. *Jus in bello*—that area of just war theory that describes moral responsibility in the conduct of war—must, therefore, address both dimensions of war's conduct. This book has attempted to fill the prevailing view's gap in *jus in bello* by describing what acting justly in war means at the strategic, war-waging level. The five war-waging principles—plus the tripartite tension inherent in waging war—more completely circumscribe the moral dimensions of war's conduct at the strategic level. Together with the traditionally recognized war-fighting principles and responsibilities, therefore, the war-waging principles and responsibilities of *jus in bello* contribute to describing justice in war more completely. Undeniably, what I have presented will be found deficient. Equally undeniable, however, is that the content of this book advances the understanding of the moral dimension of war and may stimulate more discussion about an important dimension of just war theory that the prevailing view omits.

Epilogue

As I finished writing *Just War Reconsidered,* the war in Syria continued. Starting as a series of protests that were part of the Arab Spring that originated in Tunisia in December 2011, the originally peaceful protest in Syria met a violent government response that then sparked a violent reaction that morphed into a civil war and swept in external actors. It is now both a war between Syrians and a war among states and nonstates for power, influence, and control over both territory and people. It is also a war among extremists, whether Sunni or Shia, neither of whom represent the desires of the average Syrian citizen or the average Muslim. In this sense, the war in Syria is embedded within the global war against al-Qaeda and its affiliates, the Islamic State in Iraq and Syria (ISIS), and other similar organizations. It has erased the border between Iraq and Syria—something that ISIS hopes to replicate elsewhere, thus threatening the rule-based international system. It has also spilled into other neighbors—Turkey, Jordan, and Lebanon—and Russia and Iran are involved. It has created a massive humanitarian crisis affecting the region, Europe, and the United States, threatening regional and global stability and security as well as vital US interests. As General David Petraeus said when giving testimony before the Senate Armed Services Committee on September 22, 2015: "The Las Vegas Rule does not apply. What happens in the Middle East will not stay in the Middle East."[1]

The war had another origin, however. The group that now calls itself ISIS was formerly al-Qaeda in Iraq. Between 2007 and 2011, the Surge and subsequent operations reduced the capacity of al-Qaeda in Iraq significantly. Many of its remaining leaders left Iraq for Syria, where they reconstituted and renewed their operations in Iraq after the United States left, taking advantage of the poor domestic and security policies of the Maliki administration and the lack of American involvement and interest. By 2013, al-Qaeda in Iraq had reestablished its strongholds and networks along the Euphrates River valley, and, in January 2014, it had taken control of Fallujah once again. Soon after, it rebranded itself as ISIS and launched an offensive in northern Iraq and down the Tigris River that took control of Mosul. For a time, Baghdad was threatened from the north and the west. The territory lost to these offensive actions in Iraq, and those that expanded their control over large portions of Syria, formed the self-declared caliphate.

Both antecedents of the current war in Syria emerged in 2011: the supposed ending of the US war in Iraq and the Syrian government's violent response to the Syrian manifestation of the Arab Spring.

The United States has vital interests in the Middle East, but its ability to influence the outcome of the current hostilities is now minimal. It got to where it is today not by poor war fighting but by less than satisfactory war waging. It has been relatively effective at killing and destroying, but has that fighting led to strategic effect? To answer that question, we must analyze US war-waging proficiency.

Just War Reconsidered shows that justice in the conduct of war is dual faced, but the question arises as to how this book's war-waging perspective might help in analyzing the current war.

At times, American war aims have been clear but so expansive as to be not achievable or at least not achievable by the ways and means applied. At other times, they have been absent or at least opaque to the common citizens. So the first set of questions that this book suggests concern the responsibilities of senior political and military leaders, as described in chapter 2:

1. Making the best initial decisions possible concerning war aims, strategies (domestic, diplomatic, military, and nonmilitary), policies, and campaigns.
2. Adapting initial decisions as the dynamics of war unfold.
3. Raising and allocating forces, other resources, and funds necessary to achieve those aims.
4. Engaging in adequate diplomacy.
5. Attending to the legitimacy of the war, that is, maintaining public support.

6. Making the military and nonmilitary government agencies work well enough to execute strategies and policies and attain war aims.
7. Establishing mechanisms that facilitate proper dialogue, decision making, action, and adaptation.

Are American war aims sufficiently identified? Are these aims aligned sufficiently with the strategies, policies, and campaigns that are supposed to achieve them? Or are they intellectually incoherent, the political and military leadership employing strategies, following policies, and executing campaigns that work against themselves and the stated aims, thus potentially wasting time, resources, and maybe even lives? Is the overall approach either too rigid, blindly holding on to an approach regardless of the realities as they unfold, or too fluid, reflecting the old saw, "If you don't know where you're going, any road will take you there"? Is the war being dragged out unnecessarily owing to a refusal to allocate sufficient resources—forces, funds, or strategic attention? Are the strategies, policies, and campaigns involved diminishing or creating public support? Is the leadership simply following polls or actually leading? Have the various departments, mainly the Departments of State and Defense as well as the several military headquarters involved, worked well enough together to produce the desired outcomes?

The answers to these questions will vary. Some will be satisfactory, others not so much. Of those that are not satisfactory, some will be simple mistakes that reflect the difficulty and complexity of right behavior at the strategic, war-waging level. Others, however, will be of a different category: neither unfortunate consequences of war nor examples of understandable human fallibility. Rather, they are the result of sustained imprudence, making the same mistake over and over again. This kind of error is the kind of failure that deserves moral blame, even if it does not reflect legal guilt. These kinds of errors lead naturally to a second set of questions, ones related to the principles suggested in chapter 6: continuous dialogue, final decision authority, managerial competence, legitimacy, and resignation.

Has the civil-military dialogue been adequate to the task? Or has it followed one of two common fallacies: generals and admirals who mistakenly believe that in war their only job is to execute the policy maker's war aims, requiring of them only an end state and the time and resources to accomplish the job, and political leaders who mistakenly believe that in war their job is to make policy decisions, getting from military leaders only options that are to be used in discussions from which those military leaders are excluded? Has the dialogue been too exclusive, cutting out civil or military subordinates who should participate, or cut short because content does not match ideology? Or has the dialogue really been a facsimile, useful more to provide cover for decisions already made? Has the final decision authority been more interested in control than in dialogue or more interested in an ideological outcome than in responsible use? Have civil and military leaders served the final decision authority well or been too obedient and overly compliant? Once decisions are made, have civil and military leaders managed their bureaucracies and headquarters well enough, and is there sufficient clarity of responsibility to create the unity of effort and coherence of action necessary to achieve the aims set? Or has business as usual diffracted the necessary unity and coherence? Has the dialogue continued through execution, thus setting up the right conditions for adapting as the war unfolds? Or is it too episodic to keep up with reality? Is the legitimacy of the war being lost because of the way it has been waged? Do senior political and military leaders explain and justify what they are doing on behalf of the American people? Or are they letting the polls dictate what actions to take? Finally, are lives being wasted or put at risk unnecessarily because there is little hope that current war aims can be achieved via the strategies, policies, and campaigns being executed or because there is no desire to allocate the means necessary for success?

The answers to these questions also will vary. Again, some will be satisfactory, others not so much. And, of those that are not satisfactory, some will be simple mistakes, while others will result from sustained imprudence that deserves moral blame, even if nothing illegal has been done.

The responsibilities and principles, as well as the questions that derive from them, corroborate the tripartite war-waging tension outlined in this book, that is, the inherent tension among (1) achieving coherence by setting war aims and making strategy, policy, and campaign decisions that increase the probability of achieving those war aims, (2) generating organizational capacity by translating those aims and decisions into action to achieve war aims at the least cost, in lives and resources, and the least risk to the innocent and to one's political community, then adapting decisions and actions as the vagaries of war unfold, and (3) maintaining legitimacy by doing all the foregoing while observing the war convention, sustaining public support for the war effort, and ensuring proper subordination of the military to civilian leadership.

The framework I present here is not one that will identify the right war-waging course of action to take. Rather, using the framework merely increases the probability of right conduct in waging war, just as *jus in bello*'s war-fighting principles do not guarantee but only increase the likelihood of right conduct on the battlefield. The framework is also useful in explaining, justifying, or judging war-waging behaviors and decisions—again, just as do *jus in bello*'s war-fighting principles. Therein lies *Just War Reconsidered*'s contribution to just war theory: providing not a final answer but another step toward a more complete understanding of *jus in bello*.

Notes

Prologue

1. For the purposes of this book, I have chosen to use Michael Walzer's *Just and Unjust Wars: A Moral Argument with Historical Illustrations* (1977), 5th ed. (New York: Basic, 2000) as the representative of just war theory. I made this choice not unaware of the rich history of just war theory from Plato and Aristotle to Augustine, Aquinas, and Grotius. Nor am I unaware of the richness of subsequent writings. There are shelves of books describing and reflecting on the history of just war theory. Rather, I have made this choice because Walzer's work is the contemporary standard, at least in the United States. Walzer is a much-in-demand speaker on the topic of justice in war, and *Just and Unjust Wars* has been and still is used in America's military academies and professional military education programs as well as in many colleges, universities, and national security programs. Brian Orend correctly says: "It's not much of an exaggeration to say [that Walzer's *Just and Unjust Wars*] has been to current just war theory what Grotius's *The Laws of War and Peace* was to prior centuries." Brian Orend, *The Morality of War* (Peterborough, ON: Broadview, 2006), 24.

1. *Jus in Bello*'s Missing Piece

1. The traditional *jus in bello* principles—those that I call the *tactical, warfighting principles*—are the following: the combatant/noncombatant distinction, noncombatant immunity, double effect and double intent, proportionality, and due care and due risk. In general, I use the versions of these principles found in Walzer, *Just and Unjust Wars*, 34–47, 127–232, 287–327; and Orend, *The Morality of War*, 104–59. There are numerous other articles and books that discuss, criticize, and amend these principles and the moral arguments on which they rest. The authors of these views raise significant issues, and I refer to some of those in this book. My purpose here, however, is different. I leave the discussion of the adequacy of *jus in bello*'s tactical, war-fighting principles to others, instead focusing narrowly on a missing element in *jus in bello:* the strategic, war-waging element.

2. Carl von Clausewitz, *On War,* ed. and trans. Michael Howard and Peter Paret (Princeton, NJ: Princeton University Press, 1976), 89.

3. Two of the more useful works concerning the changes in the tools and the conduct of war are Rupert Smith, *The Utility of Force: The Art of War in the Modern World* (New York: Penguin, 2006); and David Kilcullen, *Out of the Mountains: The Coming of Age of the Urban Guerrilla* (New York: Oxford University Press, 2013). See also Gordon R. Sullivan and James M. Dubik, *Envisioning Future Warfare* (Fort Leavenworth, KS: US Army Command and General Staff College Press, 1995).

4. Walzer, *Just and Unjust Wars,* 31.

5. David Rodin, *War and Self-Defense* (New York: Oxford University Press, 2002), 193–94, 199.

6. Jeff McMahan, *Killing in War* (New York: Oxford University Press, 2009), 3.

7. Ibid., 14 (see generally 1–16, 32–36).

8. Ibid., 36 (see generally 38–101, 104–21, 131–53).

9. David Luban, "Risk Taking and Force Protection," in *Reading Walzer,* ed. Yitzhak Benbaju and Naomi Sussmann (New York: Routledge, 2014), 277–301, 279.

10. Walzer, *Just and Unjust Wars,* 9, 151–59.

11. Luban, "Risk Taking and Force Protection," 283.

12. Ibid., 285, 292.

13. Orend, *The Morality of War,* 160.

14. Ibid., 204 (see generally 162–81, 190–217).

15. Mona Fixdal, *Just Peace: How Wars Should End* (New York: Palgrave Macmillan, 2012), 4, 11. George Weigel presents an interesting and compelling argument concerning how wars should end by expanding on Augustine's insight that peace is a certain kind of order within a political community—*tranquillitas ordinis*—and subsequent Catholic thought. See George Weigel, *Tranquillitas Ordinis: The Present Failure and Future Promise of American Catholic Thought on War and Peace* (New York: Oxford University Press, 1987).

16. Nancy Sherman, "The Moral Psychic Reality of War," in Benbaju and Sussman, eds., *Reading Walzer,* 302–26, 302. See also Nancy Sherman, *Afterwar: Healing the Moral Wounds of Our Soldiers* (New York: Oxford University Press, 2015).

17. Orend, *The Morality of War,* 24.

18. Walzer, *Just and Unjust Wars,* xi–xiii (quote xi).

19. Michael Norman and Elizabeth M. Norman, *Tears in the Darkness: The Story of the Bataan Death March and Its Aftermath* (New York: Farrar Straus Giroux, 2009), 4.

20. Rick Atkinson, *An Army at Dawn: The War in North Africa, 1942–1943* (New York: Henry Holt, 2002), 8.

21. Andrew Roberts, *Masters and Commanders: How Four Titans Won the War in the West, 1941–1945* (New York: HarperCollins, 2009), 122.

22. Atkinson, *An Army at Dawn,* 11.

23. John Keegan, *The Second World War* (New York: Viking, 1989), 313.

24. Roberts, *Masters and Commanders,* 223, 254–57, 260–88, 291–99, 362–64, 561, 587.

25. Williamson Murray and Allan R. Millett, *A War to Be Won: Fighting the Second World War* (Cambridge, MA: Belknap Press of Harvard University Press, 2000), 273.

26. Roberts, *Masters and Commanders,* 115.

27. Ibid., 48.

28. Walzer, *Just and Unjust Wars,* 38–39.

29. Roberts, *Masters and Commanders,* 115, 152–53. See also Forrest C. Pogue, *George C. Marshall: Ordeal and Hope, 1939–1941* (New York: Viking, 1965), 283.

30. David Kaiser, *No End Save Victory: How FDR Led the Nation into War* (New York: Basic, 2014), 16.

31. Russell F. Weigley, *Eisenhower's Lieutenants: The Campaigns of France and Germany, 1944–1945* (Bloomington: Indiana University Press, 1981), 1.

32. Among the many books dealing with this subject, Kaiser's *No End Save Victory* offers an excellent description of the organizational decisions that Roosevelt made.

33. Pogue, *George C. Marshall,* 289, 295. For a complete account of the speed, severity, and completeness of Marshall's changes, see ibid., 289–301.

34. Walzer, *Just and Unjust Wars,* 38–39; Orend, *The Morality of War,* 170–79; Geoffrey S. Corn et al., *The Law of Armed Conflict: An Operational Approach* (New York: Wolters Kluwer Law & Business, 2012), 2, 527.

35. Bernard Brodie, *War and Politics* (New York: Macmillan, 1973), 1–28; Clausewitz, *On War,* 75–88.

36. Walzer, *Just and Unjust Wars,* 316, 38–39.

37. Ibid., 292, 298, 304.

38. Ibid., 292, 302.

39. Alan H. Goldman, *The Moral Foundations of Professional Ethics* (Totowa, NJ: Rowman & Littlefield, 1980), 3–9, 290; James S. Fishkin, *The Limits of Obligation* (New Haven, CT: Yale University Press, 1982), 26–27.

40. Walzer, *Just and Unjust Wars,* 58–63. The legalist paradigm consists of six basic propositions: (1) There exists an international society of independent states. (2) This international society has a law that establishes the rights of its

members—above all the rights of territorial integrity and political sovereignty. (3) Any use of force or imminent threat of force by one state against the political sovereignty or territorial integrity of another constitutes aggression and is a criminal act. (4) Aggression justifies two kinds of violent response: a war of self-defense by the victim and a war of law enforcement by the victim and any other international society. (5) Nothing but aggression can justify war. (6) Once the aggressor state has been militarily repulsed, it can also be punished. Walzer then goes on to describe exceptions: varieties of justified intervention, preemptive strikes, and supreme emergency. Thus, the legalist paradigm is not absolute, but, absent these exceptions, it holds.

41. Ibid., 19, 31, 36, 38, 59, 61–63, 74, 85–86, 91, 95, 127, 136, 231, 245, 287, 289–92.

42. Ibid., 251–68.

43. Ibid., 21, 31 (quote), 110, 129.

44. Eliot A. Cohen, "The Unequal Dialogue: The Theory and Reality of Civil-Military Relations and the Use of Force," in *Soldiers and Civilians: The Civil-Military Gap and American National Security,* ed. Peter D. Feaver and Richard H. Kohn (Cambridge, MA: MIT Press, 2001), 429–58, 453.

45. Orend, *The Morality of War,* 105. Orend goes on to say: "Responsibility for the conduct of war . . . rests on the state's armed forces." Ibid., 106. Walzer would agree completely.

46. Mackubin Thomas Owens, *US Civil-Military Relations after 9/11: Renegotiating the Civil-Military Bargain* (New York: Continuum International, 2011), esp. chap. 3, "The Role of the Military and Military Effectiveness."

47. Bruce Riedel, foreword to Ronald E. Neumann, *The Other War: Winning and Losing in Afghanistan* (Washington, DC: Potomac, 2009), vii–x, x.

2. Describing *Jus in Bello*'s War-Waging Dimension

1. T. Harry Williams, *Lincoln and His Generals* (New York: Knopf, 1952), Kindle locations 99 (quote), 112.

2. James M. McPherson, *Tried by War: Abraham Lincoln as Commander-in-Chief* (New York: Penguin, 2008), xiii.

3. Jethro K. Lieberman, *The Enduring Constitution: A Bicentennial Perspective* (New York: West, 1987), 452, 455.

4. McPherson, *Tried by War,* 5.

5. Andrew J. Polsky, *Elusive Victories: The American Presidency at War* (New York: Oxford University Press, 2012), 35, 36.

6. McPherson, *Tried by War,* 107–8.

7. James M. McPherson, *Battle Cry of Freedom: The Civil War Era* (New York: Oxford University Press, 1988), 443.

8. Doris Kearns Goodwin, *Team of Rivals: The Political Genius of Abraham Lincoln* (New York: Simon & Schuster, 2005), 348, 365–67, 461–62, 536–37.

9. McPherson, *Battle Cry of Freedom*, 383–84 (quote 383; see generally 382–91).

10. Goodwin, *Team of Rivals*, 364.

11. Herman Hattaway and Archer Jones, *How the North Won: A Military History of the Civil War* (Champaign: University of Illinois Press, 1983), 138 (including Stanton quote).

12. Ibid., 119–24, 127–50 (quote 121).

13. McPherson, *Battle Cry of Freedom*, 857.

14. Hattaway and Jones, *How the North Won*, 101–52.

15. Polsky, *Elusive Victories*, 42, 60 (quote).

16. McPherson, *Tried by War*, 42.

17. Polsky, *Elusive Victories*, 60.

18. McPherson, *Tried by War*, 127.

19. "The Election of 1864," n.d., U.S. History: Pre-Columbian to the New Millennium, http://www.ushistory.org/us/34e.asp.

20. McPherson, *Battle Cry of Freedom*, 742.

21. Hattaway and Jones, *How the North Won*, 143–44.

22. McPherson, *Tried by War*, 6.

23. Ibid., 1–8.

24. Polsky, *Elusive Victories*, 80.

25. Ibid., 79.

26. Goodwin, *Team of Rivals*, xvi–xvii.

27. *Citizens-who-become-soldiers* is slightly awkward, but it is telling. It is a reminder that soldiers—or sailors, marines, airmen, or coast guardsmen for that matter—are not mere instruments. Of course, by entering military service, each of us becomes an instrument of the state. We are there to be used by the state. In this sense, all wars necessarily involve using lives. But we remain citizens, and I will argue later in this book that our government retains some obligation to us to ensure that our lives are used well, not wasted. In addition to being citizens, we remain human beings. As such, to use a Kantian concept, we cannot be taken as mere means. Rather, our lives retain moral value because we remain ends in ourselves. Again, I take up this argument later in the book but thought it necessary to explain why I chose to use the admittedly slightly awkward construction.

28. Don E. Fehrenbacher, ed., *Lincoln: Speeches and Writings, 1859–1865* (New York: Library of America, 1989), 536.

29. Of course no war convention existed during the Civil War in the same way the Geneva and Hague Conventions and the Law of Armed Conflict do today. For a sense of what did govern war at the time, see "Instructions for the

Government of Armies of the United States in the Field, Prepared by Francis Lieber, Promulgated by General Orders no. 100 by President Lincoln, 24 April 1863," http://avalon.law.yale.edu/19th_century/lieber.asp. For an insight as to how legal precedents set in the Civil War affected American's post-9/11 wars, see Andrew Kent, "Constitution and the Laws of War during the American Civil War, the Federal Courts, Practice and Procedure," Faculty Scholarship (New York: Fordham University Law School, 2009), http://ir.lawnet.fordham.edu/cgi/viewcontent.cgi?article=1252&context=faculty_scholarship.

30. For an excellent recent account of the successes and failures of the US strategic, war-waging performance since the attacks of September 11, 2001, see Richard D. Hooker Jr. and Joseph J. Collins, eds., *Lessons Encountered: Learning from the Long War* (Washington, DC: National Defense University Press, 2015). Although no comparisons are made to the American Civil War, chaps. 1–3 of the collection summarize a variety of actions that have a family resemblance to the lessons Lincoln, his cabinet, and his generals had to learn.

31. George W. Bush, *Decision Points* (New York: Crown, 2010), 184.

32. Ibid., 195.

33. "Text: President Bush Addresses the Nation," *Washington Post,* September 20, 2001, http://www.washingtonpost.com/wp-srv/nation/specials/attacked/transcripts/bushaddress_092001.html.

34. Bush, *Decision Points,* 184–91.

35. Michael Morell recounts how, at a National Security Council meeting just four days after the 9/11 attacks, the director of the CIA "put on the table a detailed and multifaceted plan to go after Bin Laden and al Qa'ida": "Less than two weeks later, on September 26, the Agency had its first team of CIA officers on the ground in Afghanistan." Michael Morell, *The Great War of Our Time: The CIA's Fight against Terrorism from al Qa'ida to ISIS* (New York: Hachette, 2015), 63.

36. Bob Woodward, *Bush at War* (New York: Simon & Schuster, 2002), 242–44.

37. Donald Rumsfeld, *Known and Unknown: A Memoir* (New York: Sentinel, 2011), 375.

38. Sean Naylor, *Not a Good Day to Die: Chaos and Courage in the Mountains of Afghanistan: The Untold Story of Operation Anaconda* (New York: Berkley, 2005), 10–11, 13–14, 18–19, 20, 24, 43, 48, 53, 56, 87–88, 122–33, 135–37, 149–50, 154–57, 172–74, 271–72.

39. Bush, *Decision Points,* 211, 220.

40. Neumann, *The Other War,* xi–xii.

41. Dov S. Zakheim, *A Vulcan's Tale: How the Bush Administration Mismanaged the Reconstruction of Afghanistan* (Washington, DC: Brookings Institu-

tion Press, 2011), Kindle locations 61 (first quote), 96 (second quote), 126 (third quote), 1210–1411 (fourth quote 1210), 1782–1819, 1888, 1912–36.

42. Ibid., Kindle location 548.

43. Riedel, foreword to Neumann, *The Other War,* vii–x. See also Rajiv Chandrasekaran, *Little America: The War within the War for Afghanistan* (New York: Knopf, 2012).

44. Peter Tomsen, "The Good War: What Went Wrong in Afghanistan—and How to Make It Right," *Foreign Affairs* 93, no. 6 (November/December 2014): 47–54, 49.

45. Ricardo S. Sanchez, *Wiser in Battle: A Soldier's Story* (New York: HarperCollins, 2008), 167–69.

46. Rumsfeld, *Known and Unknown,* 501.

47. Sanchez, *Wiser in Battle,* 382.

48. Michael R. Gordon and Bernard E. Trainor, *Cobra II: The Inside Story of the Invasion and Occupation of Iraq* (New York: Pantheon, 2006), 149, 152 (first and second quotes), 156 (third quote).

49. L. Paul Bremer III, *My Year in Iraq: The Struggle to Build a Future of Hope* (New York: Threshold, 2006), 5–13 (quotes 8, 11, 12).

50. Rajiv Chandrasekaran, *Imperial Life in the Emerald City: Inside Iraq's Green Zone* (New York: Knopf, 2007), 16, 21, 64, 90–94, 98–99.

51. Bush, *Decision Points,* 249–50, 257–61, 268–69.

52. Jeffrey Record, *Dark Victory: America's Second War against Iraq* (Annapolis, MD: Naval Institute Press, 2004), 116, 129.

53. Gordon and Trainor, *Cobra II,* 493 (quote), 495.

54. For more complete accounts of this period, see Ali A. Allawi, *The Occupation of Iraq: Winning the War, Losing the Peace* (New Haven, CT: Yale University Press, 2007); Bremer, *My Year in Iraq;* Chandrasekaran, *Imperial Life in the Emerald City;* Gordon and Trainor, *Cobra II;* Record, *Dark Victory;* Thomas E. Ricks, *Fiasco: The American Military Adventure in Iraq* (New York: Penguin, 2006); and Sanchez, *Wiser in Battle.*

55. Bush, *Decision Points,* 367.

56. "In Depth: Topics A to Z: Iraq," Gallup.com, n.d., http://www.gallup .com/poll/1633/iraq.aspx.

57. Bush, *Decision Points,* 363 (quote), 371. The Askariya shrine at the Golden Mosque of Samarra was one of the holiest sites in Shia Islam. On February 22, 2006, two massive explosions destroyed the mosque. The attack was an enormous provocation designed to incite a war between Shia and Sunni Iraqis. It succeeded.

58. Ibid., 210–11.

59. "In Depth Topics: A to Z: Afghanistan," Gallup.com, n.d., http://www

.gallup.com/poll/116233/Afghanistan.aspx?g_sourve-TRENDS_A_TO_Z&g_
medium=topics7g_campaign=tiles.

60. Bush, *Decision Points,* 211–17.

61. Jessica Lewis, *Al Qaeda in Iraq Resurgent, Part I* (Washington, DC: Institute for the Study of War, September 2013), *Al Qaeda in Iraq Resurgent, Part
II* (Washington, DC: Institute for the Study of War, October 2013), and *The
Islamic State of Iraq Returns to Diyala* (Washington, DC: Institute for the Study
of War, April 2014). All are available at www.understandingwar.org.

62. For the Department of Defense casualty count as of July 28, 2013, http://
www.defense.gov/news/casualty.pdf. For the dollar cost, see Daniel Trotta, "Cost
of War at Least $3.7 Trillion and Counting," *Reuters,* June 29, 2011, http://www
.reuters.com/article/2011/06/29/us-usa-war-idUSTRE75S25320110629.

63. See Walzer, *Just and Unjust Wars,* 127–59, 304–15; and Luban, "Risk
Taking and Force Protection," 277–301.

64. William T. Sherman to U. S. Grant, March 10, 1864, in William T.
Sherman, *Memoirs of General William T. Sherman* (New York: Da Capo, 1984),
399–400.

65. Michael Walzer, *Arguing about War* (New Haven, CT: Yale University
Press, 2004), 24. Luban, too, acknowledges the importance of this relationship.
See Luban, "Risk Taking and Force Protection."

66. The issue of when killing between combatants is justified has been laid
wide open by Jeff McMahan. Prior to his argument, a common view reigned.
Walzer expresses the common view that, regardless of which side they fight on,
soldiers are morally equal. Soldiers on the opposite side are enemies, but they are
not personal enemies. Because war is a relation not between persons but between
political entities and their human instruments, combatants on both sides are all,
in Walzer's words, "'poor sods like me,' trapped in a war they did not make."
They are, as a result, moral equals; all soldiers on one side can kill any soldier on
the other justifiably. See Walzer, *Just and Unjust Wars,* 36–41 (quote 36). McMahan takes exception to this. He says that Walzer, and the common view that he
adduces, is mistaken. Soldiers on both sides may be equal legally but not morally.
Political leaders cannot, just by commanding their armies to attack, cause other
people's moral rights to disappear. Soldiers on the just side retain their moral
rights; soldiers on the unjust side do not. Who is liable to be attacked by whom is,
in McMahan's view, much more complicated than the common view supposes.
In the end, McMahan argues that justifications for killing people are the same in
war as they are in other contexts. See McMahan, *Killing in War,* 1–36. But the
point I make above—that military leaders are in a morally relevant relationship
with those entrusted to their care and use—is valid in both Walzer's and McMahan's view views.

67. Stanley McChrystal, *My Share of the Task: A Memoir* (New York: Portfolio/Penguin, 2013), 183 (quote), 184.

68. Ibid., 185 (quote), 186.

69. Walzer, *Arguing about War,* 24.

70. Bush, *Decision Points,* 354–94 (quote 378).

71. Walzer, *Just and Unjust Wars,* 110.

72. Michael Walzer, *Spheres of Justice: A Defense of Pluralism and Equality* (New York: Basic, 1983), 282–84, 289.

73. Ibid., 281.

74. I do not intend to use Rawls's ideas as a full explanation of the concept of justice. See John Rawls, *A Theory of Justice* (Cambridge, MA: Harvard University Press, 1971), esp. 11–22. Rather, I use his idea of the veil of ignorance in a more limited way: to illustrate one way in which to explain the limits placed on a democratic government in terms of how it can use the lives of its citizens-who-become-soldiers.

75. Walzer, *Spheres of Justice,* 5. Walzer is summarizing Rawls, *A Theory of Justice,* 136–42.

76. Rawls, *A Theory of Justice,* 12.

3. Principals and Agents

1. Peter D. Feaver, *Armed Servants: Agency, Oversight, and Civil-Military Relations* (Cambridge, MA: Harvard University Press, 2003); Samuel P. Huntington, *The Soldier and the State: The Theory and Politics of Civil-Military Relations* (Cambridge, MA: Belknap Press of Harvard University Press, 1957).

2. Huntington, *The Soldier and the State,* 2.

3. Ibid.

4. Ibid., 80–85.

5. Ibid., 3.

6. Ibid., 80–83 (quote 81).

7. Ibid., 83–96.

8. Ibid., 191–92 (quote 192).

9. Good summaries of Huntington's position as well as the contribution that *The Soldier and the State* has made to and the influence that it has had on the US military can be found in Suzanne C. Nielsen and Don M. Snider, introduction to *American Civil-Military Relations: The Soldier and the State in a New Era,* ed. Suzanne C. Nielsen and Don M. Snider (Baltimore: Johns Hopkins University Press, 2009), 1–10, and "Conclusions," in ibid., 290–308.

10. Barry R. McCaffrey, foreword to Nielsen and Snider, eds., *American Civil-Military Relations,* xiii–xvi, xiv–xv.

11. Feaver, *Armed Servants,* 2, 7 (quote), 8–10, 55–56.

12. Ibid., 54–55 (quote 55).

13. Ibid., 8–9.

14. Ibid., 61, 64–65.

15. Ibid., 171.

16. Ibid., 171–72.

17. Ibid., 172–74 (quote 174). The conventional wisdom to which Feaver refers comes primarily from US Army officers who claim that senior military leaders were too compliant with strategies they knew were not succeeding and could not succeed—the latter being more important than the former. This episode is covered in Harry G. Summers, *On Strategy: The Vietnam War in Context* (Carlisle Barracks, PA: Strategic Studies Institute, 1981); Bruce Palmer Jr., *The 25-Year War: America's Military Role in Vietnam* (Lexington: University Press of Kentucky, 1984); and H. R. McMaster, *Dereliction of Duty: Lyndon Johnson, Robert McNamara, the Joint Chiefs of Staff, and the Lies That Led to Vietnam* (New York: HarperCollins, 1997). Feaver did not reference, but could have, one other military piece that follows suit: Douglas Kinnard, *The War Managers* (Wayne, NJ: Avery, 1985).

18. Feaver, *Armed Servants,* 172, 174–75.

19. Ibid., 175.

20. I use the dates given in Andrew F. Krepinevich Jr., *The Army and Vietnam* (Baltimore: Johns Hopkins University Press, 1986).

21. "Statistical Information about Fatal Casualties of the Vietnam War," National Archives, August 2013, http://www.archives.gov/research/military/vietnam-war/casualty-statistics.html#water.

22. I used the estimates from Stephen Daggett, *Costs of Major U.S. Wars,* Report 7-5700 (Washington, DC: Congressional Research Service, June 29, 2010), http://www.fas.org/sgp/crs/natsec/RS22926.pdf, which are based on 1965–1975 spending.

23. Feaver, *Armed Servants,* 177–78.

24. Ibid., 234–82.

25. Ibid., 283.

26. Ibid., 284.

27. Ibid., 8; Peter D. Feaver and Richard H. Kohn, "Conclusion: The Gap and What It Means for American National Security," in Feaver and Kohn, eds., *Soldiers and Civilians,* 459–73, 469, 473.

28. Feaver, *Armed Servants,* 8.

29. Ibid., 302.

30. Gideon Rose, *How Wars End: Why We Always Fight the Last Battle: A History of American Intervention from World War I to Afghanistan* (New York: Simon & Schuster, 2010), 266.

31. Ibid., 267.

32. Record, *Dark Victory*, 98.

33. Feaver, *Armed Servants*, 298.

34. Lewis Sorley, *Honorable Warrior: General Harold K. Johnson and the Ethics of Command* (Lawrence: University Press of Kansas, 1988), 222–23.

35. McMaster, *Dereliction of Duty*, 61, 89, 325. For another account of the civil-military relationship during the Vietnam War, see Matthew Moten, *Presidents and Their Generals: An American History of Command in War* (Cambridge, MA: Belknap Press of Harvard University Press, 1997), 271–311.

36. Record, *Dark Victory*, 98.

37. Bush, *Decision Points*, 92.

38. Matthew Moten, "A Broken Dialogue: Rumsfeld, Shinseki, and Civil-Military Tension," in Nielsen and Snider, eds., *American Civil-Military Relations*, 42–71 (quote 54).

39. Ibid., 63.

40. Feaver, *Armed Servants*, 54–55, 72–73 (quote), and see generally 72–78, 83–88, 95, 286, 318–19.

41. Ibid., 83.

42. The statistics of two studies are revealing: "Study Shows Employee Theft a Big Problem for U.S. Companies," Xinhua News Agency, August 11, 1999, http://www.investigation.com/press/press4.htm; and "Employee Theft Statistics," Statistic Brain Research Institute, September 7, 2015, http://www.statisticbrain.com/employee-theft-statistics.

43. Feaver, *Armed Servants*, 83.

44. Walzer, *Just and Unjust Wars*, 21–32, 110, 287–96.

45. Colin Powell, *My American Journey* (New York: Random House Large Print, 1995), 790–97. See also George Bush and Brent Scowcroft, *A World Transformed: The Collapse of the Soviet Union, the Unification of Germany, Tiananmen Square, and the Gulf War* (New York: Knopf, 1998), 480–92; Michael R. Gordon and Bernard E. Trainor, *The Generals' War: The Inside Story of the Conflict in the Gulf* (Boston: Little, Brown, 1995), 400–403; and Lawrence Freedman and Efraim Karsh, *The Gulf Conflict, 1990–1991: Diplomacy and War in the New World Order* (Princeton, NJ: Princeton University Press, 1993), 403–4.

46. Ronald Dworkin, *Taking Rights Seriously* (Cambridge, MA: Harvard University Press, 1978), 198.

47. Feaver, *Armed Servants*, 65.

48. Ibid., 6, 8, 171, 177.

49. Feaver and Kohn, "Conclusion," 464–65, 468.

50. Article II, Section 2, US Constitution. US Constitution, art. 2, sec. 2, cited in Lieberman, *The Enduring Constitution*, 455.

51. 10 U.S.C. §§ 113, 162, 3011, 5011, 8011.

52. The National Security Council is chaired by the president. Its statutory members, in addition to the president, are the vice president and the secretaries of state and defense. The chairman of the Joint Chiefs of Staff is the statutory military adviser to the council, and the director of central intelligence is the intelligence adviser. The secretary of the Treasury, the US representative to the United Nations, the assistant to the president for national security affairs, the assistant to the president for economic policy, and the chief of staff to the president are invited to all meetings of the council. The attorney general and the director of the Office of National Drug Control Policy attend meetings pertaining to their jurisdiction. Other officials are invited as appropriate. See "Membership of the National Security Council," n.d., http://clinton4.nara.gov/WH/EOP/NSC/html/NSC_Membership.html.

53. US Constitution, art. 1, sec. 8, cited in Lieberman, *The Enduring Constitution,* 452–53.

54. Fishkin, *The Limits of Obligation,* 26–27. See also Goldman, *The Moral Foundations of Professional Ethics,* 3–9, 290–93.

55. Dworkin, *Taking Rights Seriously,* 188.

56. The official title of the Pentagon Papers was "Report of the Office of the Secretary of Defense Vietnam Task Force," commissioned by Secretary McNamara in 1967 and leaked by Daniel Ellsberg to the *New York Times* in 1971. The full text is available at http://www.archives.gov/research/pentagon-papers.

57. Rose, *How Wars End,* 239.

58. Mark Perry, *Four Stars: The Inside Story of the Forty-Year Battle between the Joint Chiefs of Staff and America's Civilian Leaders* (Boston: Houghton Mifflin, 1989), 162–65.

59. Feaver and Kohn, "Conclusion," 473.

4. Dialogue and the Nature of War

1. Eliot A. Cohen, *Supreme Command: Soldiers, Statesmen, and Leadership in Wartime* (New York: Anchor, 2002), 10; Clausewitz, *On War,* 75, 80–81, 86–87, 606, 608.

2. Clausewitz, *On War,* 609–10.

3. Cohen, *Supreme Command,* 2, 7, 10, 12.

4. Ibid., 77, 108, 111, 206, 208–9.

5. Ibid., 77, 108, 118.

6. Ibid., 211.

7. Clausewitz, *On War,* 100–112 (quote 100).

8. Cohen, *Supreme Command,* 173–207.

9. Ibid., 10.

10. Ibid., 173–74.

11. Ibid., 10, 12, 209.

12. Jean Hampton, *The Intrinsic Worth of Persons: Contractarianism in Moral and Political Thought,* ed. Daniel Farnham (New York: Cambridge University Press, 2007), 11, 20, 25.

13. Cohen, *Supreme Command,* 180.

14. McMaster, *Dereliction of Duty,* 275–99.

15. Perry, *Four Stars,* 148.

16. Johnson himself made ten trips. See Sorley, *Honorable Warrior,* 152.

17. Cohen, *Supreme Command,* 182 (quote), 184.

18. McMaster, *Dereliction of Duty,* 50, 84, 89–90, 116.

19. Sorley, *Honorable Warrior,* 147–48.

20. McMaster, *Dereliction of Duty,* 147.

21. Perry, *Four Stars,* 137 (quote), 141–43.

22. McMaster, *Dereliction of Duty,* 113.

23. Perry, *Four Stars,* 146 (quote), 157, 159.

24. Cohen, *Supreme Command,* 179.

25. Feaver, *Armed Servants,* 171.

26. Palmer, *The 25-Year War,* 172–73.

27. For example, Brian Orend describes two of the tests one considers in determining whether to go to war—"probability of success . . . and proportionality." With respect to probability of success, he says: "It remains important that communities contemplating war . . . consider whether such an extreme measure has any reasonable probability of success. That is the least . . . that they owe themselves." With respect to proportionality, he says: "A state considering a just war must weigh the expected universal (not just selfish national) benefits of doing so against the expected universal costs." Orend, *The Morality of War,* 60, 62. Both, he concludes, are difficult but necessary judgments associated with the decision to go to war.

28. Sorley, *Honorable Warrior,* 304.

29. Clarke D. Forsythe, *Politics for the Greatest Good: The Case for Prudence in the Public Square* (Downer's Grove, IL: InterVarsity, 2009), 16; Aristotle, *Nicomachean Ethics,* trans. Martin Oswald (Indianapolis: Bobbs-Merrill, 1962), 152–73.

30. Dwight D. Eisenhower, *Crusade in Europe* (New York: Doubleday, 1948), 220–52.

31. Clausewitz, *On War,* 100–112; Cohen, *Supreme Command,* 173–207.

32. Cohen, *Supreme Command,* 10, 173–224.

33. For another useful look at collaboration and discourse, see Mark Perry, *Partners in Command* (New York: Penguin, 2007), which explores the relationship and exchanges between George Marshall and Dwight Eisenhower.

34. Peter Baker, *Days of Fire: Bush and Cheney in the White House* (New York: Doubleday, 2013), Kindle locations 5089–5102.

35. Ibid., Kindle locations 5206 (first quote), 5221 (second quote). See also Gordon and Trainor, *Cobra II,* 101–4.

36. Baker, *Days of Fire,* Kindle locations 5205, 5221. See also Ricks, *Fiasco,* 96–100.

37. Gordon and Trainor, *Cobra II,* 311–14 (quote 311).

38. James Kitfield, "My Iraq War," *National Journal* 45, nos. 12–13 (March 21, 2013): 3, http://www.nationaljournal.com/s/82349/my-iraq-war.

39. Baker, *Days of Fire,* Kindle locations 6069. Also in Woodward, *State of Denial: Bush at War, Part III* (New York: Simon & Schuster, 2006), 373.

40. Sanchez, *Wiser in Battle,* 347–60; Baker, *Days of Fire,* Kindle locations 6678–6722, 765 (quote), 7881, 7971–7984.

41. Woodward, *State of Denial,* 368–69.

42. Michael Gordon and Bernard Trainor, *The Endgame: The Inside Story of the Struggle for Iraq, from George W. Bush to Barack Obama* (New York: Pantheon, 2012), 130–32.

43. Woodward, *State of Denial,* 387–90.

44. Gordon and Trainor, *The Endgame,* 132–33, 135–36.

45. Woodward, *State of Denial,* 397.

46. Ibid., 426–27 (quote 426).

47. Gordon and Trainor, *The Endgame,* 158–62.

48. Woodward, *State of Denial,* 423–24 (quote). See also Baker, *Days of Fire,* Kindle locations 8899–8929 (same quote 8899).

49. Gordon and Trainor, *The Endgame,* 163.

50. Ibid., 189–90.

51. George W. Casey, *Strategic Reflections: Operation Iraqi Freedom, July 2004–February 2007* (Washington, DC: National Defense University Press, 2012), 94 (first quote), 96 (second quote).

52. Baker, *Days of Fire,* Kindle locations 9270–9303; Casey, *Strategic Reflections,* 98; Gordon and Trainor, *The Endgame,* 192–95; Bob Woodward, *The War Within: A Secret White House History, 2006–2008* (New York: Simon & Schuster, 2008), 107–9.

53. Casey, *Strategic Reflections,* 113–16.

54. Four articles illustrative of the mood in the United States in 2007 are Michael Crowley, "Can Lobbyists Stop the War?" *New York Times Magazine,* September 9, 2007, http://www.nytimes.com/2007/09/09/magazine/09antiwar-t.html?_r=0; William G. Howell and John C. Pevehouse, "When Congress Stops Wars," *Foreign Affairs* 86, no. 5 (September/October 2007): 95–107; and Jim Vandehei and John F. Harris, "Dems Could Do Far More to End Iraq War,"

Politico, September 27, 2007, http://www.politico.com/news/stories/0907/6048 .html. See also a compilation of videos put together by the US Institute of Peace describing the situation in Iraq at the beginning of 2007: "WT_Iraq War Perceptions," http://www.youtube.com/watch?v=u6_xTnoTKTI.

55. Robert M. Gates, *Duty: Memoirs of a Secretary at War* (New York: Knopf, 2014), 16–17.

56. Baker, *Days of Fire,* Kindle locations 9517, 9529, 2940, 2967, 3463, 5356, 5498, 6982, 7113, 8178, 9490, 10024, 10026–37 (quotes).

57. Ibid., Kindle location 9504.

58. The debate of late 2006/early 2007 that led to the increase in US forces and the change in strategy known as *the Surge* is well documented. For four of the more complete accounts, see Woodward, *The War Within,* 3–13, 53–312; Gordon and Trainor, *The Endgame,* 267–328; Thomas E. Ricks, *The Gamble: General David Petraeus and the American Military Adventure in Iraq, 2006–2008* (New York: Penguin, 2009), 74–148; and Baker, *Days of Fire,* Kindle locations 9517, 9529, 9620, 9658, 9672, 9854, 9999, 10129, 10142, 10589, 10695, 10733.

59. Gates, *Duty,* 25.

60. There are multiple accounts of the events, arguments, briefings, and maneuverings that led to Bush's decision to surge in Iraq in 2007. Among the more complete are Gates, *Duty,* 27–79; Gordon and Trainor, *The Endgame,* 267–328; Ricks, *The Gamble,* 3–127; and Woodward, *The War Within,* 3–13, 42–321.

61. Gordon and Trainor, *The Endgame,* 329–504; Ricks, *The Gamble,* 127–293; Woodward, *The War Within,* 374–425; Baker, *Days of Fire,* Kindle locations 10757–11401, 11730–12318; James M. Dubik, "Operational Art in Counterinsurgency" (Washington, DC: Institute for the Study of War, May 2012); David Petraeus, "How We Won in Iraq: And Why All the Hard-Won Gains of the Surge Are in Grave Danger of Being Lost Today," *Foreign Policy,* October 30, 2013, http://www.foreignpolicy.com/articles/2013/10/29/david_petraeus_how_ we_won_the_surge_in_iraq#sthash.bV18Kydz.dpbs. Of course, the debate over how successful the Surge of 2007–2008 was remains active. For arguments representing opposing positions, see Peter Beinart, "The Surge Fallacy," *Atlantic,* September 2015, 13–15; and James M. Dubik, "A Lesson of the Iraq War and the Surge," *Army Magazine,* November 12, 2015, http://www.armymagazine .org/2015/11/12/a-lesson-of-the-iraq-war-and-the-surge. These two are representative of many more. There is no argument, however, over whether the strategy and outcome of the Surge period improved the situation in Iraq compared to the strategy and outcome of the period 2003–2006. And there is no argument that the quality of the dialogue between senior political and military leaders in these two periods mattered.

5. The Decision-Execution Regime

1. Clausewitz, *On War*, 119, 121.

2. Ibid., 119–21. Also considered sources of friction but treated in different chapters of *On War* are danger, physical effort, and the friction inherent in just finding out what is going on in the battle area, i.e., intelligence in war. See ibid., 113–14, 115–16, and 117–18, respectively.

3. Richard H. Kohn, "Building Trust: Civil-Military Behaviors for Effective National Security," in Nielsen and Snider, eds., *American Civil-Military Relations*, 264–89, 271.

4. Gates, *Duty*, 19–20, 24, 50, 60–61, 84–86, 440, 575.

5. Ibid., 307.

6. Ibid., 8, 16–17, 19–20, 24, 31, 33, 38, 40–45, 50, 56–57, 59–61, 63–64, 67–72, 74, 81, 84–86, 93–94, 96, 101, 103, 120, 134, 147, 151, 200, 208, 221–22, 228–30, 231, 233, 236, 266, 268–69, 278, 283, 289–91, 297–300, 307, 323, 337–38, 348–49, 352, 354–57, 361–71, 373, 378–79, 381–83, 422, 440, 464, 474–81, 512, 514–15, 518, 539, 547–48, 562–65, 575.

7. Cohen, *Supreme Command*, 77, 99, 208.

8. Ibid., 10.

9. Gates, *Duty*, 120, 369, 574.

10. Ibid., 134.

11. Ibid., 84.

12. Ibid., 370.

13. Cohen, *Supreme Command*, 77 (quote), 99.

14. Ibid., 209.

15. Gates, *Duty*, 353, 367ff.

16. Ibid., 83.

17. Cohen, *Supreme Command*, 8, 12 (quote).

18. Gates, *Duty*, 335–86.

19. Jason Reifler, Christopher Gelpi, and Peter Feaver, "Success Matters: Casualty Sensitivity and the War in Iraq," ScholarWorks/Political Science Faculty Publications, no. 10 (Atlanta: Georgia State University, Winter 2006), http://scholarworks.gsu.edu/cgi/viewcontent.cgi?article=1070&context=political_science_facpub. This essay continues work done several years earlier on the same topic and published in Peter D. Feaver and Christopher Gelpi, *Choosing Your Battles: American Civil-Military Relations and the Use of Force* (Princeton, NJ: Princeton University Press, 2004).

20. Gates, *Duty*, 25.

21. The explicit link between the dialogue and the execution is derived from Larry Bossidy and Ram Charan, *Execution: The Discipline of Getting Things Done* (New York: Crown Business, 2002).

22. Cohen, *Supreme Command.*

23. R. W. Komer, *Bureaucracy Does Its Thing: Institutional Constraints on U.S.-GVN Performance in Vietnam* (Santa Monica, CA: Rand, 1972).

24. Ibid., v.

25. Gates, *Duty,* 115.

26. Komer, *Bureaucracy Does Its Thing,* v–xiii.

27. See also Neil Sheehan, *A Bright Shining Lie: John Paul Vann and America in Vietnam* (New York: Random House, 1988); Krepinevich, *The Army and Vietnam;* Kinnard, *The War Managers;* Sorley, *Honorable Warrior;* McMaster, *Dereliction of Duty;* and J. Powers, ed., *The Pentagon Papers,* recently abridged ed. for the Millennial Generation (Los Angeles: PowerPlayz.com, 2012).

28. Komer, *Bureaucracy Does Its Thing,* xii, 156.

29. Ibid., 151.

30. Gates, *Duty,* 366.

31. Bush, *Decision Points,* 378. "The situation in Iraq is unacceptable to the American people—and it is unacceptable to me. Our troops in Iraq have fought bravely. They have done everything we asked them to do. . . . It is clear that we need to change our strategy in Iraq."

32. Gates, *Duty,* 116 (quote), 126–27, 133, 147.

33. Ibid., 447.

34. Ibid., 126–27.

35. Ibid., 370, 375.

36. Gates, *Duty,* 384–85 (first two quotes), 475 (third quote). On the strategy and resource debates, see ibid., 335–86.

37. Bossidy and Charan, *Execution,* 21, 23.

38. Brodie, *War and Politics,* 6, 473.

39. Reifler, Gelpi, and Feaver, "Success Matters," 8 (second quote), 20 (first quote).

40. Ibid., 11–16, 24–26, 44–45.

41. Brodie, *War and Politics,* 440.

42. Kohn, "Building Trust," 267–69 (quote 268).

43. Ibid., 269.

6. *Jus in Bello*'s War-Waging Principles

1. As a reminder, the traditional just war theory *jus in bello* principles—those that I call *jus in bello's tactical, war-fighting principles*—are the following: the combatant/noncombatant distinction, the principle of noncombatant immunity, the principle of double effect and double intent, the principle of proportionality, and the principle of due care and due risk.

2. Walzer, *Just and Unjust Wars,* 152.

3. Two quick references for the time lines associated with the 1990–1991 Gulf War are "Timeline of the Gulf War," Wikipedia, n.d., http://en.wikipedia.org/wiki/Timeline_of_the_Gulf_War; and "Gulf War Fast Facts," CNN Library, updated November 16, 2015, http://www.cnn.com/2013/09/15/world/meast/gulf-war-fast-facts.

4. Bush and Scowcroft, *A World Transformed,* 341, 383, 399, 484.

5. Gordon and Trainor, *The Generals' War,* 37–101, 123–202, 372–438; Bush and Scowcroft, *A World Transformed,* 302–492; Dick Cheney, *In My Time: A Personal and Political Memoir* (New York: Threshold, 2001), 181–239; and Powell, *My American Journey,* 696–817.

6. Gordon and Trainor, *The Generals' War,* 414–15.

7. Bush and Scowcroft, *A World Transformed,* 425.

8. Ibid., 328, 353, 358, 380–81, 383, 390–91, 393, 395, 397, 401, 417, 428, 432, 446, 461–69, 468, 473, 477, 482, 484–87.

9. Ronald Heifetz, Alexander Grashow, and Marty Linsky, *The Practice of Adaptive Leadership* (Boston: Harvard Business Press, 2009), 24.

10. Two of the best definitions and descriptions of the difference between technical and adaptive problems can be found in Ronald A. Heifetz, *Leadership without Easy Answers* (Cambridge, MA: Belknap Press of Harvard University Press, 1994), 74–76; and Heifetz, Grashow, and Linsky, *The Practice of Adaptive Leadership,* 19–28.

11. Heifetz, Grashow, and Linsky, *The Practice of Adaptive Leadership,* 19.

12. Heifetz, *Leadership without Easy Answers,* 69–150, 183–206.

13. Heifetz, Grashow, and Linsky, *The Practice of Adaptive Leadership,* 19.

14. Heifetz, *Leadership without Easy Answers,* 75.

15. Ryan Crocker, conversation with the author, fall 2011.

16. Heifetz, *Leadership without Easy Answers,* 84–88.

17. Ibid., 75.

18. Heifetz, Grashow, and Linsky, *The Practice of Adaptive Leadership,* 19.

19. Ibid., 26–27.

20. Ibid., 31.

21. Gates, *Duty,* 120, 369 (quote).

22. Bush, *Decision Points,* 184.

23. Feaver, *Armed Servants,* 65.

24. Gates, *Duty,* 369, 366–85 (quote 368).

25. Ibid., 370.

26. Kohn, "Building Trust," 269.

27. Gates, *Duty,* 384.

28. Two of the many good business books on this topic are Bossidy and Charan, *Execution;* and Stephen P. Bradley and Richard L. Nolan, *Sense and*

Respond: Capturing Value in the Network Era (Boston: Harvard Business School Press, 1998). Though called something different, performance gap–adaptation regimes are exactly what Heifetz, Grashow, and Linsky describe in *The Practice of Adaptive Leadership* as necessary in any adaptive leadership situation. On the war-waging context, see Gates, *Duty*, 362–63.

29. Bush, *Decision Points,* 363.

30. Gordon and Trainor, *The Endgame,* 208.

31. Reifler, Gelpi, and Feaver, "Success Matters," 8.

32. Gallup poll, February 14, 2014, http://www.gallup.com/poll/116233/afghanistan.aspx.

33. Martin Blumenson, "Kasserine Pass, 30 January–22 February 1943," in *America's First Battles: 1776–1965,* ed. Charles E. Heller and William A. Stofft (Lawrence: University Press of Kansas, 1986), 226–65, 226.

34. Atkinson, *An Army at Dawn,* 533. See also Jean Edward Smith, *Eisenhower in War and Peace* (New York: Random House, 2012), Kindle locations 3761–4881.

35. Albert O. Hirschman, *Exit, Voice, and Loyalty: Responses to Decline in Firms, Organizations, and States* (Cambridge, MA: Harvard University Press, 1979), 1–61, 76–126.

36. Ibid., 92–93.

37. Ibid., 93–96.

38. Ibid., 115–16.

39. Ibid, 117.

40. Sorley, *Honorable Warrior,* 268.

41. Ibid., 304.

42. Walzer, *Just and Unjust Wars,* 311.

43. Hirschman, *Exit, Voice, and Loyalty,* 116.

44. Gates, *Duty,* 370.

45. Maxwell D. Taylor, *The Uncertain Trumpet* (New York: Harper & Bros., 1959), 4.

46. Taylor's conduct in the narrow instance used in this example is, I believe, an accurate illustration of the proper use of voice while one is on and off active duty. His role in the dysfunctional civil-military relationship of the Johnson administration, however, is another matter.

47. Kohn, "Building Trust," 282.

48. Walzer, *Just and Unjust Wars,* xiii, xv.

49. Ibid., 44.

50. Jeff McMahan provides another perspective. For him, rights are never lost; they are forfeited in relation to another person in a particular context. His view is that a person forfeits his or her right not to be attacked by posing an illegitimate threat. Walzer's view is more of a class action: because soldiers enter the

class of dangerous persons, their right to life is lost or significantly altered. From this position, Walzer then argues that, in this sense, soldiers—whether fighting a just war or an unjust one—are morally equal. McMahan does not agree. Soldiers, for him, may be legal equals but not moral equals. The forfeit of the right not to be attacked is not a class action but one based on individual action and related to the justice of one's cause. See McMahan, *Killing in War*. In this study, I stuck to Walzer's view in that his represents the still-prevailing position, even if McMahan's challenge may ultimately create a new prevailing view.

51. Walzer, *Just and Unjust Wars*, 54 (quote), 136. Elsewhere, I have a more complete analysis of Walzer's use of rights in his just war theory. See James M. Dubik, "Human Rights, Command Responsibility, and Walzer's Just War Theory," *Philosophy and Public Affairs* 11, no. 4 (Fall 1982): 354–71.

52. Walzer, *Just and Unjust Wars*, 136. This is the specific view that McMahan challenges.

53. Ibid., 137, 156.

54. The following four reports summarize the stay-the-course discussion: "Rumsfeld Agrees Bush Is 'Not Backing Away from Staying the Course,'" ThinkProgress, October 24, 2006, http://thinkprogress.org/security/2006/10/24/8252/rumsfeld-stay-course/#; "Hume Reported Bush 'Has Stopped Using the Phrase "Stay the Course,"' Ignored Rumsfeld's Denial Earlier That Day, Administration's Previous Flip-Flops," MediaMatters for America, October 26, 2006, http://mediamatters.org/research/2006/10/26/hume-reported-bush-has-stopped-using-the-phrase/137080; Jim Rutenberg and David S. Cloud, "Bush Abandons the Phrase 'Stay the Course' on Iraq," *New York Times*, October 24, 2006, http://www.nytimes.com/2006/10/24/world/middleeast/24policy.html?pagewanted=print&_r=0; and Sean Alfano, "Bush Drops 'Stay the Course' Phrase," CBSNews.com, October 24, 2006, http://www.cbsnews.com/news/bush-drops-stay-the-course-phrase.

55. Of the many articles, reports, monographs, and books on Abu Ghraib, the following are sufficient for our purposes: Phillip Carter, "The Road to Abu Ghraib: The Biggest Scandal of the Republican Administration Began at the Top," *Washington Monthly*, November 2004, http://www.washingtonmonthly.com/features/2004/0411.carter.html; George R. Mastroianni, "Looking Back: Understanding Abu Ghraib," *Parameters* 43, no. 2 (Summer 2013): 53–65, http://strategicstudiesinstitute.army.mil/pubs/parameters/Issues/Summer_2013/6_Mastroianni_Article.pdf; and "Bush Policy 'Led to Abu Ghraib,'" BBCNews.com, April 22, 2009, http://news.bbc.co.uk/2/hi/8012036.stm.

56. A. John Simmons, *Moral Principles and Political Obligations* (Princeton, NJ: Princeton University Press, 1979), 12–13; Rawls, *A Theory of Justice*, 114–17, 333–42.

57. Simmons, *Moral Principles and Political Obligations,* 12–13.

58. Ibid., 16–21.

59. Walzer, *Just and Unjust Wars,* 34–47, 127–59.

60. Marvin Kalb and Deborah Kalb, *Haunting Legacy: Vietnam and the American Presidency from Ford to Obama* (Washington, DC: Brookings Institution Press, 2011), Kindle locations 56, 125.

61. Walzer, *Just and Unjust Wars,* xiii.

Epilogue

1. "U.S. Policy in the Middle East," Testimony Before the US Senate Armed Services Committee, September 22, 2015, http://www.c-span.org/video/?328261-1/former-cia-director-david-petraeus-testimony-us-middle-east-policy&start=840.

Bibliography

Adler, Mortimer. *How to Think about War and Peace.* 1944. New York: Fordham University Press, 2005.

Allawi, Ali A. *The Occupation of Iraq: Winning the War, Losing the Peace.* New Haven, CT: Yale University Press, 2007.

Aristotle. *Nicomachean Ethics.* Translated by Martin Oswald. Indianapolis: Bobbs-Merrill, 1962.

Atkinson, Rick. *An Army at Dawn: The War in North Africa, 1942–1943.* New York: Henry Holt, 2002.

Bailyn, Bernard, ed. *The Debate on the Constitution.* New York: Literary Classics of the United States, 1993.

Baker, Peter. *Days of Fire: Bush and Cheney in the White House.* New York: Doubleday, 2013.

Barfield, Thomas. *Afghanistan: A Cultural and Political History.* Princeton, NJ: Princeton University Press, 2010.

Barker, Earnest. *Social Contract: Locke, Hume, Rousseau.* New York: Oxford University Press, 1980.

Bennis, Warren, and Burt Nanus. *Leaders: Strategies for Taking Charge.* New York: HarperCollins, 1985.

Bergen, Peter L. *The Longest War: The Enduring Conflict between America and Al Qaeda.* New York: Free Press, 2011.

———. *Manhunt: The Ten-Year Search for Bin Laden from 9/11 to Abbottabad.* New York: Crown, 2012.

Betts, Richard K. "Pick Your Battles: Ending America's Era of Permanent War." *Foreign Affairs* 93, no. 6 (November/December 2014): 15–24.

Blumenson, Martin. "Kasserine Pass, 30 January–22 February 1943." In *America's First Battles: 1776–1965,* ed. Charles E. Heller and William A. Stofft, 226–65. Lawrence: University Press of Kansas, 1986.

Boll, Michael M. *National Security Planning: Roosevelt through Reagan.* Lexington: University Press of Kentucky, 1988.

Bonekemper, Edward H., III. *A Victor, Not a Butcher: Ulysses S. Grant's Overlooked Military Genius.* Washington, DC: Regnery, 2004.

Boot, Max. *Invisible Armies: An Epic History of Guerrilla Warfare from Ancient Times to the Present*. New York: Liveright, 2012.

———. "More Small Wars: Counterinsurgency Is Here to Stay." *Foreign Affairs* 93, no. 6 (November/December 2014): 5–14.

Bossidy, Larry, and Ram Charan. *Execution: The Discipline of Getting Things Done*. New York: Crown Business, 2002.

Bradley, Stephen P., and Richard L. Nolan. *Sense and Respond: Capturing Value in the Network Era*. Boston: Harvard Business School Press, 1998.

Bremer, L. Paul, III. *My Year in Iraq: The Struggle to Build a Future of Hope*. New York: Threshold, 2006.

Brennan, Rick. "Withdrawal Symptoms: The Bungling of the Iraq Exit." *Foreign Affairs* 93, no. 6 (November/December 2014): 25–36.

Brodie, Bernard. *War and Politics*. New York: Macmillan, 1973.

Brown, Davis. *The Sword, the Cross, and the Eagle: The American Christian Just War Tradition*. Lanham, MD: Rowman & Littlefield, 2008.

Burk, James. "Responsible Obedience by Military Professionals." In *American Civil-Military Relations: The Soldier and the State in a New Era*, ed. Suzanne C. Nielsen and Don M. Snider, 149–71. Baltimore: Johns Hopkins University Press, 2009.

Burke, Jason. *The 9/11 Wars*. New York: Penguin, 2011.

Bush, George, and Brent Scowcroft. *A World Transformed: The Collapse of the Soviet Union, the Unification of Germany, Tiananmen Square, and the Gulf War*. New York: Knopf, 1998.

Bush, George W. *Decision Points*. New York: Crown, 2010.

Byman, Daniel, and Jeremy Shapiro. "Homeward Bound? Don't Hype the Threat of Returning Jihadists." *Foreign Affairs* 93, no. 6 (November/December 2014): 37–46.

Casey, George W. *Strategic Reflections: Operation Iraqi Freedom, July 2004–February 2007*. Washington, DC: National Defense University Press, 2012.

Chandrasekaran, Rajiv. *Imperial Life in the Emerald City: Inside Iraq's Green Zone*. New York: Knopf, 2007.

———. *Little America: The War within the War for Afghanistan*. New York: Knopf, 2012.

Cheney, Dick. *In My Time: A Personal and Political Memoir*. New York: Threshold, 2001.

Clarke, Richard A. *Against All Enemies: Inside America's War on Terror*. London: Simon & Schuster, 2004.

Clausewitz, Carl von. *On War*. Edited and translated by Michael Howard and Peter Paret. Princeton, NJ: Princeton University Press, 1976.

Cockburn, Patrick. *Muqtada: Muqtada al-Sadr, the Shia Revival, and the Struggle for Iraq*. New York: Scribner, 2008.

Codevilla, Angelo M. *Advice to War Presidents: A Remedial Course in Statecraft*. New York: Basic, 2009.

Cohen, Eliot A. "The Unequal Dialogue: The Theory and Reality of Civil-Military Relations and the Use of Force." In *Soldiers and Civilians: The Civil-Military Gap and American National Security*, ed. Peter D. Feaver and Richard H. Kohn, 429–58. Cambridge, MA: MIT Press, 2001.

———. *Supreme Command: Soldiers, Statesmen, and Leadership in Wartime*. New York: Anchor, 2002.

Cohen, Eliot A., and John Gooch. *Military Misfortunes: The Anatomy of Failure in War*. New York: Free Press, 1990.

Cohen, Marshall, Thomas Nagel, and Thomas Scanlon. *War and Moral Responsibility: A Philosophy and Public Affairs Reader*. Princeton, NJ: Princeton University Press, 1974.

Coll, Steve. *Ghost Wars: The Secret History of the CIA, Afghanistan, and Bin Laden, from the Soviet Invasion to September 10, 2001*. New York: Penguin, 2004.

Collins, Jim. *Good to Great*. New York: HarperCollins, 2001.

Corn, Geoffrey S., et al. *The Law of Armed Conflict: An Operational Approach*. New York: Wolters Kluwer Law & Business, 2012.

Craig, Gordon A. "The Political Leader as Strategist." In *Makers of Modern Strategy*, ed. Peter Paret, 481–509. Princeton, NJ: Princeton University Press, 1986.

Crowley, Michael. "Can Lobbyists Stop the War?" *New York Times Magazine*, September 9, 2007. http://www.nytimes.com/2007/09/09/magazine/09antiwar-t.html?_r=0.

Daggett, Stephen. *Costs of Major U.S. Wars*. Report 7-5700. Washington, DC: Congressional Research Service, June 29, 2010. http://www.fas.org/sgp/crs/natsec/RS22926.pdf.

Daniels, Norman, ed. *Reading Rawls: Critical Studies of "A Theory of Justice."* New York: Basic, 1975.

Dörner, Dietrich. *The Logic of Failure: Recognizing and Avoiding Error in Complex Situations*. Cambridge, MA: Perseus, 1996.

Drew, Dennis M., and Donald M. Snow. *Making Strategy: An Introduction to National Security Processes and Problems*. Maxwell Air Force Base, AL: Air University Press, 1988.

Drucker, Peter. *The Effective Executive*. New York: Harper & Row, 1985.

Dubik, James M. "Human Rights, Command Responsibility, and Walzer's Just War Theory." *Philosophy and Public Affairs* 11, no. 4 (Fall 1982): 354–71.

———. "Operational Art in Counterinsurgency." Washington, DC: Institute for the Study of War, May 2012.

Dworkin, Ronald. *Taking Rights Seriously*. Cambridge, MA: Harvard University Press, 1978.

Eisenhower, Dwight D. *Crusade in Europe.* New York: Doubleday, 1948.

Ellsberg, Daniel. *Secrets: A Memoir of Vietnam and the Pentagon Papers.* New York: Penguin, 2002.

Elshtain, Jean Bethke. *Just War against Terror: The Burden of American Power in a Violent World.* New York: Basic, 2003.

Evans, Martin. *Afghanistan: A Short History of Its People and Politics.* New York: Harper Perennial, 2002.

Fallows, James. *Blind into Baghdad: America's War in Iraq.* New York: Vintage, 2006.

Faust, Drew Gilpin. *This Republic of Suffering: Death and the American Civil War.* New York: Vintage, 2008.

Feaver, Peter D. *Armed Servants: Agency, Oversight, and Civil-Military Relations.* Cambridge, MA: Harvard University Press, 2003.

Feaver, Peter D., and Christopher Gelpi. *Choosing Your Battles: American Civil-Military Relations and the Use of Force.* Princeton, NJ: Princeton University Press, 2004.

Feaver, Peter D., and Richard H. Kohn. "Conclusion: The Gap and What It Means for American National Security." In *Soldiers and Civilians: The Civil-Military Gap and American National Security,* ed. Peter D. Feaver and Richard H. Kohn, 459–73. Cambridge, MA: MIT Press, 2001.

———, eds. *Soldiers and Civilians: The Civil-Military Gap and American National Security.* Cambridge, MA: MIT Press, 2001.

Fehrenbacher, Don E., ed. *Lincoln: Speeches and Writings, 1859–1865.* New York: Library of America, 1989.

Feinberg, Joel. *Rights, Justice, and the Bounds of Liberty: Essays in Social Philosophy.* Princeton, NJ: Princeton University Press, 1980.

Fenner, Lorry M., Mark E. Stout, and Jessica L. Goldings. *Ten Years Later: Insights on Al-Qaeda's Past and Future through Captured Records.* Washington, DC: National Defense University, 2011.

Fishkin, James S. *The Limits of Obligation.* New Haven, CT: Yale University Press, 1982.

Fixdal, Mona. *Just Peace: How Wars Should End.* New York: Palgrave Macmillan, 2012.

Forsythe, Clarke D. *Politics for the Greatest Good: The Case for Prudence in the Public Square.* Downer's Grove, IL: InterVarsity, 2009.

Fotion, Nicholas G. *Military Ethics: Looking toward the Future.* Stanford, CA: Hoover Institution Press, 1990.

Fotion, Nicholas G., and Gerard Elfstron. *Military Ethics: Guidelines for Peace and War.* Boston: Routledge & Kegan Paul, 1986.

Franks, Tommy. *American Soldier.* New York: HarperCollins, 2004.

Fredrick, Jim. *Black Hearts: One Platoon's Descent into Madness in Iraq's Triangle of Death*. New York: Random House, 2010.

Freedman, Lawrence, and Efraim Karsh. *The Gulf Conflict, 1990–1991: Diplomacy and War in the New World Order*. Princeton, NJ: Princeton University Press, 1993.

Frum, David. *An End to Evil: How to Win the War on Terror*. New York: Random House, 2003.

Fukuyama, Francis. *State-Building: Governance and World Order in the 21st Century*. Ithaca, NY: Cornell University Press, 2004.

Gaddis, John Lewis. *Surprise, Security, and the American Experience*. Cambridge, MA: Harvard University Press, 2004.

Gates, Robert M. *From the Shadows: The Ultimate Insider's Story of Five Presidents and How They Won the Cold War*. New York: Simon & Schuster, 1996.

———. *Duty: Memoirs of a Secretary at War*. New York: Knopf, 2014.

Ghani, Ashraf, and Clare Lockhart. *Fixing Failed States: A Framework for Rebuilding a Fractured World*. New York: Oxford University Press, 2008.

Gillroy, John Martin, and Maurice Wad, eds. *The Moral Dimensions of Public Policy Choice*. Pittsburgh, PA: University of Pittsburgh Press, 1992.

Glantz, Aaron. *How America Lost Iraq*. New York: Penguin, 2005.

Goldman, Alan H. *The Moral Foundations of Professional Ethics*. Totowa, NJ: Rowman & Littlefield, 1980.

Goldsmith, Jack. *Power and Constraint: The Accountable Presidency After 9/11*. New York: Norton, 2012.

Goodwin, Doris Kearns. *Team of Rivals: The Political Genius of Abraham Lincoln*. New York: Simon & Schuster, 2005.

Gordon, Michael R., and Bernard E. Trainor. *The Generals' War: The Inside Story of the Conflict in the Gulf*. Boston: Little, Brown, 1995.

———. *Cobra II: The Inside Story of the Invasion and Occupation of Iraq*. New York: Pantheon, 2006.

———. *The Endgame: The Inside Story of the Struggle for Iraq, from George W. Bush to Barack Obama*. New York: Pantheon, 2012.

Gray, J. Glenn. *The Warriors: Reflections of Men in Battle*. New York: Harper & Row, 1970.

Gray, John. *Mill on Liberty: A Defense*. Boston: Routledge & Kegan Paul, 1983.

Griffith, Samuel B., trans. *Sun Tzu: The Art of War*. New York: Oxford University Press, 1963.

Grotius, Hugo. *On the Law of War and Peace*. 1612. Edited by Stephen C. Neff. New York: Cambridge University Press, 2012.

Gul, Imtiaz. *The Most Dangerous Place: Pakistan's Lawless Frontier*. New York: Viking, 2010.

Gunaratna, Rohan. *Inside Al Qaeda: Global Network of Terror*. New York: Berkley, 2002.

Haas, Richard N. *War of Necessity, War of Choice*. New York: Simon & Schuster, 2009.

Habeck, Mary. *Knowing the Enemy: Jihadist Ideology and the War on Terror*. New Haven, CT: Yale University Press, 2006.

Haeckel, Stephan H. *Adaptive Enterprises: Creating and Leading Sense-and-Respond Organizations*. Boston: Harvard Business Press, 1999.

Hampshire, Stuart, ed. *Public and Private Morality*. New York: Cambridge University Press, 1978.

———. *Morality and Conflict*. Cambridge, MA: Harvard University Press, 1983.

Hampton, Jean. *The Intrinsic Worth of Persons: Contractarianism in Moral and Political Thought*. Edited by Daniel Farnham. New York: Cambridge University Press, 2007.

Hartle, Anthony. *Moral Issues in Military Decision Making*. Lawrence: University Press of Kansas, 1989.

Hashim, Ahmed S. *Insurgency and Counter-Insurgency in Iraq*. Ithaca, NY: Cornell University Press, 2006.

Hattaway, Herman, and Archer Jones. *How the North Won: A Military History of the Civil War*. Champaign: University of Illinois Press, 1983.

Heifetz, Ronald A. *Leadership without Easy Answers*. Cambridge, MA: Belknap Press of Harvard University Press, 1994.

Heifetz, Ronald A., Alexander Grashow, and Marty Linsky. *The Practice of Adaptive Leadership*. Boston: Harvard Business Press, 2009.

Hirschman, Albert O. *Exit, Voice, and Loyalty: Responses to Decline in Firms, Organizations, and States*. Cambridge, MA: Harvard University Press, 1979.

Hooker, Richard D., Jr., and Joseph J. Collins, eds. *Lessons Encountered: Learning from the Long War*. Washington, DC: National Defense University Press, 2015.

Howell, William G., and John C. Pevehouse. "When Congress Stops Wars." *Foreign Affairs* 86, no. 5 (September/October 2007): 95–107. http://www.foreignaffairs.com/articles/62831/william-g-howell-and-jon-c-pevehouse/when-congress-stops-wars.

Hume, David. *A Treatise of Human Nature*. Edited by L. A. Selby-Bigge. New York: Oxford University Press, 1978.

Huntington, Samuel P. *The Soldier and the State: The Theory and Politics of Civil-Military Relations*. Cambridge, MA: Belknap Press of Harvard University Press, 1957.

Ignatieff, Michael. *The Warrior's Honor: Ethnic War and the Modern Conscience*. New York: Metropolitan, 1997.

————. *The Lesser Evil: Political Ethics in an Age of Terror.* Princeton, NJ: Princeton University Press, 2004.

Ikle, Fred Charles. *Every War Must End.* New York: Columbia University Press, 1991.

"Instructions for the Government of Armies of the United States in the Field, Prepared by Francis Lieber, Promulgated by General Orders no. 100 by President Lincoln, 24 April 1863." http://avalon.law.yale.edu/19th_century/lieber.asp.

Jones, Seth G. *Counterinsurgency in Afghanistan.* Santa Monica, CA: Rand, 2008.

————. *In the Graveyard of Empires: America's War in Afghanistan.* New York: Norton, 2009.

Junger, Sebastian. *War.* New York: Hachette, 2010.

Kagan, Donald. *On the Origins of War and the Preservation of Peace.* New York: Doubleday, 1995.

Kagan, Kimberly. *The Surge: A Military History.* New York: Encounter, 2009.

Kaiser, David. *No End Save Victory: How FDR Led the Nation into War.* New York: Basic, 2014.

Kalb, Marvin, and Deborah Kalb. *Haunting Legacy: Vietnam and the American Presidency from Ford to Obama.* Washington, DC: Brookings Institution Press, 2011.

Kant, Immanuel. *Groundwork of the Metaphysic of Morals.* Translated by H. J. Paton. New York: Harper & Row, 1964.

Kaplan, Robert D. *Warrior Politics: Why Leadership Demands a Pagan Ethos.* New York: Random House, 2002.

Kaplan, Robert S., and David P. Norton. *The Strategy-Focused Organization.* Cambridge, MA: Harvard University Press, 2001.

Keegan, John. *The Second World War.* New York: Viking, 1989.

Kent, Andrew. "Constitution and the Laws of War during the American Civil War, the Federal Courts, Practice and Procedure." Faculty Scholarship. New York: Fordham University Law School, 2009. http://ir.lawnet.fordham.edu/cgi/viewcontent.cgi?article=1252&context=faculty_scholarship.

Kepel, Gilles. *Jihad: The Trail of Political Islam.* Cambridge, MA: Belknap Press of Harvard University Press, 2002.

Kilcullen, David. *Out of the Mountains: The Coming of Age of the Urban Guerrilla.* New York: Oxford University Press, 2013.

Kinnard, Douglas. *The War Managers.* Wayne, NJ: Avery, 1985.

Kitfield, James. "My Iraq War." *National Journal,* vol. 45, nos. 12–13 (March 21, 2013). http://www.nationaljournal.com/s/82349/my-iraq-war.

Klaidman, Daniel. *Kill or Capture: The War on Terror and the Soul of the Obama Presidency.* New York: Houghton Mifflin Harcourt, 2012.

Kohn, Richard H. "Building Trust: Civil-Military Behaviors for Effective National Security." In *American Civil-Military Relations: The Soldier and the State in a New Era,* ed. Suzanne C. Nielsen and Don M. Snider, 264–89. Baltimore: Johns Hopkins University Press, 2008.

Komer, R. W. *Bureaucracy Does Its Thing: Institutional Constraints on U.S.-GVN Performance in Vietnam.* Santa Monica, CA: Rand, 1972.

Krepinevich, Andrew F., Jr. *The Army and Vietnam.* Baltimore: Johns Hopkins University Press, 1986.

Kuhn, Thomas S. *The Structure of Scientific Revolutions.* Chicago: University of Chicago Press, 1970. http://avalon.law.yale.edu/19th_century/lieber.asp.

Labovitz, George, and Victor Rosansky. *The Power of Alignment: How Great Companies Stay Centered and Accomplish Extraordinary Things.* New York: Wiley, 1997.

Lewis, Jessica. *Al Qaeda in Iraq Resurgent, Part I.* Washington, DC: Institute for the Study of War, September 2013.

———. *Al Qaeda in Iraq Resurgent, Part II.* Washington, DC: Institute for the Study of War, October 2013.

———. *The Islamic State of Iraq Returns to Diyala.* Washington, DC: Institute for the Study of War, April 2014.

Liddell-Hart, B. H. *Strategy.* New York: Praeger, 1967.

Lieberman, Jethro K. *The Enduring Constitution: A Bicentennial Perspective.* New York: West, 1987.

Luban, David. "Risk Taking and Force Protection." In *Reading Walzer,* ed. Yitzhak Benbaju and Naomi Sussmann, 277–301. New York: Routledge, 2014.

Luttwak, Edward N. *Strategy: The Logic of War and Peace.* Cambridge, MA: Belknap Press of Harvard University Press, 1987.

Mann, James. *Rise of the Vulcans: The History of Bush's War Cabinet.* New York: Penguin, 2004.

Mardini, Ramzy. *Violent Landscape: Iraq and Its Insurgent Movements.* Washington, DC: Jamestown Foundation, 2010.

Marten, Kimberly Zisk. *Enforcing the Peace: Learning from the Imperial Past.* New York: Columbia University Press, 2004.

Masr, Vali. *The Shia Revival: How Conflicts within Islam Will Shape the Future.* New York: Norton, 2006.

Mastroianni, George R. "Looking Back: Understanding Abu Ghraib." *Parameters* 43, no. 2 (Summer 2013): 53–65. http://strategicstudiesinstitute.army.mil/pubs/parameters/Issues/Summer_2013/6_Mastroianni_Article.pdf.

McChrystal, Stanley. *My Share of the Task: A Memoir.* New York: Portfolio/Penguin, 2013.

McMahan, Jeff. *Killing in War*. New York: Oxford University Press, 2009.

McMaster, H. R. *Dereliction of Duty: Lyndon Johnson, Robert McNamara, the Joint Chiefs of Staff, and the Lies That Led to Vietnam*. New York: Harper-Collins, 1997.

McPherson, James M. *Battle Cry of Freedom: The Civil War Era*. New York: Oxford University Press, 1988.

———. *Abraham Lincoln and the Second American Revolution*. New York: Oxford University Press, 1991.

———. *Tried by War: Abraham Lincoln as Commander-in-Chief*. New York: Penguin, 2008.

Melden, A. I. *Rights and Persons*. Berkeley: University of California Press, 1977.

Mill, John Stuart. *Utilitarianism, On Liberty, Essay on Bentham*. Edited by Mary Warnock. New York: Meridian, 1970.

Morell, Michael. *The Great War of Our Time: The CIA's Fight against Terrorism from al Qa'ida to ISIS*. New York: Hachette, 2015.

Moten, Matthew. *Presidents and Their Generals: An American History of Command in War*. Cambridge, MA: Belknap Press of Harvard University Press, 1997.

——— "A Broken Dialogue: Rumsfeld, Shinseki, and Civil-Military Tension." In *American Civil-Military Relations,* ed. Suzanne C. Nielsen and Don M. Snider, 42–71. Baltimore: Johns Hopkins University Press, 2009.

———, ed. *Between War and Peace: How America Ends Its Wars*. New York: Free Press, 2011.

———. Moyar, Mark. *A Question of Command: Counterinsurgency from the Civil War to Iraq*. New Haven, CT: Yale University Press, 2009.

Murray, Williamson, and Allan R. Millett. *A War to Be Won: Fighting the Second World War*. Cambridge, MA: Belknap Press of Harvard University Press, 2000.

Murray, Williamson, and Robert H. Scales. *The Iraq War: A Military History*. Cambridge, MA: Belknap Press of Harvard University Press, 2003.

Nance, Malcolm. *An End to Al Qaeda: Destroying Bin Laden's Jihad and Restoring America's Honor*. New York: St. Martin's, 2010.

Naylor, Sean. *Not a Good Day to Die: Chaos and Courage in the Mountains of Afghanistan: The Untold Story of Operation Anaconda*. New York: Berkley, 2005.

Neumann, Ronald E. *The Other War: Winning and Losing in Afghanistan*. Washington, DC: Potomac, 2009.

Nielsen, Suzanne C., and Don M. Snider, eds. *American Civil-Military Relations: The Soldier and the State in a New Era*. Baltimore: Johns Hopkins University Press, 2009.

Norman, Michael, and Elizabeth M. Norman. *Tears in the Darkness: The Story of the Bataan Death March and Its Aftermath.* New York: Farrar Straus Giroux, 2009.

Nozick, Robert. *Anarchy, State, and Utopia.* New York: Basic, 1974.

Nye, Joseph S., Jr. *The Paradox of American Power: Why the World's Only Superpower Can't Go It Alone.* New York: Oxford University Press, 2002.

O'Connor, John J. *In Defense of Life.* Boston: Daughters of St. Paul, 1981.

Orend, Brian. *The Morality of War.* Peterborough, ON: Broadview, 2006.

Owens, Mackubin Thomas. *U.S. Civil-Military Relations after 9/11: Renegotiating the Civil-Military Bargain.* New York: Continuum International, 2011.

Palmer, Bruce, Jr. *The 25-Year War: America's Military Role in Vietnam.* Lexington: University Press of Kentucky, 1984.

Perry, Mark. *Four Stars: The Inside Story of the Forty-Year Battle between the Joint Chiefs of Staff and America's Civilian Leaders.* Boston: Houghton Mifflin, 1989.

———. *Partners in Command.* New York: Penguin, 2007.

Petraeus, David. "How We Won in Iraq: And Why All the Hard-Won Gains of the Surge Are in Grave Danger of Being Lost Today." *Foreign Policy,* October 30, 2013. http://www.foreignpolicy.com/articles/2013/10/29/david_petraeus_how_we_won_the_surge_in_iraq#sthash.bV18Kydz.dpbs.

Pfeffer, Jeffrey, and Robert I. Sutton. *The Knowing-Doing Gap: How Smart Companies Turn Knowledge into Action.* Cambridge, MA: Harvard University Press, 2000.

Plato. "Crito." In *Five Dialogues,* trans. G. M. A. Grube, 45–57. Indianapolis: Hackett, 1981.

Pogue, Forrest C. *George C. Marshall: Ordeal and Hope, 1939–1941.* New York: Viking, 1965.

Pollack, Kenneth M. *A Path Out of the Desert: A Grand Strategy for America in the Middle East.* New York: Random House, 2008.

Polsky, Andrew J. *Elusive Victories: The American Presidency at War.* New York: Oxford University Press, 2012.

Powell, Colin. *My American Journey.* New York: Random House Large Print, 1995.

Powers, J., ed. *The Pentagon Papers.* Recently abridged ed. for the Millennial Generation. Los Angeles: PowerPlayz.com, 2012.

Rashid, Ahmed. *Taliban: Militant Islam, Oil, and Fundamentalism in Central Asia.* New Haven, CT: Yale University Press, 2000.

———. *Descent into Chaos: The United States and the Failure of Nation Building in Pakistan, Afghanistan, and Central Asia.* New York: Penguin, 2008.

Rawls, John. *A Theory of Justice.* Cambridge, MA: Harvard University Press, 1971.

———. "Fifty Years After Hiroshima." In *Moral Philosophy, A Reader* (4th ed.), ed. Louis P. Pojman and Peter Tramel, Kindle locations 14455–613. Indianapolis: Hackett, 2009.

Record, Jeffrey. *Dark Victory: America's Second War against Iraq.* Annapolis, MD: Naval Institute Press, 2004.

Reidell, Bruce. Foreword to Ronald E. Neumann, *The Other War: Winning and Losing in Afghanistan,* vii–x. Washington, DC: Potomac, 2009.

Reifler, Jason, Christopher Gelpi, and Peter Feaver. "Success Matters: Casualty Sensitivity and the War in Iraq." ScholarWorks/Political Science Faculty Publications, no. 10. Atlanta: Georgia State University, Winter 2006. http://scholarworks.gsu.edu/cgi/viewcontent.cgi?article=1070&context=political_science_facpub.

Ricks, Thomas E. *Fiasco: The American Military Adventure in Iraq.* New York: Penguin, 2006.

———. *The Gamble: General David Petraeus and the American Military Adventure in Iraq, 2006–2008.* New York: Penguin, 2009.

———. *The Generals: American Military Command from World War II to Today.* New York: Penguin, 2012.

Riedel, Bruce. *The Search for Al Qaeda: Its Leadership, Ideology, and Future.* Washington, DC: Brookings Institution Press, 2008.

Rob, John. *Brave New War: The Next Stage of Terrorism and the End of Globalization.* Hoboken, NJ: Wiley, 2007.

Roberts, Andrew. *Masters and Commanders: How Four Titans Won the War in the West, 1941–1945.* New York: HarperCollins, 2009.

Robin, David, and Henry Shue, eds. *Just and Unjust Warriors: The Moral and Legal Status of Soldiers.* New York: Oxford University Press, 2008.

Rodin, David. *War and Self-Defense.* New York: Oxford University Press, 2002.

Rose, Gideon. *How Wars End: Why We Always Fight the Last Battle: A History of American Intervention from World War I to Afghanistan.* New York: Simon & Schuster, 2010.

Rose, Gideon, and Jonathan Tepperman. "A Hard Education: Learning from Afghanistan and Iraq." *Foreign Affairs* 93, no. 6 (November/December 2014): 2.

Rothkopf, David. *Running the World: The Inside Story of the National Security Council and the Architects of American Power.* Cambridge, MA: Perseus, 2004.

Rousseau, Jean-Jacques. *The First and Second Discourses.* Edited by Roger D. Masters. Translated by Roger D. Masters and Judith R. Masters. New York: St. Martin's, 1964.

Roy, Oliver. *Islam and Resistance in Afghanistan.* New York: Cambridge University Press, 1990.

————. *Globalized Islam: The Search for a New Ummah.* New York: Columbia University Press, 2004.

Rumsfeld, Donald. *Known and Unknown: A Memoir.* New York: Sentinel, 2011.

Sanchez, Ricardo S. *Wiser in Battle: A Soldier's Story.* New York: HarperCollins, 2008.

Sanger, David E. *Confront and Conceal: Obama's Secret Wars and Surprising Use of American Power.* New York: Crown, 2012.

[Scheuer, Michael.] *Imperial Hubris: Why the West Is Losing the War on Terror.* Washington, DC: Brassey's, 2004.

Schlesinger, Arthur M., Jr. *War and the American Presidency.* New York: Norton, 2004.

Senge, Peter M. *The Fifth Discipline: The Art and Discipline of the Learning Organization.* New York: Doubleday Dell, 1990.

Sheehan, Neil. *A Bright Shining Lie: John Paul Vann and America in Vietnam.* New York: Random House, 1988.

Sherman, Nancy. "The Moral Psychic Reality of War." In *Reading Walzer,* ed. Yitzhak Benbaju and Naomi Sussmann, 302–27. New York: Routledge, 2014.

————. *Afterwar: Healing the Moral Wounds of Our Soldiers.* New York: Oxford University Press, 2015.

Sherman, William T. *Memoirs of General William T. Sherman.* New York: Da Capo, 1984.

Simmons, A. John. *Moral Principles and Political Obligations.* Princeton, NJ: Princeton University Press, 1979.

Sky, Emma. *The Unraveling: High Hopes and Missed Opportunities in Iraq.* New York: PublicAffairs, 2015.

Smith, Jean Edward. *Eisenhower in War and Peace.* New York: Random House, 2012.

Smith, Rupert. *The Utility of Force: The Art of War in the Modern World.* New York: Penguin, 2006.

Snider, Don M., and Lloyd Mathews. *The Future of the Army Profession.* New York: McGraw-Hill, 2005.

Sorley, Lewis. *Honorable Warrior: General Harold K. Johnson and the Ethics of Command.* Lawrence: University Press of Kansas, 1998.

Straus, Barry S., and Josiah Ober. *The Anatomy of Error: Ancient Military Disasters and Their Lessons for Modern Strategists.* New York: St. Martin's, 1990.

Sullivan, Gordon R., and James M. Dubik. *Envisioning Future Warfare.* Fort Leavenworth, KS: US Army Command and General Staff College Press, 1995.

Summers, Harry G. *On Strategy: The Vietnam War in Context.* Carlisle Barracks, PA: Strategic Studies Institute, 1981.

Taylor, Maxwell D. *The Uncertain Trumpet*. New York: Harper & Bros., 1959.

Tomsen, Peter. *The Wars of Afghanistan: Messianic Terrorism, Tribal Conflicts, and the Failures of Great Powers*. New York: PublicAffairs, 2011.

———. "The Good War: What Went Wrong in Afghanistan—and How to Make It Right." *Foreign Affairs* 93, no. 6 (November/December 2014): 47–54.

Tong, Rosemarie. *Ethics in Policy Analysis*. Englewood Cliffs, NJ: Prentice-Hall, 1986.

Vandehei, Jim, and John F. Harris. "Dems Could Do Far More to End Iraq War." *Politico*, September 27, 2007. http://www.politico.com/news/stories/0907/6048.html.

Wakin, Malham M., ed. *War, Morality, and the Military Profession*. Boulder, CO: Westview, 1979.

Walzer, Michael. *Obligations: Essays on Disobedience, War, and Citizenship*. Cambridge, MA: Harvard University Press, 1970.

———. *Just and Unjust Wars: A Moral Argument with Historical Illustrations*. 1977. 5th ed., New York: Basic, 2000.

———. *Spheres of Justice: A Defense of Pluralism and Equality*. New York: Basic, 1983.

———. *Exodus and Revolution*. New York: Basic, 1985.

———. *Arguing about War*. New Haven, CT: Yale University Press, 2004.

Weigel, George. *Tranquillitas Ordinis: The Present Failure and Future Promise of American Catholic Thought on War and Peace*. New York: Oxford University Press, 1987.

Weigley, Russell F. *Eisenhower's Lieutenants: The Campaigns of France and Germany, 1944–1945*. Bloomington: Indiana University Press, 1981.

Whiteley, C. H. "On Duties." In *Moral Concepts*, ed. Joel Feinberg, 53–59. New York: Oxford University Press, 1969.

Williams, T. Harry. *Lincoln and His Generals*. New York: Knopf, 1952.

Woodward, Bob. *Bush at War*. New York: Simon & Schuster, 2002.

———. *Plan of Attack*. New York: Simon & Schuster, 2004.

———. *State of Denial: Bush at War, Part III*. New York: Simon & Schuster, 2006.

———. *The War Within: A Secret White House History, 2006–2008*. New York: Simon & Schuster, 2008.

———. *Obama's Wars*. New York: Simon & Schuster, 2010.

Wright, Lawrence. *The Looming Tower: Al Qaeda and the Road to 9/11*. New York: Vintage, 2006.

Zakheim, Dov S. *A Vulcan's Tale: How the Bush Administration Mismanaged the Reconstruction of Afghanistan*. Washington, DC: Brookings Institution Press, 2011.

Index

Bush, George W. *(cont.)*
68; on Rumsfeld's power and
control, 72; on sending Americans
to war, 145; war in Afghanistan
and, 37–38, 40, 47; war in Iraq
and, 42, 44, 46–47; war-waging
responsibilities of senior leaders
and, 128
bypass regime, 151, 154

Casey, George W., 45, 46, 106–7, 110,
153
Central Intelligence Agency (CIA),
38–39
change regime, 151, 154
Cheney, Dick, 106
Churchill, Winston, 15, 16, 17, 18, 121
citizens-who-become-soldiers: concept
of, 27n183; as moral agents, 51;
relationship to civil-military
leadership, 53–56; unequal
dialogue framework and, 93–94;
value of the lives of, 74–78; war
as life and death, 35, 48, 50,
51; war-waging decisions and
responsibility for the lives of, 83,
87–88, 93–94. *See also* soldiers;
soldiers' lives
civilian control: by constitutional
form, 59; by government
institution, 59; police patrol
monitoring analogy of civilian
control, 74–75; principal-agent
theory and (*see* principal-agent
theory); right to be wrong, 78–87
(*see also* right to be wrong); by
social class, 59; subjective, 58–59
civil-military dialogue: broken
dialogues, 119–20; Eliot
Cohen on the importance of,
90; dialogue-execution regime
and, 124; during the First Gulf
War, 139–41; focus on output,

123–24; impact of leaks on,
147–48; importance in strategic
war-waging, 35; during the Iraq
War, 102–11; issues of protected
space and public discussion, 120;
Richard Kohn on the impact of
dysfunctional relationships upon,
149; as multiple sets of dialogues,
117–24; principle of continuous
dialogue, 138–49; requirement of
directed focus and attention, 121–
23; unequal dialogue concept,
91–95 (*see also* unequal dialogue
framework); war-waging and, 89;
war-waging principles and the
current war in Syria, 175–76
civil-military leadership: adaptive
problems and adaptive leadership,
141, 142–47; challenges of
bureaucracies for, 113–14; friction
in war and, 115–17; importance of
recognizing the complete account
of *jus in bello,* 171; interference
with the right to be wrong,
discussion of, 83–87; managerial
competence and bureaucracies,
150–55; as moral agents, 160;
need for guiding principles of
war-waging responsibilities,
135; North African invasion
during World War II and,
15–21; principle of final decision
authority, 149–50; principle of
resignation, 157–64; relationship
and responsibilities to citizens-
who-become-soldiers, 53–56;
requirements of a performance-
oriented dialogue-execution
regime, 130–32; responsibilities in
war-waging, 34–37, 48–50; stakes
at risk in war, 89–90; strategic
war-waging in the American Civil
War, 27–37; usefulness of war-